Applied Decision Support

Applied Decision Support

MICHAEL W. DAVIS

PRENTICE HALL, Englewood Cliffs, New Jersey 07632

Library of Congress Cataloging-in-Publication Data

DAVIS, MICHAEL W.
Applied decision support.

Includes index.
1. Decision support systems. I. Title.
T58.62.D38 1988 658.4'03 87-25876
ISBN 0-13-040072-6

Editorial/production supervision
and interior design: *Robert C. Walters*
Cover design: *20/20 Services, Inc.*
Manufacturing buyer: *Barbara Kelly Kittle*

Printed in the United States of America
10 9 8 7 6 5 4 3 2 1

ISBN 0-13-040072-6 01

Prentice-Hall International (UK) Limited, *London*
Prentice-Hall of Australia Pty. Limited, *Sydney*
Prentice-Hall Canada Inc., *Toronto*
Prentice-Hall Hispanoamericana, S.A., *Mexico City*
Prentice-Hall of India Private Limited, *New Delhi*
Prentice-Hall of Japan, Inc., *Tokyo*
Simon & Schuster Asia Pte. Ltd., *Singapore*
Editora Prentice-Hall do Brasil, Ltda., *Rio de Janeiro*

To the pillars of my life:
Karen, Sean and Craig

Contents

5

Special Considerations and Aspects of DSS Applications 59

6

Composition of A DSS 74

7

Database Management Capabilities 83

10

Software Considerations 143

11

Creating DSS Capabilities 168

Preface

Most would agree that computer technology has gone through massive changes since its beginning. We have seen the cost, size, and capacity of computers improve one hundred fold. Practically every segment of our lives has benefited from the technological progress of automation, including the way we manage and run our business affairs. The computer's ability to process large amounts of information in the "wink of an eye" has made it a valuable asset in virtually every aspect of the management process. Whether it be controlling a complicated production process, coordinating the nationwide distribution of a large scale manufacturing and sales operation, or planning multibillion dollar investments, managers have become highly dependent on automation.

The explosion of computer applications in the business world has caused similar growth in the types of information systems used to process and analyze information on the computer. This book is concerned with one special area of information processing known as "Decision Support Systems" or DSS. The term DSS generally applies to systems that are designed to help managers evaluate and analyze complex situations. The phrase "generally applies" is used here because one of the major issues confronting this field is just what distinguishes a DSS from other Information Processing Systems. Ask someone to explain the concept and application of DSS and the answer given will most often depend on who you ask.

Even the majority of literature available today discusses the topic of DSS in rather vague concepts. Open virtually any book and the reader is barraged by an assortment of "buzz words" and confusing terminology (Management Information Systems, Expert Systems, Management Support Systems, Knowledge Based Systems, . . .). To make matters worse, the reader usually has to pause every other sentence to translate some nebulus idea or phrase into every day English. The most simple concepts become couched in abstract terms. This book was designed to provide a user's viewpoint of decision-support applications. The text was written in a nontechnical manner to help the reader understand how topics such as distributed systems, quantitative models, user friendliness, conversational systems, Natural Language Processing, DBMS, ad hoc data query, financial planning, risk analysis, resource allocations, production planning, Expert Systems, Artificial Intelligence, Fourth Generation Lanaguages, and an assortment of other terms fit in the scheme of decision-support applications. There are no prerequisites to understanding the material, nor is any presumption made about the reader's background or experience. The content is targeted to meet the needs of a broad audience in the commercial, military, and public service sector across a wide range of professional endeavors, including:

- Business students requiring an introduction into the concept of decision support and its potential application to real world problems.
- Mid- and line-level managers responsible for coordinating the development, acquisition, and implementation of a DSS.
- Executives searching for a more quantitative approach to solving some of the more difficult problems.

This text provides a broad coverage of the field of DSS. The objective is to establish a general understanding of what a DSS is (and is not), how it is used to support decisions, and what factors contribute to a successful application. The material is designed to help the reader:

- Understand the properties that distingush a decision-support application from other automation efforts.
- Examine the various factors that comprise the decision-making environment and how they affect the required characteristics of a DSS.
- Appreciate the variety of applications where decision support is applicable and the role it plays in reaching complex decisions.
- Understand the various components of a DSS and what must be considered to satisfy a particular requirement.
- Examine the process by which a DSS is developed and implemented.
- Explore some of the pitfalls that must be avoided if the DSS is to become an effective management tool.
- Examine the quantitative and modeling aspects of decision support.
- Finally to survey some actual successful (and unsuccessful) applications and some of the currently available commercial packages.

Michael W. Davis

1

Introduction

There was a time when managers could make it through the day without consulting their electronic guru—the computer. Today, however, few organizations can survive without the assistance of automation. The complexity of modern decisions has caused managers to become increasingly dependent on the computer's ability to quickly process large quantities of data while acting as an immense reservoir for an endless stream of information. Try to visualize a modern nationwide operation functioning without the use of automation. Imagine coordinating the complex activities of a manufacturing process that ships millions of products, along thousands of routes, from production to warehouse to customers; or a military logistics system that distributes hundreds of thousands of different supplies around the globe daily.

Since the early seventies there has been significant progress in the development of information processing systems, especially in areas where managers have to struggle with complicated decisions. A special breed of computerized systems, known as "Decision Support Systems," have evolved for the specific purpose of helping decision makers reach difficult and "messy" decisions. To understand how Decision Support Systems (DSS) differ from other automated information systems, we need to examine how computer technology, and its application to the management process, has evolved.

TECHNOLOGICAL PROGRESS

Advancements in the field of computer applications can be attributed to three movements: progress in the operational characteristics of computer hardware, improvements in the way computers and humans interact, and an increase in the variety and quantity of applications. The rate at which computer applications have grown is not just a result of these three movements alone, but also the way they stimulate and influence each other to create an "endless circle" of progress (Exhibit 1–1). This relationship will become clear as we examine the progress of computer science over the last few decades.

In the last 25 years, the operational capabilities and features of computers have grown exponentially in three areas: reduction in physical size, increase in speed and storage capacity, and a substantial decrease in cost. Improvements in these areas have occurred in three major "leaps" or stages: mainframe dominance, introduction of minicomputers, and the "micro" revolution.[1] Let us briefly compare the original dinosaurs that used "tubes" to prove digital machines possible, with today's "electronic wonders" that store millions of pieces of information (referred to as "bytes" of data) on a chip the size of your thumb [2,3,12,20].

The ENIAC developed in 1946 at the University of Pennsylvania (often considered to be the first large scale computer) and the UNIVAC I (installed in 1951 as the first commercially available computer) filled entire rooms. By the 1960s computer science had passed into a regime of practical and marketable products. The early "mainframes" were much smaller than the computers of the 1950s, and had increased their computational speed and capacity many fold. However, the cost of these systems (like the IBM 360 in 1964 and the IBM 370 in 1970) was so high (in the millions of dollars) that only the largest organizations could afford their own system. In the early 1970s a new line of minicomputer products was introduced. Mini systems (like the DEC 10/20, HP3000, PRIME, and VAX) could provide almost the equivalent capabilities of the mainframes but at a fraction of the cost (under $500,000) and a significant reduction in size.

Finally, in 1977, the microcomputer revolution was born. Although the early microsystems (APPLE, TRS, etc.) were limited in their capacity, they still signaled the beginning of a new era of automation by placing significant computational power on the desktop of the manager. In just a few years, microcomputers quickly advanced to roughly the same capacity and speed as the mini and mainframe systems of the late 1970s by providing core memory exceeding several million bytes for a cost of $4,000

---

[1]Because of our "here today-gone tomorrow" technology the dividing line between these three classes has become very fuzzy and continually debated. Generally speaking, there are four properties that can be used to assess which class a computer belongs to: memory capacity, speed, size, and cost. Today, however, many microcomputers possess practically the same speed and memory capacity of mainframe and minicomputers of the late 1970s. By today's changing standards, the only method that can be used to group computers into "general" classes is to use their cost and size. The following "rule of thumb" is offered for categorizing computer applications: Microsystems—Systems for under $50,000 that can be placed on a desktop and used by less than ten users (operating simultaneously); Minisystems—Computers priced at under $500,000 that service the needs of a small to moderate sized operation; Mainframe—Large scale computers costing more than $500,000 that satisfy the automation requirements of many organizations.

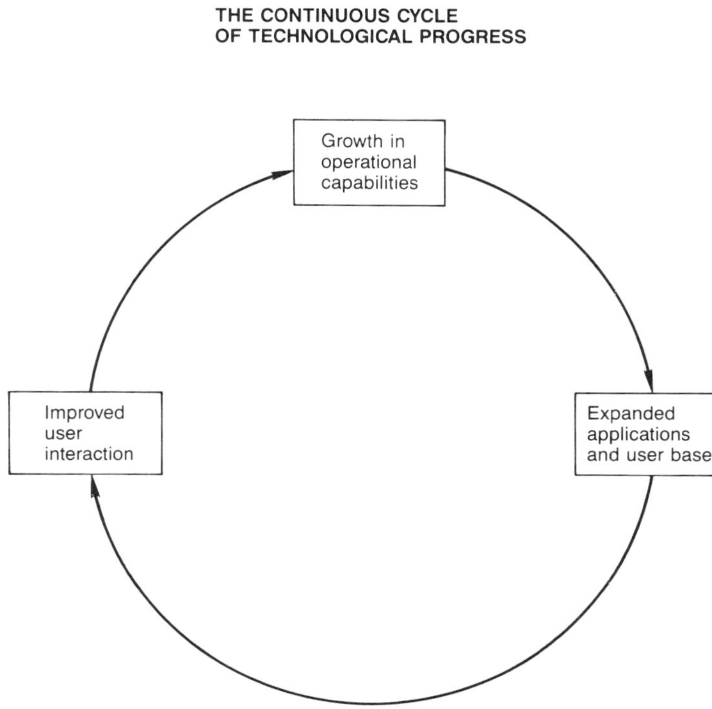

EXHIBIT 1–1 The Continuous Cycle of Technological Progress.

to $50,000. Thus, in a period of roughly 30 years, computer technology moved from a condition where a room full of million dollar hardware was required to obtain 12,000 bytes of memory (for example, the UNIVAC I) to the modern desktop microcomputers that provide two million bytes of main memory for under $10,000.

Remember that originally computers were reserved for scientific analysis and engineering design. Users, for the most part, were highly trained technical experts. Their analytical background made them more tolerant of the complicated procedures (and jargon) required to use and operate computers of that era. Subsequently, the freedom and opportunity provided by the improved generation of computers caused a significant increase in the demand for new and innovative kinds of information processing systems. Organizations soon realized the potential cost saving and productivity improvements that were possible by using computers to process the large volumes of data associated with managing their activities. However, the initial application of computers to the business world was limited to systems analysts and programmers. The operating environment was still extremely technical and confined to "batch processing," often requiring hours, or even days, to obtain results. This form of Information Processing System was still too elementary to allow direct application to the management process.

The idea soon flourished that computerized information systems could be used more effectively if the operating environment would permit use by "nontechnical" individuals and if solutions could be obtained in "real-time." Interactive systems were developed to allow each user to share the computer facility and obtain (almost) immediate results. The decreasing cost and size of computers made them more attractive and practical for a larger base of users. This, in turn, coupled with improvements in the way computers interacted with the user, resulted in a new breed of Management Information Systems (MIS) that could be more readily applied to help organizations process, store, and retrieve large quantities of data.

THE BIRTH OF DSS

For years MIS prevailed as the primary media for applying computerized systems to the management process. In areas where large amounts of information had to be accessible for easy review (financial accounting, inventory tracking, production coordination, etc.), MIS became an effective tool. However, the fixed structure of MIS applications [5,13,16,17,19] and the abundance of information that could be recalled led to another obstacle. In the more complex operational settings, managers soon became saturated by the amount of available information. A mechanism was required to somehow "cull out" or consolidate the barrage of data into a concise and readily useful form. To this end, a new MIS "offshot" appeared to allow managers to easily focus on selected sets of information germane to the particular decision. For some of the more difficult applications, analytical and mathematical procedures were merged within the MIS framework to provide managers with more quantitative and integrated results.

In the early 1970s the term "Decision Support System" (DSS) was coined for that segment of information systems primarily intended for use in supporting complex decisions. The concept was that DSS applied in situations where the decision maker was immersed in an environment of complex issues and interrelated factors at such a level that it exceeded human abilities to "weed through the chaff" and visualize the best course of action. In the years that followed, a variety of interpretations have been applied to the concept, purpose, and distinguishing properties of decision support applications ([18] surveys the various perspectives and views applied to DSS).

The evolutionary path from which today's decision support applications emerged was not a clear-cut process. Opinions as to what distinguished DSS from other automated systems was often predicated on the background of the individual making the distinction. Those specializing in the development of information systems viewed the realm of DSS with a slant toward applications that allowed the manager to interactively query large reservoirs of data and to isolate information that was of particular interest to a specific problem on an ad hoc (as needed) basis (often referred to as an "ad hoc data query"). Similarly, individuals with a financial background envisioned financial planning to be the central focus for DSS [10,15]. At the other end of the spectrum, professionals who used analytical procedures and mathematical models to analyze complex problems, began to recognize the potential for placing quantitative automated tools in the hands of the manager. By direct involvement in the decision process, the intuitive insight of the decision maker could be combined with the power of quantitative procedures. These individuals perceived that the major thrust of DSS was toward more complex and difficult problems [21]. In reality, the distinction between DSS and other automated systems

stems not from the internal procedural mechanism of the system (Data Base Management, analytical procedures, etc.), but from the purpose of the application and how it is used to help formulate decisions, analyze policies, or evaluate alternative courses of action.

The multiple evolutionary paths under which DSS has evolved is likely to have contributed to the significant confusion about the concept of DSS, what distinguishes it from other information systems, and in what areas decision support is applicable. Much of the problem can also be attributed to the rate of technological change, and the "free for all" process by which "catch" phrases became popular and misused. The tendency to misinterpret the intent of DSS also caused an initial barrier to the successful application and growth of the DSS concept. The promise of "true user friendliness" was never realized in the early systems. As a result, many of the potential users viewed the concept as another "bandwagon" fad and were put off. In recent years, however, a renewed awareness and interest in "real" DSS applications has burgeoned. Although imposters still exist, the merit of true decision support has resulted in a variety of successful efforts.

Later, we will discuss the concept and application of DSS in detail. For the moment, consider that the purpose of a DSS is to establish an integrated framework between the problem, the machine, and the decision maker. The DSS couples the speed and thoroughness of automation with the insight of human experience and, where appropriate, a proper blend of quantitative support (Exhibit 1–2). We can characterize the distinction between DSS and other information systems as:

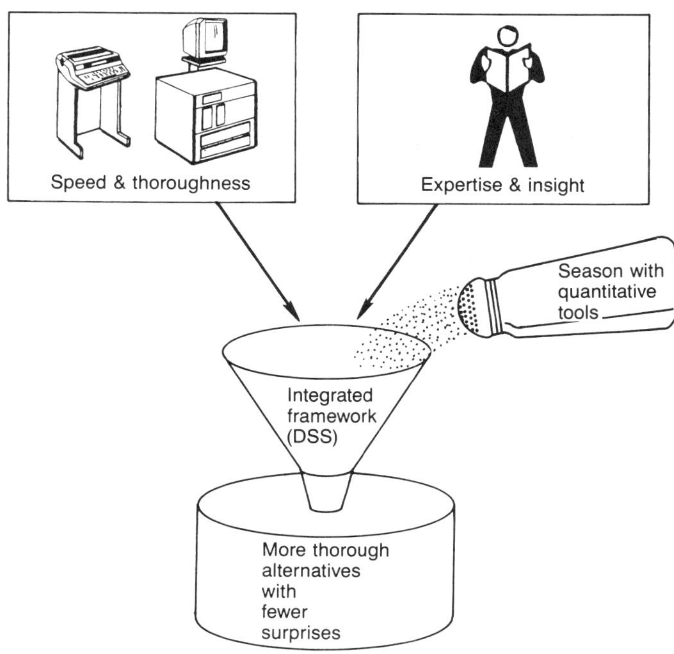

EXHIBIT 1–2 Decision Support—Providing an Integrated Framework.

- ☐ Being readily accessible to the decision maker.
- ☐ The flexibility with which the system can be tailored by the user to the changing needs and environment of the problem.
- ☐ The ease and freedom with which the system can be directly applied in reaching decisions.
- ☐ For the more complicated problems, the use of quantitative models for manipulating complex information into a consolidated form.

SCOPE—WHAT THE BOOK IS ABOUT

It is important that the reader understand the difference between the objectives of this text and some of the other more theoretical or research-oriented literature in this field. Involvement in a decision-support application occurs at three[2] basic levels of interest: the designer, the implementer, and the user. Designers are obviously those individuals that possess the technical skills necessary to develop the software and any analytical procedures that may be required. Implementers are the individuals responsible for merging the system within the particular organization and decision process being supported. Finally, the user encompasses the executive, manager or administrator that depends on the DSS to help reach difficult decisions. This text is oriented toward the latter audience.

When newcomers first encounter the field of automation, they are bombarded by a maze of new terminology. Each technology is replete with its own special jargon and, in this respect, the area of decision support is no different. Within this text a descriptive explanation is provided whenever a new topic is introduced. A brief survey, however, of some of the terminology associated with DSS will prepare the reader for subsequent discussions.

In studying information systems, it helps to classify topics into three related areas: *the building tools* (what techniques and facilities are used to build the automated product), *the automated system* (the computerized products that will be operated by the user), and *the application* (the requirement that is being supported or satisfied by the system). The reader should review Exhibit 1–3, note those topics that will be discussed in this text, and observe the role each plays in establishing decision-support capability.

The material in this text deals solely with decision-support applications. There is a multitude of literature available to those interested in the broader class of Management Information Systems [6,7,8 are examples]. The contents of this text do not focus on any single aspect of DSS but instead provide an overview, from a users perspective, of the total field of decision-support applications from concept to development to implementation. The intent here is to provide a basic understanding and appreciation for the potential value of DSS applications, as well as the steps required for successful implementation. The text is organized into thirteen chapters (Exhibit 1–4):

---

[2]Some partition DSS involvement into more refined layers of participation [16] but, for our purposes, three will suffice.

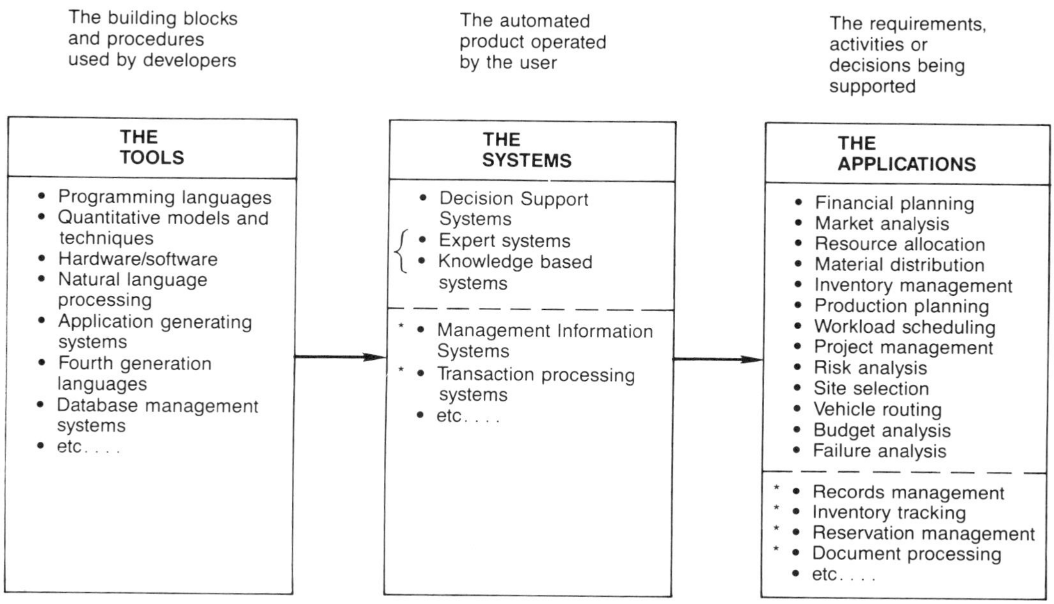

* These topics are not within the scope of this text.

EXHIBIT 1–3 Information Systems Terminology.

- ☐ Chapter 2 looks at the role DSS plays in the decision process and some example areas of application.
- ☐ Chapter 3 then examines the decision process itself, including the various types of decisions, and what conditions influence the process.
- ☐ Chapter 4 explores the when, where and how of decision support, analyzes the different properties and characteristics of DSS, and how they relate to the decision-making environment.
- ☐ Chapter 5 discusses some of the special aspects and considerations that pertain to decision support applications.
- ☐ Chapter 6 examines the makeup and composition of a DSS. This, in turn, leads to a detailed discussion of the major DSS components including: database management facilities (Chapter 7), user interface (Chapter 8), the quantitative models and techniques used by the system (Chapter 9), and eventually the software aspects of a DSS (Chapter 10).
- ☐ In Chapter 11 the step-by-step process for developing and implementing a DSS is introduced.
- ☐ In Chapter 12 we examine a few case studies to help bring things together.
- ☐ We conclude in Chapter 13 with a brief discussion of the future outlook and direction for the field of DSS.
- ☐ Appendix A summarizes some of the commercially available DSS packages.
- ☐ Appendix B provides answers to the exercises found at the conclusion of each chapter.

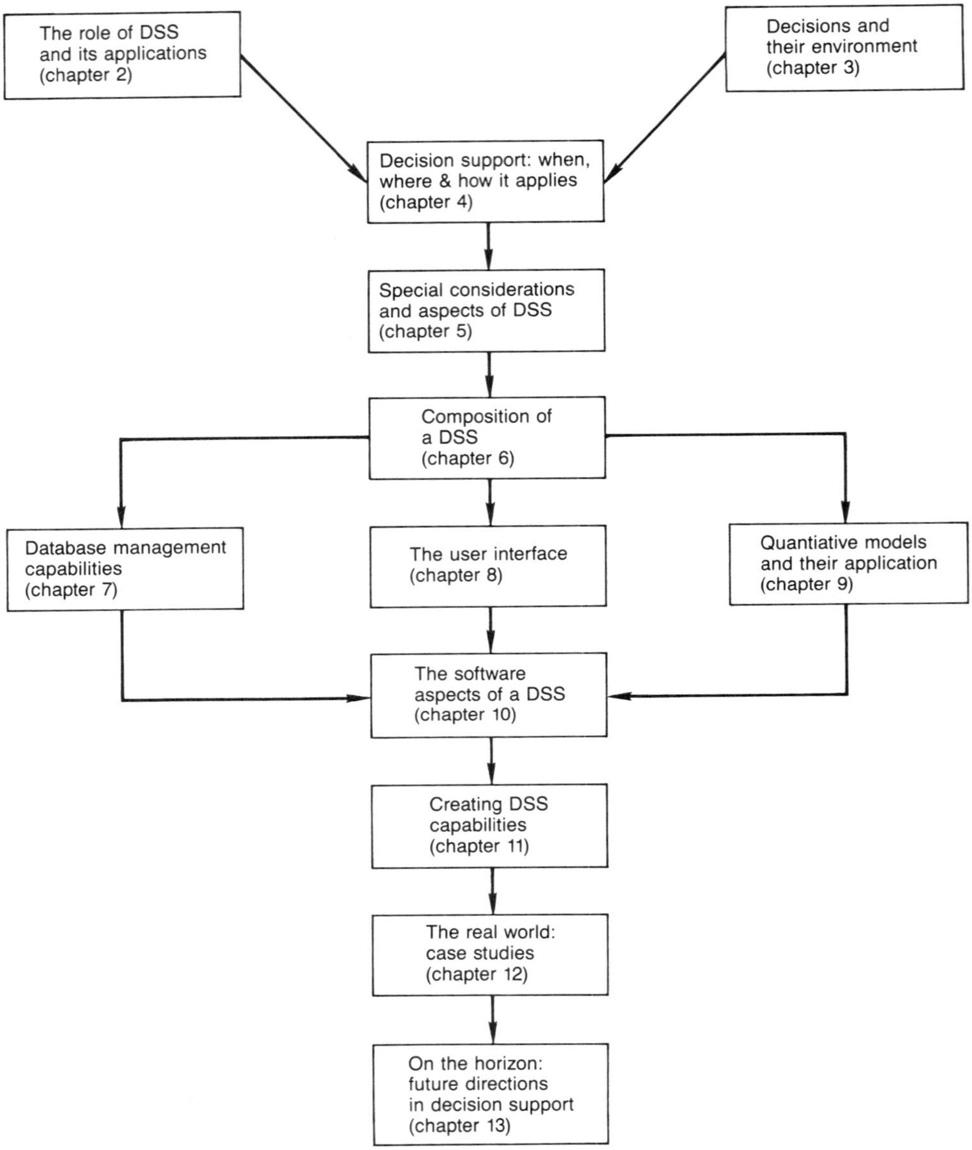

EXHIBIT 1–4 Scope and Relationship of Topics.

We previously noted that the application of computers to the decision process has not been an "exact" science. As a result, many of the concepts and techniques are not greeted with a total consensus by practitioners and academia. In areas where there is significant controversy, literature voicing both sides of the debate will be noted, and a final assessment provided by the author based on his experiences.

EXERCISES

1. In recent years users have voiced discontent with many of the systems promoted as truly oriented toward the manager. The basic contention is that the systems are not really designed for use in a real-world environment by managers experienced in making decisions, not in struggling with a technically oriented device. Consider the different perspectives of management, systems designers, and product vendors.
   a. List some of the possible reasons for the disparity between these three groups.
   b. State some of the precautions that a manager can employ to reduce the risk of eventual dissatisfaction with the system.
2. Review some of the current periodical literature on information systems (that is, Computerworld, Computer Decisions, Datamation, Infosystems, etc.) and select three or four marketed systems that are promoted as DSS. Examine their features and capabilities and note those systems you feel are really aimed at decision-support applications. Also note those systems where it is difficult to assess their true nature from the promotional material.
3. Many have viewed the inception of microcomputers as a major impetus to a more direct and broader application of computer support to the decision process. The assumption is that with hardware and software resources becoming so readily available (minimum investment costs), that managers will find DSS to be a more viable and cost effective tool. Define the advantages and disadvantages that can result from the increased freedom and economic considerations of applying microbased DSS applications.
4. We noted at the end of Chapter 1 that it often helps to step back and look at how an information system concept, topic or terminology fits into the overall scheme of developing, packaging and applying automated support to real world problems. For each of the following phrases, state whether you feel it represents: a set of *tools* or *techniques* used in the development of a computerized product; a class of information systems (*products*) that will be used by a manager; or a group of related activities, decisions or requirements that will be supported by the system (an area of *application*):
   a. Computer Assisted Manufacturing (CAM) systems
   b. Human Resource Management
   c. Statistical Models
   d. Prototyping
   e. Linear Programming

REFERENCES AND SUGGESTED READING

1. Alter, S., *Decision Support Systems: Current Practice and Continuing Challenge.* Reading, Mass.: Addison-Wesley, 1980.
2. Augarten, S., *Bit by Bit: An Illustrated History of Computers.* New York, N.Y.: Tickner and Fields, 1984.
3. Bell, G., "The MULTI in Historical Perspective," *Indepth/Computer Museum,* Computerworld, October 14, 1985.

4. Bonczek, R., C. Hollsapple & A. Whinston, "Future Directions for Developing Decision Support Systems," *Decision Science,* November 11, 1980.

5. Davis, M., "The Antonomy of Decision Support," *Datamation,* June 15, 1984.

6. Hicks, J., *Management Information Systems: A User's Perspective.* St. Paul, Minn.: West Publishing, 1984.

7. Hodge B., R. Fleck & B. Honess, *Management Information Systems,* Reston Publishing Co., Reston, Va.: 1984.

8. Kenter, J., *Management Information Systems.* Englewood Cliffs, N.J.: Prentice-Hall, 1984.

9. King, W., "Achieving the Potential of Decision Support Systems," *Journal of Business Strategy,* Winter, 1983.

10. Lasden, M., "Enriching the Decision-Making Process," *Computer Decisions,* November, 1983.

11. Leighton, R., "Decision Support Systems," *Journal of Systems Management,* February, 1981.

12. Lukoff, H., *From Dits to Bits: A Personal History of Electronic Computers,* Beaverton, Or.: Robotics Press, 1979.

13. Morton, M. and A. McCosh, *Management Decision Support Systems.* New York, N.Y.: Wiley & Sons, 1978.

14. Morton, M., "Management Decision Systems: Computer Based Support for Decision Making," *Harvard University,* Cambridge, Mass.: 1971.

15. Snyder, C., "The Allure of Decision Support Systems," *ICP Administrative and Accounting Software,* Winter, 1984.

16. Sprague, R. and E. Carlson, *Building Effective Decision Support Systems.* Englewood Cliffs, N.J.: Prentice-Hall, 1982.

17. Sprague, R. and H. Watson, "MIS Concepts" in House, W. (ed.), *Interactive Decision Oriented Database Systems.* Princeton, N.J.: Petrocelli, 1977.

18. Stohr, E. and M. Ginzberg, "Decision Support Systems: Issues and Perspectives," in Ginzberg, E., W. Reitmand and E. Stohr (eds.); *Decision Support Systems.* New York, N.Y.: North Holland, 1981.

19. Thierauf, R., *Decision Support Systems for Effective Planning and Control.* Englewood Cliffs, N.J.: Prentice-Hall, 1982.

20. Williams, G. and M. Welch, "A Microcomputer Timeline," *BYTE,* September, 1985.

21. Wynne, B., "A Domination Sequence—MS/OR, DSS," *INTERFACES,* May–June, 1984.

22. Zalud, B., "Decision Support Systems," *Data Management,* January, 1981.

2

The Role of DSS and Its Applications

We mentioned earlier that there is much confusion as to exactly what a DSS is and is not. Many have voiced concern [6,9,11,12,13] that the misunderstanding and misuse of the DSS concept will lead to its eventual demise as a distinctive management tool. In today's "high technology" world of instantaneous and global communication, how is it possible for a profession to exist in such a state of confusion? Is there not some divine leadership that coordinates the overall direction and paths we take in the advancement of science? Unfortunately not. Technological progress is an impure process. Differences in our professional experience and backgrounds can cause the same concept to be discovered and applied in many areas only by different names. It takes a long time to realize that a "Rose is a Rose" by any name. Add to this the hyper-rate at which are "here today, gone tomorrow" technology appears to be marching forward and we begin to understand how concepts can be misinterpreted.

The manager is rarely concerned with the title used to classify an automated system. The important criteria is whether the system provides the features and capabilities necessary to support a particular process. It is the professionals involved in the development and implementation of information systems that struggle with distinctive nomenclature that can be used to categorize each type of system. To complicate things even more, we often find ourselves confronted with two types of definitions: the theoretical definition established by academia and research professionals, and the more user-oriented view that evolves from real-world experience. The central theme of this chapter focuses on the latter definition to clarify just "what is a DSS," how is it distinguished from other systems, and how it is applied to the decision process [references 2 and 7 provide additional contrast between the two views].

DISTINGUISHING DSS—WHAT'S IN A NAME

One of the more frequent difficulties managers face in reaching complex decisions is how to deal with the floodgate of available data. Computers have made information so accessible that the decision maker can easily become saturated. Automation supports the management process in two ways: by helping the manager to process large volumes of information, and by helping the decision maker to perform complicated numerical operations. We can formulate these two activities more specifically as follows:

1. *Information Management.* The function of storing, handling, maintaining and reporting information in a form that is convenient to the user.
2. *Data Quantification.* The activity by which large bundles of data are consolidated or mathematically manipulated into a few meaningful indicators that depict the true (hidden) meaning of the information.

Virtually all information processing systems provide the user with some degree of information management capabilities for maintaining, tracking, tabulating, and displaying large bundles of data (accounting and billing, records management, inventory tracking, etc.). However, there are many situations where simply recalling and reporting information in a fixed form will not suffice. The problem at hand is so broad and complex that the decision maker needs help in weeding through the abundance of data in order to evaluate the alternatives. In these situations the major benefit and reason for applying automated support to the decision process is to search for the best course of action among the spectrum of possibilities, quickly analyze the complicated relationships, and build upon the qualitative insight of management experience in making the final choice.

Here lies the major distinctions between a Decision Support System designed to help reach difficult decisions and those systems intended primarily for managing and reporting information. The DSS must be capable of analyzing complicated issues and relationships in a manner that can be applied directly by the decision maker. This requires that the DSS be an active component in the decision process and that the results are in a form readily accessible for management review and interpretation (not a three-inch stack of computer printouts).

Although the term "DSS" is applied freely in today's promotional literature to virtually every type of information system, it is generally accepted [2,7,8,11] that true decision-support applications exhibit certain distinctive properties and characteristics, specifically:

- ☐ The structure and environment of the problem is not rigid or constant but instead is susceptible to change.
- ☐ The exchange (interaction) between the user and the computer is interactive in nature and in a dialogue that is informative, tolerant, and does not cause apprehension to the user.
- ☐ The system provides the user with the capability to examine different situations, evaluate various scenarios, and answer a variety of "what if" questions.
- ☐ The user is afforded the flexibility to adapt the system to his preferences, or changes in conditions, that influence the decision (changing resource levels, costing factors, interest rates, terminology, policies, etc.).

The realm of activities that benefit from such capabilities covers a broad spectrum of decision-support applications (Exhibit 2–1). As we move from the simpler require-

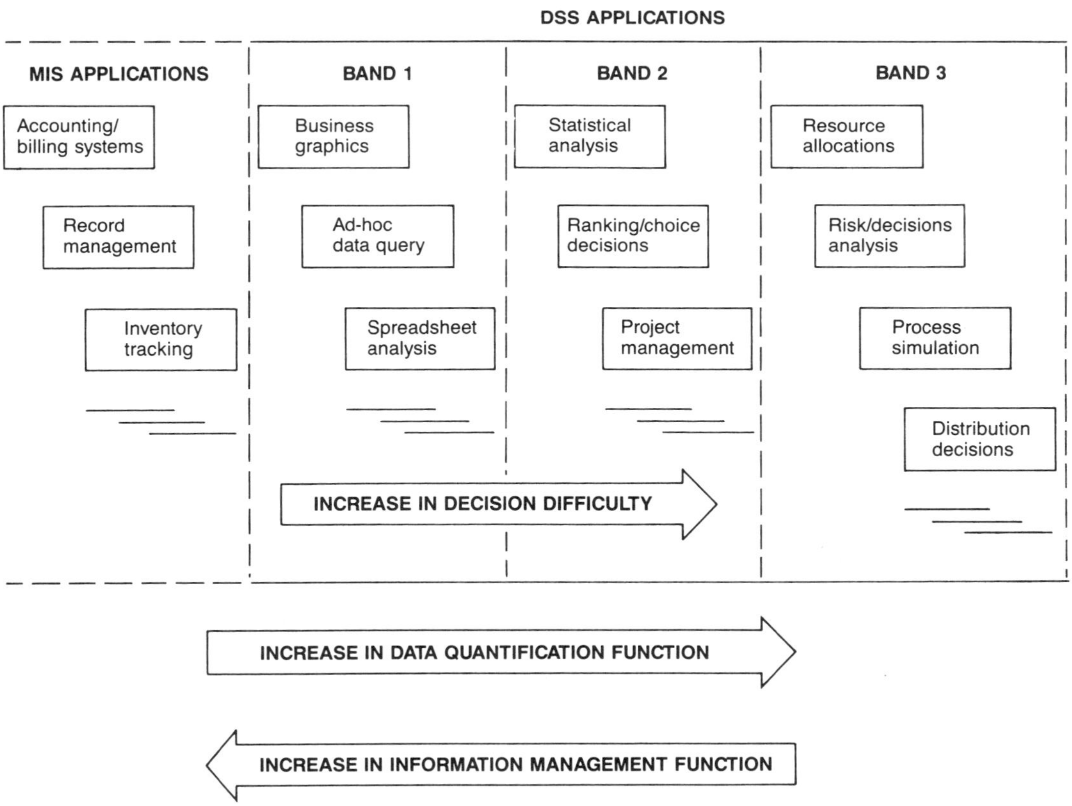

EXHIBIT 2–1 The Spectrum of DSS Applications.

ments (ad hoc data query, spreadsheet analysis, etc.), to the more sophisticated problems (risk analysis, resource allocations, etc.), the needs of the decision maker shift more from information management to the data quantification features provided by automation (Chapter 4 discusses the types of problems associated with each level or "band" of DSS application).

Often the dividing line between DSS and other information systems is "fuzzy" and applying a specific label to an application is not clear cut. The characteristics and features of the system may not provide a pure "demarcation line" but instead reflects a blend of both worlds. To illustrate, consider an information system used by a manufacturing firm to manage their product delivery and shipping operations. A large portion of the system will be dedicated to handling and processing data that reflects day-to-day status (customer demand, stock levels, resource availability, shipping capacity and costs, etc.). Line level personnel use the system to generate status reports, track progress and backlogs, maintain proper inventory levels, manage vehicle usage and maintenance records, track vehicle availability, coordinate dispatch activities, and so forth. We could refer to this system as an MIS since, in this role, it does perform the function of information management. Indeed, if this were the only purpose served by the system, the term MIS would appropriately apply.

But what about the task of planning and scheduling all parts of the operation so that things run smoothly and cost efficiently? How can we make sure that the inventory will meet demands, the qualifications of available personnel match task requirements, the best shipping routes are selected, and that vehicles are available with the proper capacity and configuration? We could try to do it by hand. However, determining the best match of personnel, vehicles, routes and customers for a large nationwide distribution system would quickly become unwieldy. There are literally billions of ways that you can ship, for example, 50 product lines from five plants to 20 regional warehouses and 100,000 customers along thousands of different routes. Trying to visualize the most cost efficient combination is humanly impossible. In such an environment we would be dealing with a decision-support application that uses quantitative procedures to integrate all these factors, search for the best solution, and allow direct intervention by operational personnel and line level managers. In essence, we have a hybrid application that provides capabilities and features associated with both the MIS and DSS domain (Exhibit 2–2).

HOW THE PROCESS WORKS

Now that we hopefully understand how a DSS differs from other information systems, we need to examine the role a DSS plays in the decision process and how it all fits together. Remember that in order for the DSS to work effectively, two things must be satisfied: it must be capable of being directly applied to the decision process, and it must present results in a form that are readily usable by the decision maker. This imposes some rather stringent requirements. Unlike other information systems, the DSS will most likely be used by personnel with neither the time nor the inclination to become proficient in

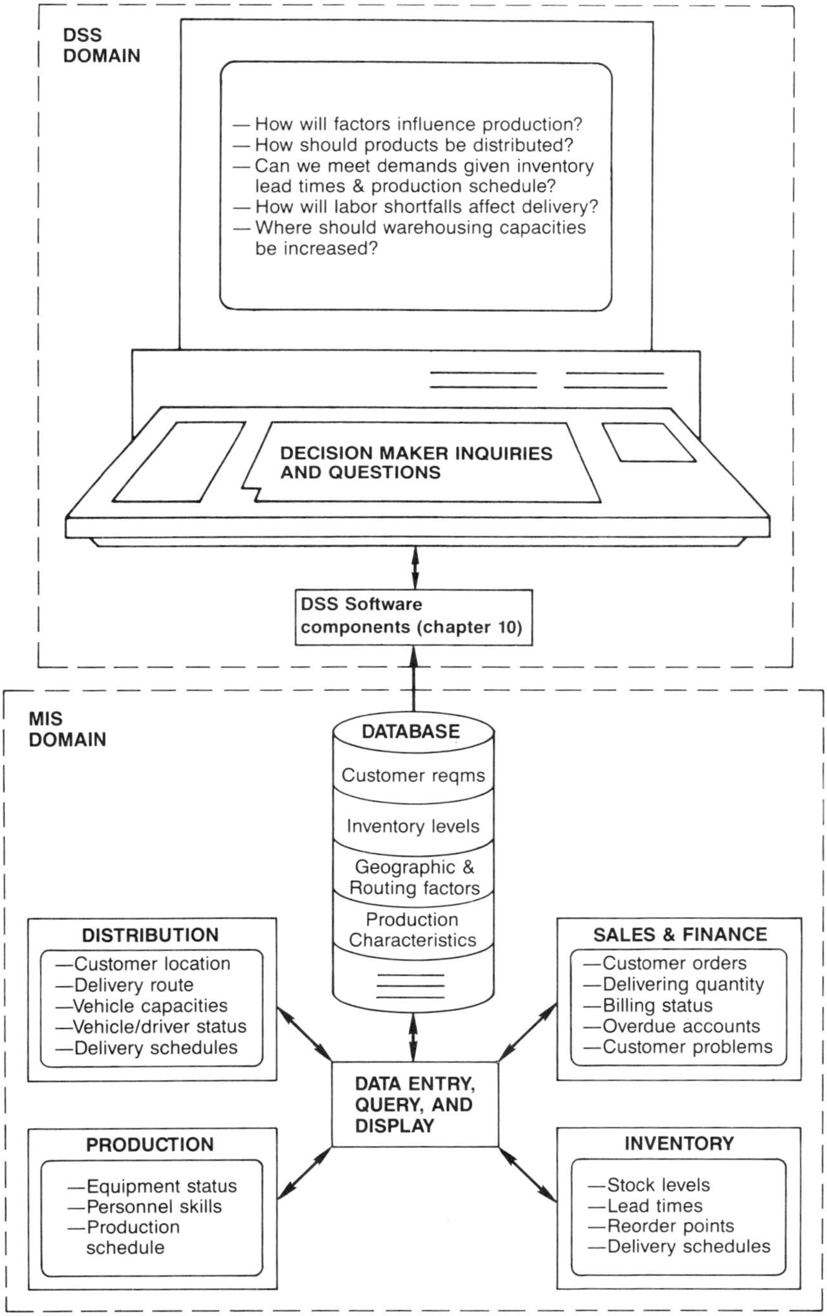

EXHIBIT 2–2 A Hybrid MIS/DSS Application in a Manufacturing Environment.

"computerese" jargon or technical procedures. The purpose of the DSS is to become a natural extension of the decision maker. This means that the system must operate as a "Black Box" (Exhibit 2–3). The manager generally knows what questions need to be asked, understands the conditions and issues that influence the problem, and has a basic feeling for the appropriateness or range of answers. The difficulty is in putting it all together and making sense of the results. Here lies the role of the DSS: allow the user to input his questions, identify the state of his problem, and examine the results without regard for the complexity or internal workings of the system.

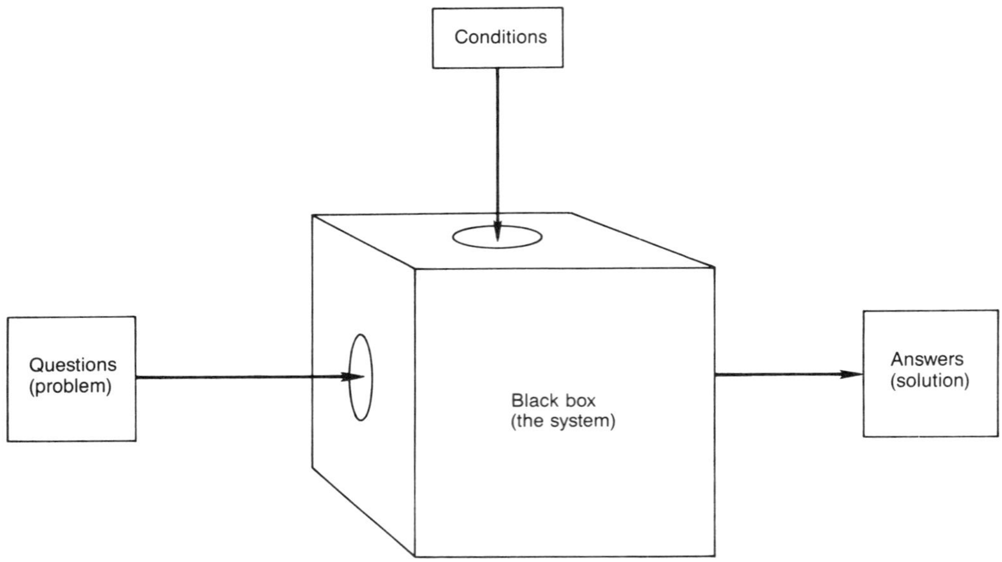

EXHIBIT 2–3 The "Black Box" Approach.

Not all agree that the DSS should behave in analogous to a Black Box. Some believe that the manager should understand how the system operates internally in order to have confidence in the result. In a practical sense, however, the decision maker cannot afford the effort required to comprehend the operational mechanism and functioning of the system. It is only essential that the decision maker be comfortable with how well the system reflects reality.

Given that the DSS must function as a Black Box, we can understand how the total process works by examining the way decisions are ideally formulated (Exhibit 2–4). The decision maker must determine how an organization or physical system can be expected to behave under a variety of different circumstances. Management objectives, organizational issues, historical data, operational conditions, external factors, resource considerations, and so forth, are analyzed and combined quantitatively to provide various indicators of performance, risk and cost. Management then uses human experience and insight, to weed out unacceptable alternatives and to propose new ones.

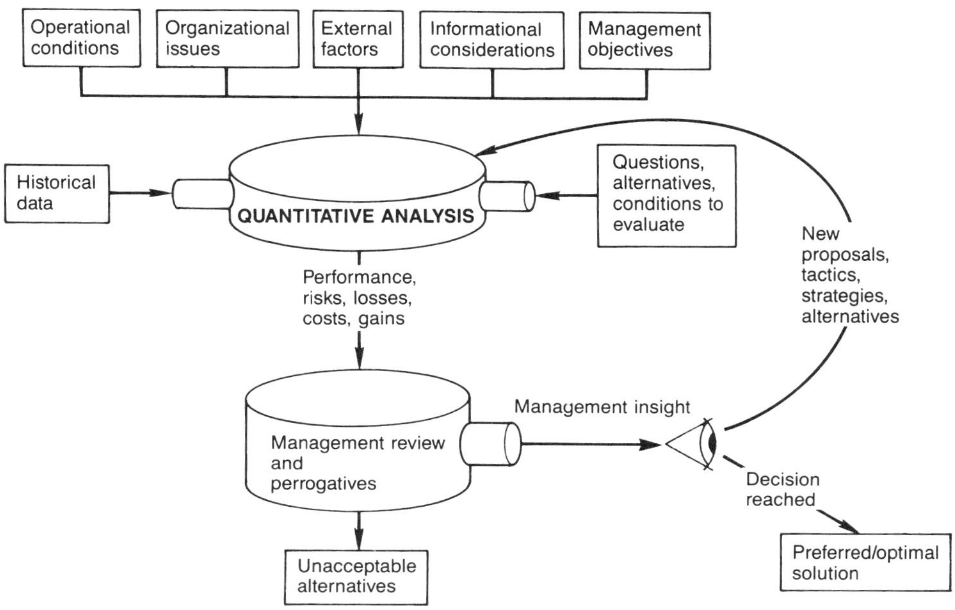

EXHIBIT 2–4 How Decisions Are "Ideally" Formulated.

The process is continued until an acceptable course of action is found. In this way, the DSS permits the manager to explore more possibilities, and expand his perspective and knowledge as to the effects of his decisions.

To sense what a decision-support application looks like from a users perspective, it will help to examine several DSS in action, see how they are used to help formulate policies, and the way they can be used to analyze complex problems. Exhibits 2–5 through 2–10 provide a sampling of systems that span the total spectrum of decision-support applications, especially:

- ☐ Exhibit 2–5 demonstrates how an interactive system can be used to query a database for a selected set of information using an everyday English dialogue.
- ☐ In Exhibit 2–6 a commercially available microcomputer package is used to graphically project sales data. The user selects which data is to be analyzed (top figure) and the results are portrayed in both a bar (middle) and pie chart (bottom).
- ☐ In Exhibit 2–7 a DSS helps an organization manage and project its workforce level and expenditures. The manager states what the prevailing conditions are (annual attrition, current recruiting actions, etc.), what the policies will be (ceilings, budget constraints, freeze policies, etc.), and then evaluates the resulting projections (workforce levels, funding expenditures, etc.).
- ☐ Exhibit 2–8 depicts a DSS being used to schedule the relocation and refurbishment of office facilities based on the required moves and renovations, and the available resources (work crews, shift duration, overtime, etc.).

Show me what percent of total salaries is for managers in each department.

PRINT A PERCENTAGE OF THE TOTAL ANNUAL SALARY IN EACH DEPARTMENT OF ALL EMPLOYEES WITH EEO=MANAGER.

DEPARTMENT	SALARY	PERCENT
ACCOUNTING	$25,560.00	1.94
ADMINISTRATION	$162,924.00	12.37
CUSTOMER SERVICE	$56,880.00	4.32
DATA PROCESSING	$224,808.00	17.07
FINANCIAL PLANNING	$45,000.00	3.42
HUMAN RESOURCES	$20,400.00	1.55
RESEARCH	$39,600.00	3.01
SALES & MARKETING	$368,820.00	28.01
STORES	$341,940.00	25.97
TRAINING	$30,909.00	2.35
OVERALL	$1,316,841.00	100.00

EXHIBIT 2–5 Adhoc Query of a Database in an English Dialogue. *Courtesy of Artificial Intelligence, Inc.*

SPECIFY LINE/OR GRAPH

MTA: SALES.FORECAST

ADVERTISING
BUDGET
EXPENSE
INDUSTRY.SALES
PRICE
SALES
SALES.FORECAST
SHARE
UNITS

Select type of graph

LINE BAR STACKED BAR X

Layout	Dimensions	Selection(s)
ACROSS	MONTH	JUN86 TO DEC86
BREAKOUT	DISTRICT	ATLANTA BOSTON CHICAGO
PACKD BY	PRODUCT	ALL

VIEW PRINT PLOT SELECT UTILITIES DONE

Database DEMO Input Choices Local

The menu and options screen of Easy Express

EXHIBIT 2–6 Projecting Sales Graphically with a Microcomputer Product. *Courtesy of Information Resources Massachusetts, Inc.*

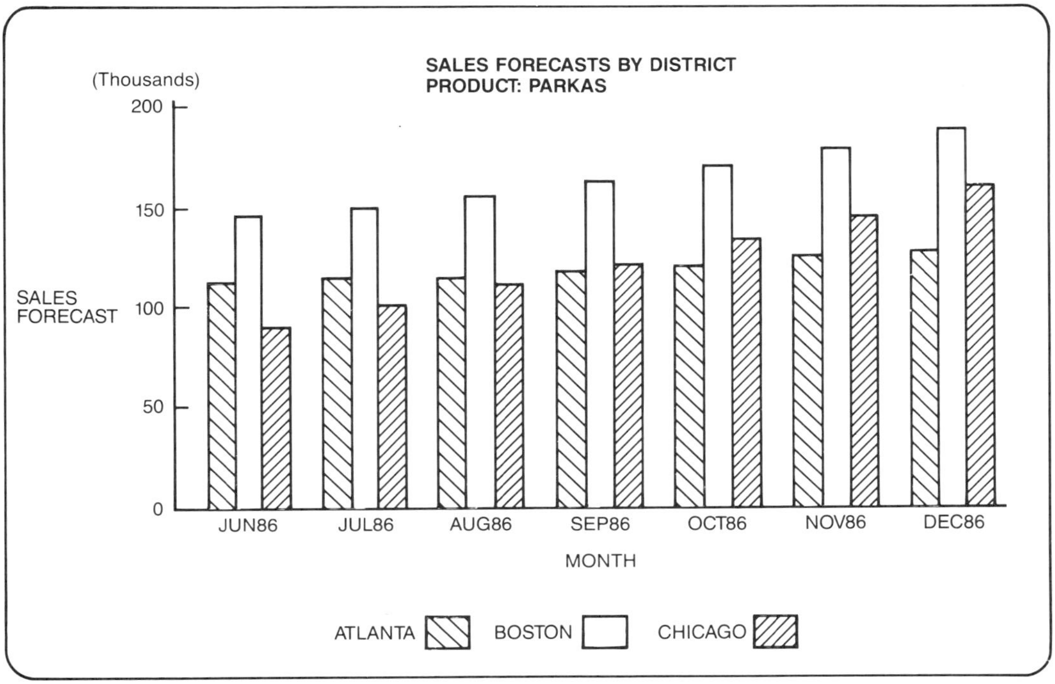

The integration of analysis and display tools means clear, quick representation of results. Here, a product manager can see separate graphs (screens) for each product.

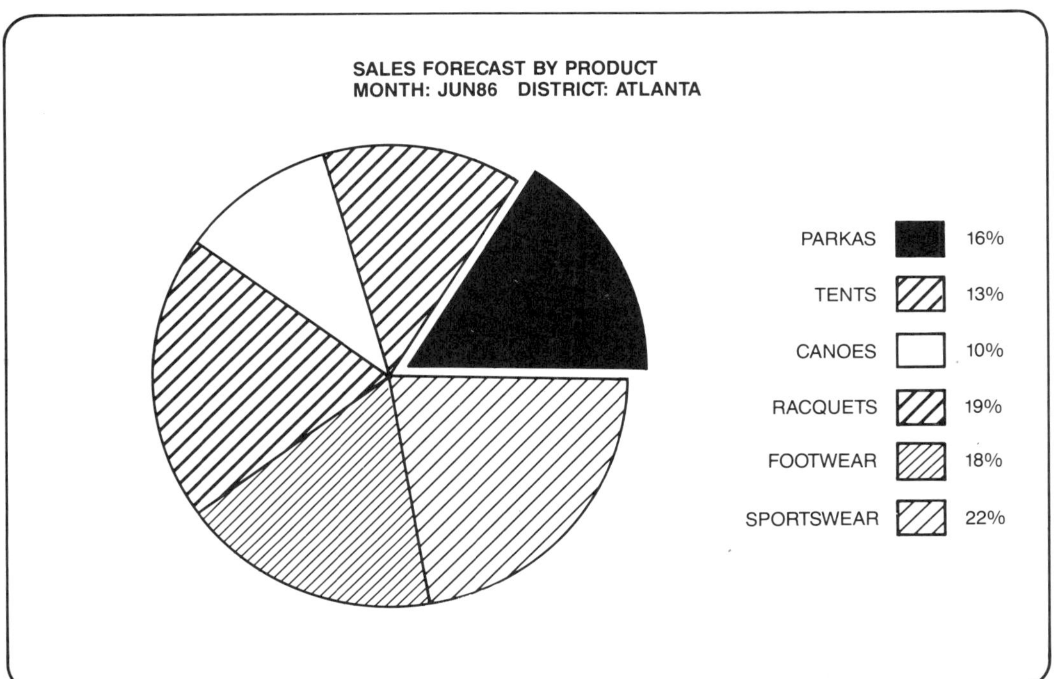

Alternatively, a district manager can see separate graphs for each district.

EXHIBIT 2–6 (Continued)

```
ENTER THE EXPECTED ANNUAL ATTRITION (enter blank return when finished):
  % Attrition  |  from      |  to
>     10          10/1/85     1/10/86
>      8          1/11/86     9/30/86
>

ENTER YOUR FREEZE POLICY (lose 1 gain 0 is total freeze, 1 for 1 is no freeze):
  lose | gain | from      |  to
>  1       1    10/1/85     2/1/86
>  1       0     2/2/86     9/30/86
>
IDENTIFY YOUR BUDGET AND ALLOWABLE DEVIATION (below budget end of year)
  budget   |   % allowable deviation

> 9800000        6 %
>

ENTER THE AUTHORIZED WORKFORCE LEVEL (awl)
  awl  |  from     |  to
> 480     10/1/85     2/1/86
> 440      2/1/85    10/1/86
>

HOW MANY RECRUITING ACTIONS ARE CURRENTLY IN PROGRESS
> 38

WHICH GRAPHS WOULD YOU LIKE TO SEE ?
(Number on Board [NOB], Funding [FUNDS], Monitoring Envelopes [MONITOR])
> NOB  FUNDS
```

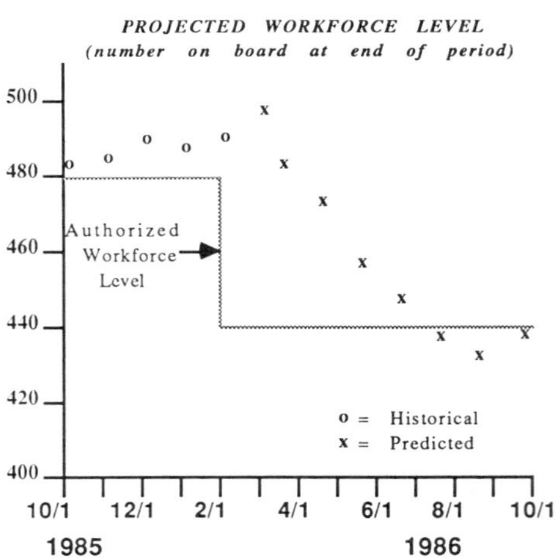

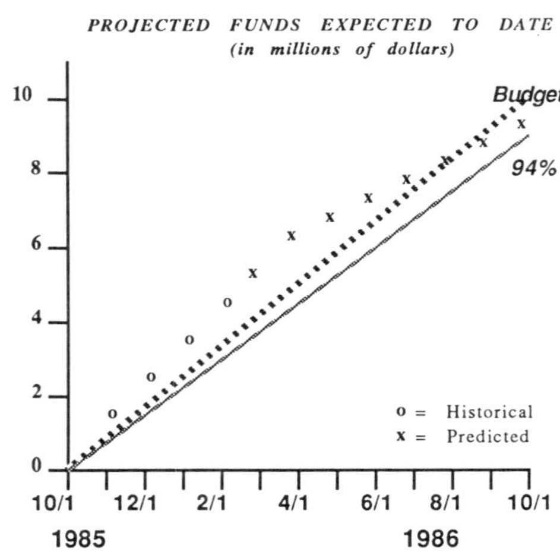

EXHIBIT 2–7 Predicting the Level and Expenditures of a Workforce.

```
     Which clients or organizations do you want to schedule?

> Davis.corp   DIM.Institute   CMI.Commission

     Should I use the standard task durations and costs?

> yes

     Which crews do you wish to assign?

> Team4   Team3   Team6

     How many hours in each workshift?

> 8      8      10

     Should weekends and/or holidays be considered?

> no

     Do you want to change any of the planned moves or renovations?

> yes

     ENTER DESIRED CHANGES (client name, building, room, renovations):

> Davis.corp   North  301  moveout paint carpet movein
> DIM.Institute Adam 1024 telephone moveout wall.partition paint movin

     When should the moves begin (month/day/year)?

> 10/1/86

          OFFICE RELOCATION AND RENOVATION SCHEDULE FOR DAVIS.CORP

  TEAM  !         !     !          OCTOBER                    !      NOVEM.
ASSIGNED!BUILDING!ROOM!1        !8       !15      !21      !28 !1       !8...
    4      NORTH     406  OP-PCI
    3      NORTH     210  OW---WTP-PC-CI
    6      MASON     101  OI
    3      NORTH     135   OTI
    6      MASON     210   O   W---WP-PC-CI
    4      NORTH     012                OP-PI
    4      NORTH     246                    OW---WP-PC-CI
    3      TOWERS    1002   OTP-PI
    6      NORTH     334          OW---WP-PTI
           -                          -                       -
           -                          -                       -
```

EXHIBIT 2–8 A DSS for Scheduling Facility Moves and Renovations.

- ☐ Exhibit 2–9 shows how a DSS can be used to estimate the most profitable production plan for a given amount of funds, staff and material at a processing plant.
- ☐ Exhibit 2–10 illustrates an application where a resource manager must estimate how much it will take to accomplish a specific workload (number of tasks, products, projects, etc.).

```
     What is the title of your problem?

> PRODUCTION PLAN FOR STATION 3 IN MARCH

     What is your objective?

> MAXIMIZE PROFITS

     What is the equation for total profit?

> 80 PRODUCT1  +  34 PRODUCT2  +  23 PRODUCT3  +  16 PRODUCT4

     What are your constraints?

>BUDGET 35PRODUCT1 + 64PRODUCT2 + 82PRODUCT3 + 42PRODUCT4 < 80005
>MATERIAL  25PRODUCT1 + 50PRODUCT2 + 50PRODUCT3 + 100PRODUCT4 < 450000
>STAFF.TIME  1PRODUCT1 + 2PRODUCT2 + 4PRODUCT3 + 5PRODUCT4 < 20000
>MACHINE.TIME  5PRODUCT1 + 14PRODUCT2 + 2PRODUCT3 + 12PRODUCT4 < 120000

     Enter the minimum and maximum amounts to be produced:

> PRODUCT1     0     800
> PRODUCT2   100     200
> PRODUCT3   350     500
> PRODUCT4   700    1000

     YOUR SOLUTION IS AS FOLLOWS:

          *********************************************
          *                                           *
          *  PRODUCTION PLAN FOR STATION 3 IN MARCH   *
          *                                           *
          *********************************************

   PROFIT FOR OPTIMUM SOLUTION:  58090 DOLLARS

   LEVEL OF PRODUCTION:
            443 PRODUCT1                350 PRODUCT3
            100 PRODUCT2                700 PRODUCT4

   UNUSED RESOURCES:
                 THIS CONSTRAINT  * HAD THIS LEFT OVER
                   2. MATERIAL          346425 POUNDS
                   3. STAFF.TIME         14457 MINUTES
                   4. MACHINE.TIME      100985 MINUTES

   POSSIBLE IMPROVEMENTS:
         AN INCREASE IN THIS  * MAY BE EXPECTED TO IMPROVE
       CONSTRAINT BY ONE UNIT * THE PROFIT BY THIS AMOUNT
          1. BUDGET                 2.29 DOLLARS
```

EXHIBIT 2–9 A DSS for Production Planning.

```
     You may enter:

     RESOURCES  - To  estimate  the resources needed for  a  specified
                  workload
     WORKLOAD   - To  predict how much can be done with  a  specified
                  amount of resources
     RATES      - To change the rate at which resources are  consumed
                  by each organization
     END        - To end this session


> resources


     On each line identify how many of each product, task, or projects
     you plan to work on next year (i.e, 500 publications):


> 220  audits
> 8000   inspections
> 40  site.reviews
> 12000 loan.applications
> 12  accident.investigations
> 16000  public.inquiries




     TO  SATISFY THIS LEVEL OF WORK WILL REQUIRE THE FOLLOWING AMOUNTS
     OF RESOURCES:
```

DIVISION	STAFF YEARS	FUNDS (millions) SALARIES	EXPENSES	SUPPORT CONTRACTS	TRAVEL (trips)	COMPUTER TIME (access-hours)
TRAVEL	8	.16	3.1	4	12	504
ACCOUNTING	32	.9	.26	8	17	763
TRANSPORTATION	16	.2	.9	3	0	44
ADMINISTRATION	21	.42	.12	18	67	1221
FACILITIES	14	.18	4.5	22	6	183
PUBLIC.AFFAIRS	47	1.7	1.4	0	23	1628
OPERATIONS	102	4.6	1.8	37	306	7334

EXHIBIT 2–10 A DSS for Projecting an Organization's Resource Requirements.

AREAS OF APPLICATION

We have noted that DSS are applied in areas where the complexity of the process exceeds human abilities to visualize the affects and implications of a decision. Such problems are typically characterized by three conditions:

1. The operation or system consists of many interdependent activities.
2. There are a multitude of complex factors and issues that influence the system's behavior.
3. The relationship between the parts of the system and factors that affects its performance are extremely complicated and intertwined (like trying to untangle a snarled fishing line, loosen one end and the mess becomes tangled somewhere else).

Such complications are experienced in virtually every type of business activity and operation carried out in the commercial, military and public service sectors. We can group DSS applications by the management function they support and look at a few examples of how they are used.

Operations Planning and Management

In carrying out the routine affairs of an organization, there are a variety of activities that warrant decision support. DSS have been used to help organizations plan and manage such diverse operations as:

- Product and material distribution.
- Production planning and control.
- Personnel and workshift scheduling.
- Inventory management.
- Logistics planning.
- Petroleum and natural gas processing and distribution.
- Project management and control.
- Vehicle routing and disbursing.
- Electric power distribution.
- Waterway management.
- Blood storage and distribution planning.

Resource Allocation and Acquisition

One of the major functions of management is to determine the most effective allocation of an organization's scarce resources. It requires that the decision maker trade-off between various programs and operations within his preview and arrive at the best balance of limited resources. Areas where DSS have been used effectively to support such decisions include:

- Financial planning and analysis.
- Portfolio planning.
- Workforce allocation.
- Personnel assignment selection.
- Budgetary planning.
- Mining and oil exploration planning.
- Target assignment and selection during military operations.
- Patient bed and operating room assignments.

Workload and Demand Forecasting

Before resources can be allocated to the appropriate activities, an estimation of the expected workload and demand to be placed on the organization is in order. The quantitative support provided by a DSS can be valuable in forecasting demands in the following areas:

- Identifying near term and long range staffing requirements.
- Projecting the potential market response and customer demands.
- Determining the maintenance workload in vehicle and equipment servicing facilities.
- Estimating the material and budget requirements for a manufacturing process.
- Projecting the stock replenishment requirements for long lead time systems.

Process Evaluation and Analysis

Because of the dynamic nature of modern organizations, decision makers frequently have to make adjustments in the policies and tactics governing the operation. The effective manager evaluates the effects of proposed policies and procedures before they are implemented. When the processes in question are structurally diverse and complex in scope, DSS provides a valuable tool for analyzing the situation before decisions are enacted. Examples of successful applications in this area include:

- Hazard evaluation in the toxic chemical and nuclear industry.
- Organizational analysis to assess the performance and implications of various policies (delegation of authority, structural layout, division support and interaction. etc.).
- Force analysis to evaluate the effectiveness of force makeup, system performance and command, and control policies under different combat scenarios.
- Intelligence analysis to assess the value, validity and need for intelligence information.
- Vulnerability assessments to estimate an organization's accessibility to fraud, waste, abuse, espionage, catastrophic damage, and so forth.
- Data disclosure analysis to determine the sensitivity of confidential information to misuse and intrusion.
- Analyzing the appropriate strategies for consolidating large scale field structures for drug enforcement, agricultural service offices, nationwide logistic systems, and so on.

This list summarizes but a few of the many areas where decision support can and has been successfully applied. Chapters 4, 5, 9, 10 and 12 provide samples of actual applications.

EXERCISES

1. Based on the discussion in Chapter 2, which of the following information systems could be classified as a DSS:
   a. A system used to process and transfer funding transactions at a banking institution.
   b. A system that schedules vehicle maintenance based on task duration and the available resources (personnel, facility space, working hours, etc.).
   c. A system used to predict customer demands for heating oil from historical records

of consumption rates and the average daily temperature, and that assigns daily deliveries based on truck capacity, on-hand inventories, and available manpower.

d. An office system that processes correspondence, maintains an inventory of documents, keeps track of executive schedules, and helps to automate other administrative routines.

e. A system that helps an organization select investments based on interest rates, return rates, investment periods, etc.

f. A system that maintains customer reservations for products or services (airlines, car rentals, etc.).

g. A system that helps an organization to determine the best routes for shipping products from storage to customer.

h. A system that projects retail sales by region and by product line for a seasonal product (swimwear, winter clothes, etc.) to evaluate positive or negative trends, promotional campaigns, and so forth.

i. A system that helps an organization analyze the affects of funding allocations (budget cuts, staff reductions, etc.).

j. A system that analyzes the affects of proposed policies (inspection frequency, safety programs, manager training, etc.) on the accident incidence rate and hazards to employees in a large organization.

2. Consider the statement:

> "A DSS does not reduce the workload of a manager but increases it. Managers must deal with this reality up front otherwise the application is doomed to failure."

Answer the following questions:

a. How can a system designed to support the decision process increase the manager's workload?

b. In situations where it applies, is this a shortcoming or fallacy in trying to support complex decisions with automation (explain your answer)?

c. In what situations would this be more likely, and in what type of applications would you not expect it to occur?

3. At the end of Chapter 2 we grouped various applications under the management function they supported (operations planning and management, resource allocation and acquisition, workload and demand forecasting, and process evaluation and analysis). For those systems you classified as a DSS in Exercise 1, note which management function they support.

REFERENCES AND SUGGESTED READING

1. Keen, P., "Value Analysis: Justifying Decision Support Systems," *MIS Quarterly,* March, 1981.
2. Keen, P. and M. Morton, *Decision Support Systems: An Organizational Perspective,* Reading, Mass.: Addison-Wesley Publishing, 1977.

3. Keen, P. and G. Wagner, "DSS: An Executive Mind-Support System," *Datamation,* November, 1979.

4. Hogan, J. and H. Watson, "Management's Role in the Approval and Administration of Decision Support Systems," *MIS Quarterly,* June, 1983.

5. Klein, R., "Computer-Based Financial Modeling," *Journal of Systems Management,* May, 1982.

6. Naylor, T., "Decision Support Systems or Whatever Happened to MIS," *INTERFACES,* August, 1979.

7. Sprague, R. and E. Carlson, *Building Effective Decision Support Systems,* Englewood Cliffs, N.J.: Prentice-Hall, 1982.

8. Stohr, E., W., Reitman and M. Ginzberg (Ed.), *Decision Support Systems, New York, N.Y.:* North Holland, 1982.

9. Vazonyi, A., "Decision Support Systems, Computer Literacy and Electronic Models," *INTERFACES,* February, 1982.

10. Wagner, G., "Optimizing Decision Support Systems," *Datamation,* May, 1980.

11. Wagner, G., "Decision Support Systems: The Real Substance," *INTERFACES,* April, 1981.

12. Watson, H. and M. Hill, "Decision Support Systems or What Didn't Happen with MIS," *INTERFACES,* October, 1983.

13. Wynne, B., "Decision Support Systems—A New Plateau of Opportunity or More Emperor's Clothing?" *INTERFACES,* February, 1982.

14. Wysong, E., "MIS in Perspective," *Journal of Systems Management,* October, 1985.

3

Decisions and Their Environment

Recall that the basic role of decision support is to provide an effective mechanism for condensing the complication of the world in such a manner that the manager can exercise his corporate insight. Decision support acts as a focal pont (Exhibit 3–1) that concentrates the experience of the decision maker onto the complexities of the real world, resulting in "better" solutions to our problems. Thus decision-support applications can be partitioned into three segments: the human element, automation, and the problem or physical system in question (an organization, market base, logistic system, battle-front, etc.).

Our goal is so establish guidelines and principles that can help to identify the best combination and matchup between decision-automation-problems in each setting. Subsequent discussions center on the "automation" side. Because understanding the decision process is so essential to designing a system to support the process, this chapter examines the various aspects of the decision-making environment, namely: What makes up a decision, what factors and conditions influence the process, and what governs the degree of difficulty in each case? Those interested in a more focused and theoretical discussion of the decision-making process should consult the suggested literature at the end of the chapter [1,2,3,4].

DECISION-MAKING PHILOSOPHIES

Each individual approaches a problem differently depending on his background, surrounding environment, experience and inherent psychological conditioning. There are

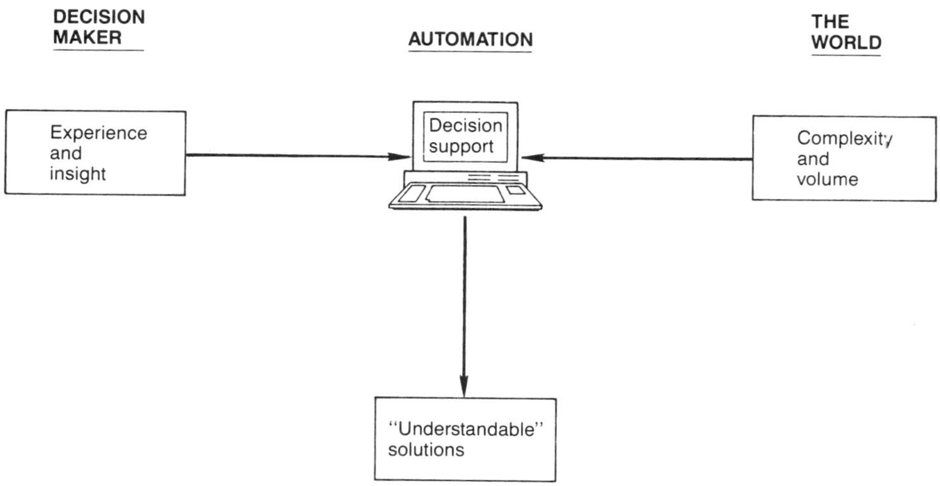

EXHIBIT 3–1 Decision Support as a Focal Point.

a number of models that describe the philosophy or style with which decisions are made. Three of the more classical models can be summarized as follows:

Rational Model

The rational approach is characterized by viewing decision making as a very structured process where an individual or group reduces a problem into a set of measurable factors (cost, production rates, market share, consumption rates, etc.) that influence the outcome. The relative merit of each outcome can be determined quantitatively and the ultimate goal is to select the alternative that results in the most profitable or productive outcome.

Organizational Model

In the organizational model the decision maker is more concerned with following established policies or guidelines than with evaluating all of the relevant factors in a quantitative fashion. The decision maker behaves on a personal level to take actions and make choices that preserve his position or posture in the organization. The individual avoids uncertainty and follows a "safe" path in reaching decisions.

Political Model

The political setting is one where decisions result from group interactions with each individual exercising his persuasive abilities or organizational power to satisfy subjective goals. Under this process there is no "absolutely" best decision. The goal is to select the alternative that provides the most "acceptable solution."

In the real world, decisions are reached not by any single philosophy but often by a combination. In situations where a *rational* approach is reasonable and is used, the quantitative support afforded by a DSS provides the greatest opportunity for benefit and success from a decision support application. Although *organizational* and *political* conditions must be accounted for and combined with the quantitative insights provided by a DSS, decisions that are dominated by these two styles are not as well suited to obtainig benefit from automated support as the *rational* process. Reference [6] provides further discussion as to the implications of each decision-making philosophy on the development and successful implementation of a DSS.

DECISION-MAKING—WHAT IS IT?

It is appropriate that we now concern ourselves with "just what is the decision-making process" and what steps do we go through each time a choice must be made between two or more competing alternatives. Whether it is personal, recreational, or business related, decision making plays a vital role in our day-to-day affairs. Most of the decisions we make are done without any awareness that our mental process is actually going through a "give and take" battle. Should I buy brand A or brand B? Which job offers the best opportunity? Which candidate will make the best president (or cause the least damage)? In each case we evaluate our possible choices and select that which "appears" to provide the best alternative.

Consider five examples that range from being relatively simple to fairly difficult:

- ☐ The child that must decide which piece of cake will make him the victor in a "sibling war."
- ☐ The shopper trying to determine which automobile is the best buy.
- ☐ The program manager toiling over how this year's limited resources should be allocated across the organization.
- ☐ The field officer struggling with the best tactical deployment of his forces.
- ☐ The legislative branch battling over whether or not a bill should be passed.

Although the scope and difficulty varies in each case, the underlying process by which a decision is reached is essentially the same (Exhibit 3–2). In each situation the decision maker must:

- ☐ Identify (or formulate) what alternatives are available to choose from.
- ☐ Examine all the factors that influence the value, risk or acceptability of each candidate proposal.
- ☐ Evaluate and analyze each alternative in terms of some set of objectives or requirements.
- ☐ Compare and rank the possible outcomes.
- ☐ Select the alternative that provides the best, or most acceptable, course of action.

Consider the car buyer who wants to purchase a vehicle that is attractive, reasonably priced, gas conscious, provides adequate power, reliable, easy to maintain, and so forth.

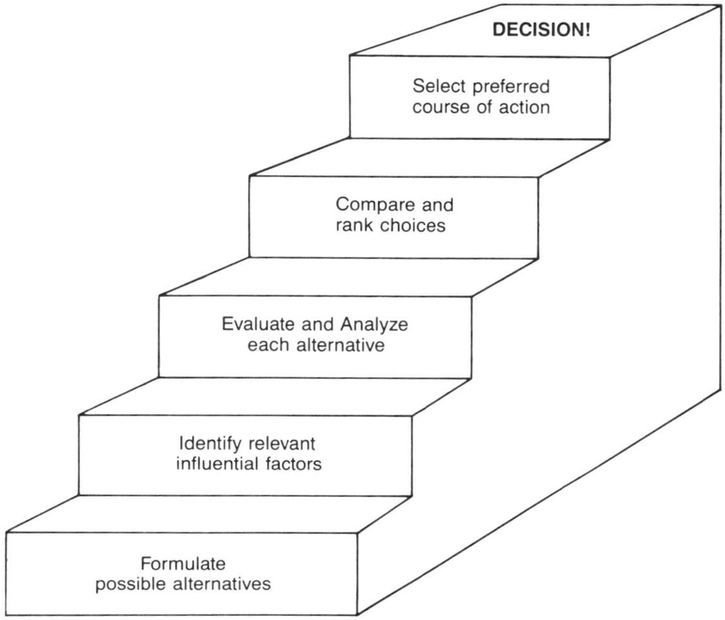

EXHIBIT 3–2 Steps in the Decision Process.

In addition to these objectives the buyer must take into account such factors as loan rates, available funds, consumer reports, spouse inputs, distance to the dealer for future service calls, service reputation, delivery time (that is, in stock or eight weeks), and so on. Each car model is examined and evaluated to weed out those candidates that are unacceptable from those that are "in the running." Ideally, the survivors are ranked and the best overall vehicle is purchased (unfortunately the individual typically falls into a "feeding frenzy" and loses out to buyer impulse).

The program manager goes through a similar but somewhat more involved process in trying to develop the most reasonable annual operating plan. The intention is to allocate the organization's limited resources in a manner that will meet most, if not all, milestones, minimize overall cost, and reduce the amount of personnel shifts. Beyond these management objectives, the program manager must consider such relevant factors as satisfying preferred customers, utilizing in-house skills and expertise, conforming to executive policies (affirmative action, priority programs. . .), what operations are most economical, and similar concerns. Various allocations will be evaluated and those violating the minimum requirements will be discarded. The remaining possibilities will then be reviewed to find out which assignment of funds, personnel and material will result in the best end-of-year accomplishments.

In the case of the field officer, the ultimate goal is to inflict the maximum damage on the enemy while reducing the risk of loss to his forces. The field officer must analyze how various deployment tactics will stack up against the conjectured tactics of his opponent. In each scenario a variety of factors must be taken into account including:

geographic advantages, exchange ratios of various weapon systems under different conditions (terrain, weather, night/day), logistics considerations (supply channels, stock levels, . . .), and so forth. After all scenarios have been evaluated, that which provides the greatest chance of success (survival) will be selected.

Note that in each situation the decision maker goes through virtually the same steps. He identifies pertinent objectives and influential factors, evaluates possible choices in terms of these requirements, compares the surviving candidates, and finally selects the alternative that provides the best overall outcome in terms of the objectives. What is it then that distinguishes one decision from another?

Observe that in our examples there are three basic areas where the process differs, namely: the quantity and complexity of factors affecting the decision; the relative gain or loss that can result from the proper or incorrect choice; and the likelihood or risk associated with making the best decision. In general, as the problem complexity, potential gain, and risk increases, the evaluation procedure becomes more complicated. But at what point does the procedure become so involved that the human thought process is overwhelmed and automated support becomes necessary? To answer this question we must first understand the range of factors that constitute the decision-making environment, then examine the various facets of the evaluation procedure.

THE DECISION-MAKING ARENA

Decisions result from a give and take "tug of war" process. The decision maker performs at the center of an arena struggling to find the most acceptable trade-off and balance between a barrage of competing (and often conflicting) requirements. The various factors and issues that play a part in the decision process will naturally vary from case to case. In general, however, these considerations comprise five layers in the "Decision Making Arena" (Exhibit 3–3).

Operational Factors

There is an abundance of conditions that *directly* affect the output and performance of an operation. Operational requirements deal with the fundamental inputs and functioning mechanism of the organization. Examples include:

- ☐ Resource limitations that restrict the operation (budget constraints, workforce availability, facility capacities, skills and expertise).
- ☐ Physical conditions that influence the process (plant layout, distribution routes, physical design).
- ☐ Functional parameters that affect performance (production rates, supplier reliability, product quality, employee safety, failure rates, economics of scale).

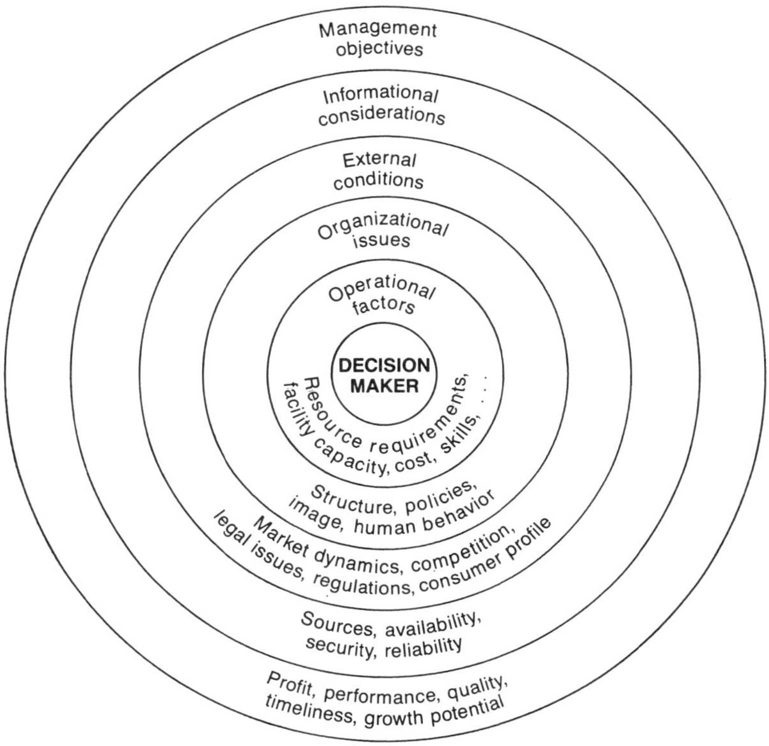

EXHIBIT 3–3 The Decision-Making Arena.

Organizational Factors

Operational requirements are generally easy to understand and visualize. Above the operational level, however, is another set of factors more difficult to grasp and quantify. Whether we are dealing with commercial activities, financial institutions, public service facilities, or the military sector: there are organizational issues that must be taken into account. Organizational requirements are crucial to the successful outcome of virtually every decision and can be grouped into the following categories (Exhibit 3–4).

- ☐ *Policies.* Procedural rules and mandates that must be complied with, such as:
  - Approval authority (procurement, contracts, payments, corporate agreements).
  - Staffing philosophies (skill mix, temporary, unions).
  - Executive directives (product expansions, market dominancy, research priorities).
- ☐ *Structure.* Issues dealing with the functional management and operational philosophy of the organization, namely:

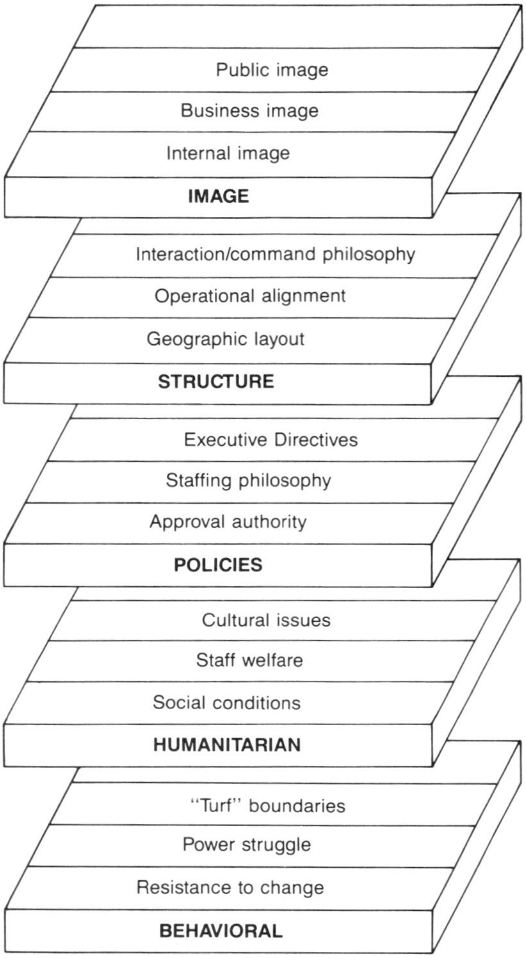

EXHIBIT 3–4 Layers of Organizational Factors.

- Geographic layout (region, state, etc.).
- Operational alignment (by market or product line, by function [engineering, R&D, service, administration], etc.).
- Interaction/Command philosophy (centralized, matrix, subsidiary, autonomy).

☐ *Image.* Impressions conveyed by the actions of the organization, such as:
- Public image (ethics, concern for the public,. . .).
- Business image (customer satisfaction, product backing, financial credibility).
- Internal image (management competency, decision consistency, concern for personnel).

☐ *Humanitarian.* Provisions and concerns dealing with human welfare, as in:
- Social conditions (area development, environmental impact).

- Staff welfare (morale, career development, job satisfaction).
- Cultural issues (affirmative action, EEO, job corp involvement).

☐ *Behaviorial.* Motivational factors dealing with human nature, such as:
- Resistance to change.
- "Turf" boundaries.
- Power struggles.

To illustrate, consider the program manager who must decide how resources will be allotted and what operations will be cut back. He must take into account the policies of the organization toward use of temporaries, maintaining certain skill levels, and guidelines toward market growth areas. He must also be concerned with how units within the organization depend upon one another and what effect cuts in one area will have in another, how will customers perceive cuts in selected functions (service, customer support, etc.), possible repercussions from union forces, will special cultural groups be affected unfairly, and so on.

External Factors

Up to this point all of the conditions and issues discussed have been more or less within the control of management. For example, if the decision maker wishes not to be confined by the productive capacity of his factory, new facilities can be procured or built; if the current field structure of a large organization has proliferated to a point where it is inefficient and unmanageable, then a policy of decentralization can be implemented; if management feels that the public image of the corporation has gone down hill and will impede upcoming efforts to expand into new markets, a campaign can be undertaken to rebuild the corporate image; and so forth. There is, however, a layer of considerations that is beyond management control which equates to "acts of god" that can be adjusted to but not changed. External factors (Exhibit 3–5) are "givens" that the decision maker must take into account in a passive sense. Examples include the following:

☐ *Legal.* Laws and regulations that must be conformed to, such as:
- Labor (age, work week, overtime).
- Hiring (union, affirmative action, quotas, . . .).
- Worker environment (noise level, safety, OSHA, . . .).
- Functioning principles (anti-trust laws, price fixing, kickbacks, foreign sales, . . .).

☐ *Economics.* Financial considerations that include:
- Funding conditions (interest rates, investor or market interest, supply of external capital).
- Regulated charges (shipping rates, minimum wage, severance/unemployment compensation, . . .).
- Taxing procedures (deductibles, incentives, credits).

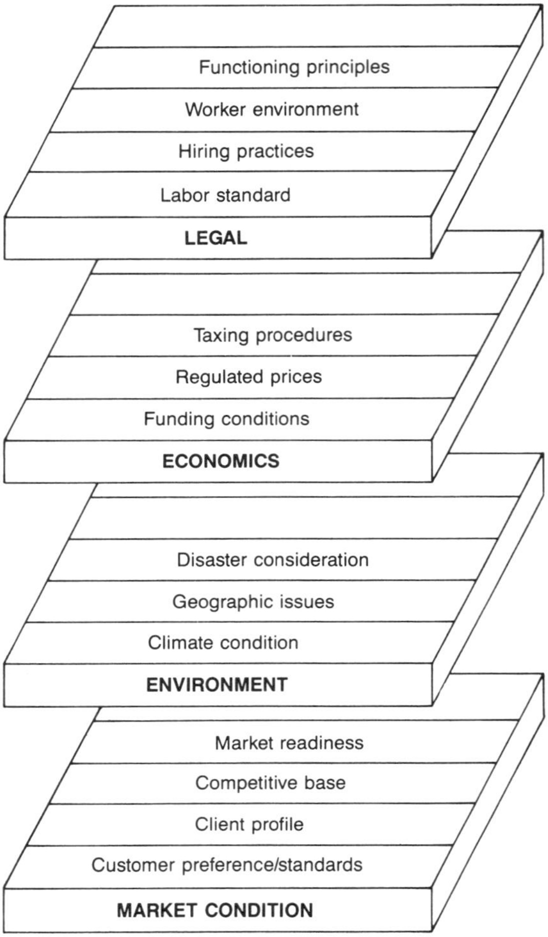

EXHIBIT 3–5 Layers of External Factors.

- ☐ *Environment.* Environmental conditions that impact the operation, such as:
  - Climate (weather, humidity, temperature).
  - Geographics (terrain, abrasive/dust atmosphere, accessibility, labor pool, existing supply/shipping facilities).
  - Disaster potential (floods, forest fires, severe storms).
- ☐ *Market Conditions.* Factors and forces influencing the demand or workload for an organization. Examples would include:
  - Competitive base (market share).
  - Market readiness (that is, requires development in other technologies, consumer preparedness [for example, like the introduction of an optical recording disk to the mass public for videos], etc.).

- Customer profile (client expertise, potential pool of consumers, customer geographic dispersion, etc.).
- Customer preference (system formats, protocols, market dominance [for example, IBM client base]; existing customer standards, etc.).

Consider the case where corporate executives have several options as to where a plant should be located for a new line of products. Potential sites include the West Coast, New England, Puerto Rico, Phillipines and India. The evaluation process must examine each alternative in terms of a variety of external issues, including:

- Tax credits for domestic development.
- Tariff costs and quotas.
- Labor rates (salary, unemployment, benefits) in that area.
- Availability of required skills mix.
- The existence of established transportation facilities and supply lines.
- The effect of prevailing climatic conditions on the quality of the production process.
- The potential for disruptive events in each area (political unrest, union strikes, etc.).

Informational Factors

The value and quality of a decision will depend significantly on the manager's knowledge and understanding of the various aspects of the "decision-making arena." The ability to visualize the role each factor plays in the final outcome will be predicated on the information available to support the evaluation. In other words, information provides the link between the decision maker, automation, and the world at each layer of influential factors. Several conditions can affect how information is used in reaching the decision (Exhibit 3–6), for example:

☐ *Availability.* How accessible is the data in terms of:
  - Sources and channels (internal, external).
  - Security/confidentiality issues.
  - Transfer requirements (computer to computer, compatibility, formats, protocol).
  - Media information (document, microfiche, punched deck, floppy disk, tape).

☐ *Reliability.* How confident can the manager be as to the data's:
  - Accuracy (human error, transfer noise).
  - Currency (two years old versus sampled last week).
  - Validity (statistical size and procedures).

☐ *Resolution.* How detailed is the information? As with the "Three bears" nursery rhyme, is the data:
  - Too elaborate.
  - Too fragmented.

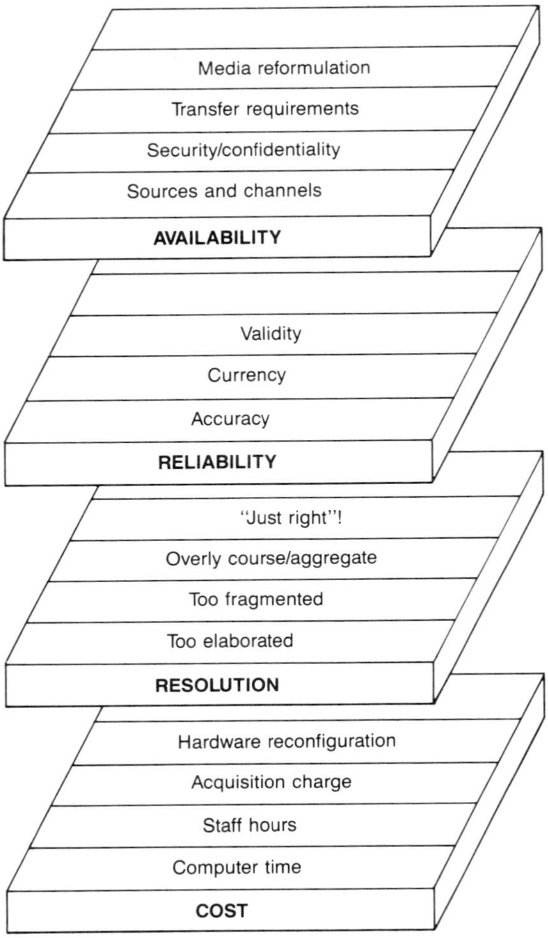

EXHIBIT 3–6 Layers of Informational Factors.

- Overly course or aggregate.
- Aligns well with the required inputs of the application (Just right!).

☐ *Cost*[1] What will it take to acquire, prepare, verify, and maintain the information in relationship to:

- Computer time.
- Staff hours.
- Acquisition price.
- Hardware reconfiguration requirements.

[1]Observe that the cost of information will be a function of each of the other factors (availability, reliability, and resolution). For example, external sources typically cost more and staff time increases if extensive verification and reprocessing is required.

Consider trying to decide whether or not an organization should expand into a new market. The decision maker will need to estimate whether the expected demand is large enough to warrant initial expenditures and eventual overhead costs. The risk of making such a decision will depend upon what data is available (current market share, customer base, etc.), the accuracy of the information (what was the sample population, does it still reflect today's trends), and what will it cost to upgrade the data to the level of detail and currency sufficient for this decision.

Management Objectives

Management objectives are the dominant forces governing the directions we search in looking for the best solution. They identify what is or is not to be accomplished in accordance with the various factors and issues pertinent to each situation. Typical objectives include: improve productivity, minimize organizational disruption and change, gain a larger share of the market, reduce cost, improve quality control, and so on.

The first step on the road to effective decision making is to define what objectives are relevant to the particular problem. The ease with which objectives are formulated (Exhibit 3–7), and how significant their contribution is to the final result, depend upon several characteristics (Exhibit 3–8), namely: their motivation, area of influence, degree of resolution, and relative clarity. The management objectives for a particular application may exhibit different characteristics in terms of their:

- ☐ *Motivation.* What is the purpose behind this action, for example:
  - Economics (minimize cost, maximize profits, reduce waste).
  - Performance (improve response time, increase productivity, reduce delays).
  - Quality (decrease rejection rates, improve customer satisfaction and service).
  - Survival (satisfy stockholders, improve business image).
- ☐ *Area of Influence.* At what level are the objectives targeted, for example:
  - Operational conditions (worker safety, reliability, production efficiency).
  - Organizational impact (better communication, structural consolidation, improved management control, reduced administrative services).
  - External issues (maximize return to shareholders, improve public image, minimize the chance of disruption from disasters, improve market share).
- ☐ *Resolution.* How quantitative is the scale of measurement, as in:
  - Numerical (minimize cost, decrease response time).
  - Subjective (improve customer satisfaction).
- ☐ *Clarity.* How easy is it to identify, understand and define an objective, for example:
  - Clear (minimize new hiring).
  - Fuzzy (follow "good" marketing strategies, support staff development).
  - Hidden (ulterior motives, power gains, visibility).

To illustrate how each characteristic affects the formulation and importance of an objective, consider a simple and a relatively difficult example:

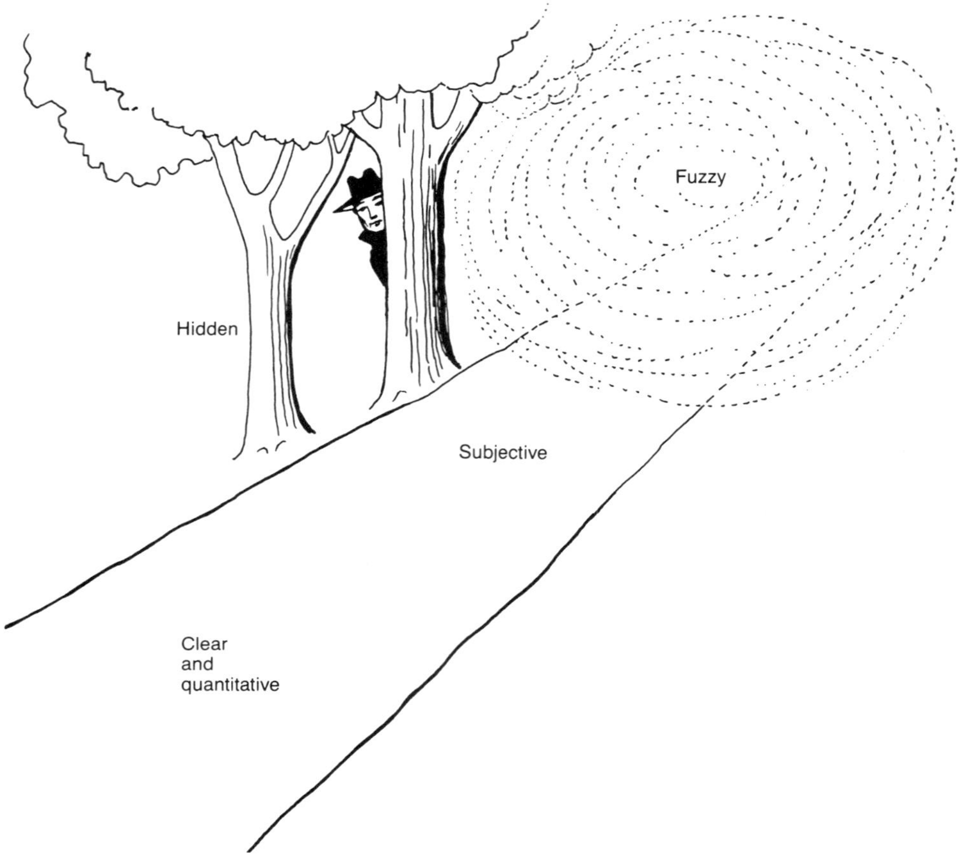

EXHIBIT 3–7 Objectives and their Formulation.

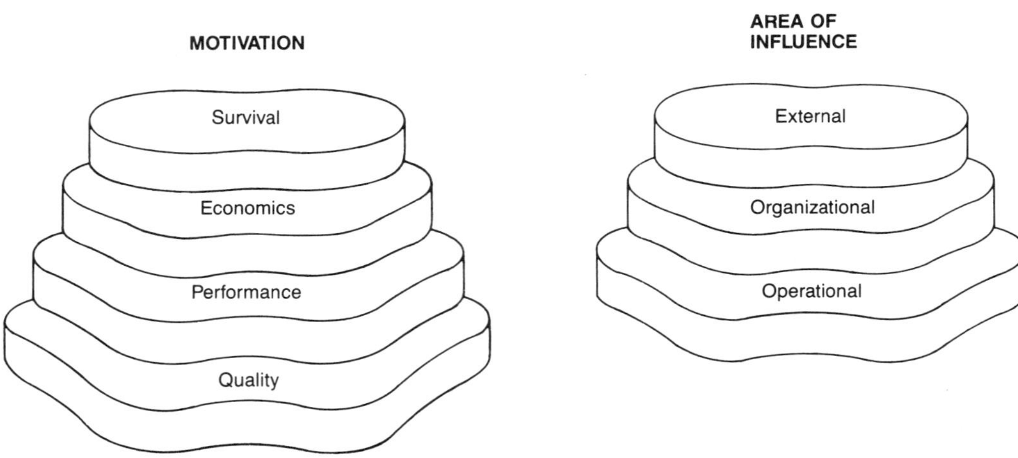

EXHIBIT 3–8 Objective Plateaus and their Importance.

1. *Improve quality control of a manufacturing process.* This objective deals with the "quality" of the operation. It can be easily formulated as a quantitative value (failures per 1,000 units produced). Its motivation is clear and to the point (minimize rejection rate).
2. *Improve our business image.* The intent of this objective is frequently one of survival and depends on a variety of external issues (competitor's activities, public perceptions, venture capitalists, etc.). It is very subjective, difficult to formulate and unclear as to what constitutes a better image. There may even be "hidden" motives (preparation for corporate takeover). Nonetheless, it is of significant importance to the future stability of the organization.

EVALUATING THE ALTERNATIVES

Assuming management can identify the variety of factors influencing the outcome of a decision, the question remains "what do we do with them?" This brings us to a point in the decision process where each alternative is analyzed and evaluated. The purpose of evaluation is to consider each relevant factor in its proper perspective, disregard those alternatives that do not satisfy the minimum requirements, then to rank the survivors according to their relative importance in terms of each management objective. Just how complicated and difficult the evaluation process is depends on three attributes of the problem in question: the variety and quantity of influential factors, the characteristics of the objectives (quantitative, subjective, clear, fuzzy), and the underlying structure and complexity of the situation being analyzed.

The evaluation procedures can be broken into three parts (Exhibit 3–9): separation of alternatives, analysis of their comparative value and attributes, and finally the ranking and selection process. The initial step is basically a weeding process. Candidates are separated into two groups—those that meet the minimum criteria and those that are unacceptable and can be disregarded from further consideration. Each acceptable alternative is then analyzed (either subjectively or using an analytical procedure) in terms of several criteria. These criteria can be grouped into three categories:

- ☐ *Economic.* Those characteristics of a solution that depict its economic status (profit, cost, rate of return, breakeven point, etc.).
- ☐ *Performance.* Conditions that describe the quality and level of outcome (productivity, response time, customer satisfaction, etc.).
- ☐ *Risk.* The likelihood that an alternative will actually result in the expected outcome (customer acceptance, political support, etc.)

Once each alternative has been analyzed, the manager is ready to score the candidates. A ranking scheme must be used that gives the proper weight to each criteria (economics, performance, risk) and places the alternatives in their proper relative order. The decision maker then exercises his experience and insight to pick that course of action which best meets "all" of the management objectives.

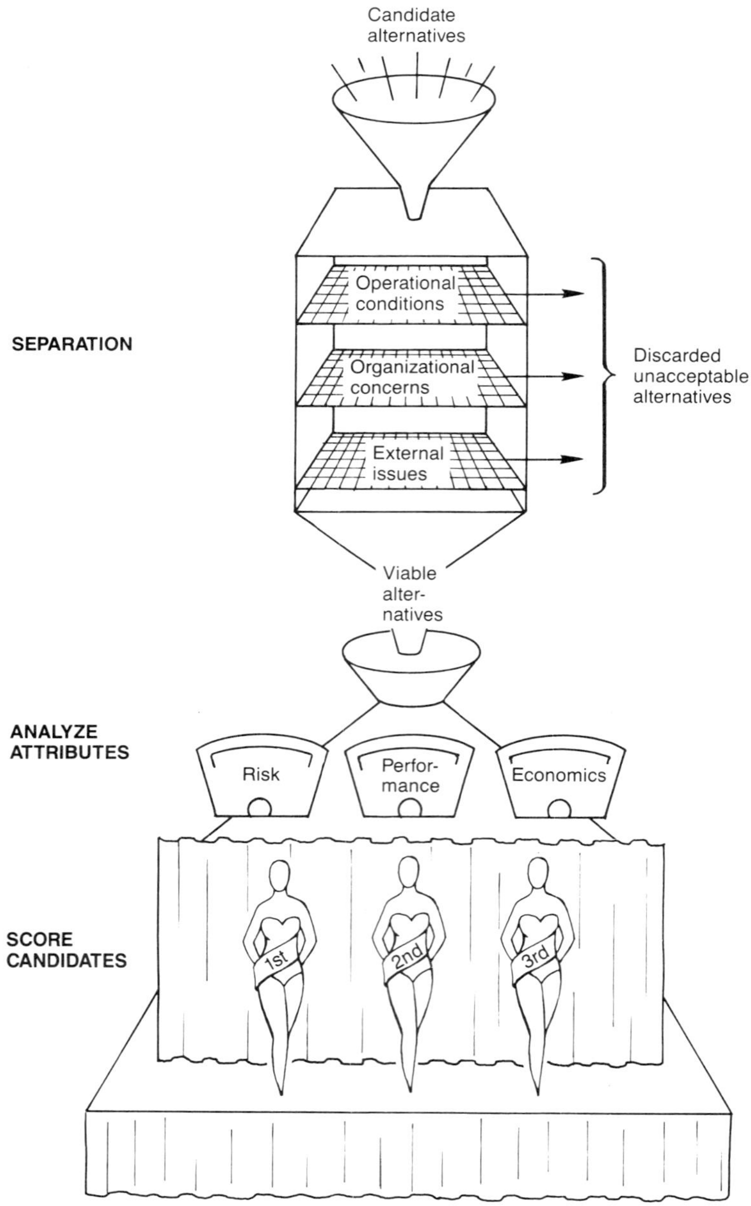

EXHIBIT 3–9 The Evaluation Procedure.

DEGREE OF DIFFICULTY

Obviously, all the decisions that managers face are not of the same caliber. Some are relatively easy, while others are extremely difficult. For example, in many cases the evaluation process can be condensed and only a simple procedure is required to score each candidate (that is, comparing the purchase price of several suppliers). Other situations require an elaborate procedure or exotic technique to analyze and rank the acceptable alternatives. The decision maker may need to score and rank a multitude of diverse objectives with different scales of measurement (cost, staffing, production rate, etc.). For larger problems the manager has to decide between millions of possible choices, each placing different demands on the limited amount of available resources (a nationwide manufacturing process, funds transfer for banking institutions, etc.).

What is it that causes one decision to be more difficult than another? Recall the examples at the beginning of this chapter. In each case the quantity and type of factors that influence the decision are quite different:

- In deciding which piece of cake should be taken, the sibling might consider a few simple factors such as which piece is larger or which has more icing. The objective is clear and to the point: maximize personal gain while inflicting the greatest loss to the sibling.
- For the prospective car buyer the choices are slightly more difficult. For each vehicle the buyer must consider cost, style, size, gas mileage, accessories, and comfort. The available information sources include buyer guides, EPA ratings, the spouses "wish" list, and so forth. The decision is not as clear as that of the sibling. The objectives are more complicated and compete with one another (style versus cost, gas mileage versus size, accessories versus price). The consequences of a bad decision are also more severe (years of discomfort, maintenance headaches, violent debates with the spouse, etc.).
- The case of the military commander is even more involved and the repercussions from the wrong choice more severe. The underlying structure and relationship between the conditions that influence the success of a military confrontation are exceedingly complex. The final outcome will depend on the combat effectiveness of each weapon system (kill ratios), terrain and weather conditions, logistics factors (stock levels, replenishment rates, supply route survival), the tactics used by one force in response to those exercised by the opponent, troop efficiency, and so on. An incorrect decision can cause increased loss of life, a lost battle, strategic impact to other fronts, or even a lost campaign. Objectives are more involved and occur in stages: win the battle; if not local victory, then delay the enemy's withdrawal; or finally to minimize the amount of lost territory.

In each of these three examples, the burden of choosing the best course of action becomes increasingly more difficult. The "degree of difficulty" can be quantified in terms of four properties that are typically associated with each decision.

1. *Structural Complexity.* The structural composition of each problem defines the relationships and interactions between its parts and determines how these parts will behave under various conditions. The structural intricacy of a problem will strongly influence the decision maker's ability to mentally "joggle" and visualize what will happen under different circumstances. Imagine the complicated structure in a manufacturing process. The operation is comprised of production plants, storage facilities, and customer's sites, overlayed by an extensive network of shipping routes (air, rail, truck, seaway), each with its own set of properties (cost, capacity,. . .). Consider a second example where the complexity stems from the functional relationship between the factors influencing the decision. In planning and managing an organization's workforce, the decision maker must be able to visualize how the workforce will respond to a variety of policies and external forces such as: seasonal attrition, time lags in the hiring process, executive freezes, recruiting policy, etc. Predicting the expenditures and level of the workforce under such diverse conditions is a formidable task.

2. *Objectives.* The quantity and characteristics of the things we wish to accomplish will affect the difficulty of the decision process, for example:

- ☐ *Quantity.* It is much simpler to make a decision when the manager need only satisfy a single objective. As the number of objectives increases, the manager must contend with satisfying many initiatives, some of which compete with one another. Simply stated, it is much easier to toss and catch one ball then to try and juggle many at one time.
- ☐ *Scale Similarity.* In the real world management objectives are frequently measured in different scales. Consider the objectives of the enthusiastic car buyer (gas efficiency, cost, maintenance) all of which are measured differently (miles per gallon, dollars, time to repair). The difficulty arises from comparing how well one alternative stacks up against its competitors. The consumer must find a way to combine "apples and oranges" so that one choice (15 miles per gallon, $9,000, two hours mean repair time) can be compared to another (18 miles per gallon, $12,000, 1.5 hours mean repair time).
- ☐ *Resolution.* Quantitative objectives can be accounted for much more readily than those that must be assigned a subjective value (low, median, high; poor, fair, good). For example, comparing a vehicle's gas mileage (18 mpg versus 15 mpg) is simpler and more precise than a "feeling" about the esthetic value of a car's outward appearance (ugly, OK, "neat").

3. *Consequence and Risk.* The extent of gain (or loss) from the correct (or wrong) decision, along with the likelihood of things happening the way we expect, affects our willingness to take chances and risk the rewards (or repercussions). For example, the decision to invest a dollar in the lottery is relatively simple. Although the chance of winning is miniscule and the loss from not winning is insignificant, the gain would be monumental. At the other end of the spectrum, consider the decision as to whether or not to commit national resources to a survival program for nuclear attack (emergency preparedness, beam weaponry, interceptor devices). Although the probability of such an exchange is hopefully small, the loss from such a confrontation would be catastrophic. The likelihood that a preparedness program would improve the survival rate is also questionable. Most would agree that such a decision is a real "gut wrencher."

4. *Dynamics and Uncertainty.* Finding safe passage through unknown channels is much easier during daylight in calm seas than on a foggy night or in a pitching storm.

The uncertainty and dynamic nature of a problem has a similar effect in trying to make the right decision. If the effect of several factors is unknown or the environment changes rapidly, the decision maker must plot the best course in a sea of darkness. Consider the decision to pick the most economical product from an assortment of competitors based solely on price. The manager simply compares the prices at the time of the purchase and picks the one which is lowest. Choosing the best long term commitment of capital is not as direct (interest rates fluctuate month to month, the stability of a new market is unclear, etc.).

This chapter focused on establishing an appreciation for the complexities of the decision process. The intention was to create a basic foundation for moving to the next logical step: Understanding when, where and how quantitative automation can be used to directly support the decision maker.

EXERCISES

1. Consider the following problems and list some of the external, organizational, and operational factors that will influence the decision and note two or three that you feel will play the more prominent part in the decision process:
   a. Your organization has just suffered a major catastrophy. At one of your processing plants an explosion has just caused major damage to the plant and the surrounding community after undergoing a revision to the production process. You must decide whether to shut down other plants that have had similar revisions until the cause for the failure can be identified, or to continue their operation on the assumption the accident was an isolated incident.
   b. You have recently been offered the opportunity to jointly market a product developed by another company. The product technology is about two years old (for example, competition will have established a two year lead). Retained earnings are not sufficient to cover your share of the venture. What will your decision be based on?
   c. Due to austere times, your organization must incur a 10 percent cutback in expenses. You provide three major lines of products: consulting contracts you must win by competition, software products that have an estimated yearly sale of 4,000 units, and existing maintenance contracts on previous sales. You must decide how the cuts will be distributed across the three product lines and what expenses will be cut (salaries, marketing, facilities, etc.)
2. For the following situations, identify some of the possible management objectives (reduce operating cost, improve morale, etc.) and their characteristics (motivation, area of influence, resolution, clarity):
   a. The objectives behind maintaining and controlling inventory levels for high cost long lead time items (aircraft components, computers, etc.).
   b. The possible reasons for establishing decision-support capabilities within an organization.
   c. The reasons for expanding into a new market.

3. For each of the situations described in Exercise 1, identify some of the uncertainties (conditions the manager is unsure about) and the potential losses at risk from making the wrong choice (the repercussions that could result from selecting the wrong alternative).

4. Of the three classical decision models discussed in this chapter (rational, organizational, political) identify which applies in the following situations and explain why:
   a. Deciding on salary increases, layoff policies, benefit plans, etc., during contract negotiations between labor and management.
   b. A manager trying to decide how to assign his staff to various projects based on executive priorities, union rules, remaining contract funds, etc.
   c. Deciding which system to procure based on cost, performance, service, etc.

5. The decision maker can rarely guarantee that the choice he makes is the right one. He can, however, minimize his risks by taking each pertinent factor or issue into account. Select one of the classic ''decisions gone wrong'' from the last 100 years of events (that is, the space shuttle accident, Vietnam war, Watergate, etc.) and for each step of the decision process (Exhibit 3–2): identify the available options (alternatives); define the relevant factors at each layer of the decision-making arena (Exhibit 3–3); and finally state what flaw or error in the process resulted in the wrong choice being made.

REFERENCES AND SUGGESTED READING

1. Harrison, F., *The Managerial Decision Making Process,* Boston, Mass.: Houghton Mifflin Co., 1981.
2. Inbar, M., *Routine Decision Making Process, Sage Publications,* 1979.
3. Simon, H. and A. Newell, *Human Problem Solving,* Englewood Cliffs, N.J.: Prentice-Hall, 1972.
4. Ungson, G. and D. Braunstein, *Decision Making—An Interdisplinary Inquiry,* Boston, Mass.: Kent Publishing, Co., 1982.
5. Taylor, R., *Behavioral Decision Making,* Glenview, Ill.: Scott, Foresman & Company, 1984.
6. Taylor, S., "Organizational Decision Making and DSS Design," in Hannan. J. (ed.), *Systems Development Management,* New York, N.Y.: Auerbach Publishers Inc., 1982.

4

Decision Support: When, Where, and How It Applies

Difficult decisions are too frequently reached through "aerial extraction" techniques (that is, pulled out of thin air) with only minimal understanding about the implications. The day-to-day pressures of putting out "brush fires" and fighting the "wolves at the door" causes many decisions to be aimed at corrective rather than preventive actions. One of the major prerequisites to the successful application of decision support in such an environment is to understand when, where and how it is used. More often than not a computerized system will be implemented without an adequate appreciation for the true need or how it can really be applied to the decision process. This chapter examines the properties and features that must be incorporated within the DSS framework if automated support is to perform as an extension to the decision makers insight. Keep in mind that a DSS never replaces the human element but instead provides a tool to expand the manager's understanding of the problem in question.

WHEN IS IT RIGHT?

Automated support provides the decision maker with the extended ability to manipulate large volumes of data, perform complicated computations and to investigate a multitude of factors that would otherwise go unnoticed. Decision support enables the manager to quickly visualize and evaluate what is likely to happen under a variety of different scenarios. By broadening the base of alternatives that can be considered, decisions are less likely to result in surprises, unexpected repercussions and missed economic opportunities.

But when does decision support become practical? What characteristics make application of a DSS valid in one area and not in another? All management decisions do not warrant the expenditures and effort necessary to implement an automated system. In many cases the use of automation is more likely to result in overkill (like shooting a fly with a cannon). In other situations the problem is so fluid and dynamic that the only reasonable approach is to make "seat of the pants" decisions. It is important that the manager be able to distinguish between when a DSS will be be beneficial and when it will be nothing more than cosmetic.

Ideally, the choice to establish automated support is based on a thorough examination of those factors that will influence whether the application is practical and likely to achieve its original goals. The following represents some of the more prominant factors that must be taken into account when considering whether a DSS is appropriate to a particular setting.

Economics

Often the dominant consideration behind establishing decision support capabilities will be one of economics. Implementing a DSS within most organizations requires a significant expenditure of funds and staff time to develop (or procure), install, and operate the system. The total cost can range anywhere between $5,000 (for a microcomputer installation) and into the millions of dollars for a large corporate application. Offsetting this cost with demonstrable savings can be the determining factor to a GO/NO GO decision.

Consequence and Risk

Frequently the driving motivation that justifies a DSS is not financial return but instead a reduction in the risk associated with the decision process. Most decisions carry the inherent risk of negative consequences from choosing the wrong course of action (Chapter 3). The degree of loss can frequently warrant the necessary effort to create decision support capabilities. Consider the loss from law suits, a damaged public image, or a shutdown in operations because of a plant explosion in the chemical industry or contamination from a nuclear incident. Improving management's ability to perceive and prevent conditions leading up to such a disaster are often sufficient justification (if nothing more than to give the appearance that a logical and "caring" thought process was used). A similiar example pertains to the development of a flight scheduling system for a military training facility. Although the savings in staff time are important, the primary reason is to reduce the risk of schedule "foul ups." If pilots are authorized to fly without the proper qualifications, the repercussions can be devastating to the commanding officer in the event of an accident.

Organizational Considerations

Frequently, the characteristics of the organization will be a key factor in determining whether a DSS is likely to succeed. Conditions such as management philosophy (authoritative versus adaptive), organizational structure (line of command, channels of communications), properties of the user populace (reluctance, background, inherent learning ability), and so forth, can be a deterrent. Consider the experience of a consulting firm that was contracted to help a large metropolitan government improve their financial management activities. The effort was to be completed in two stages. First, procedures were to be established for gathering, processing, and communicating data throughout the organization. Once this was accomplished automated support was to be developed to help manage the process. At the conclusion of the first phase, however, the contractor elected not to accept the option for the second phase. The reason reported to the media was that current staffing skills and management qualifications were insufficient to even operate manual procedures, let alone a sophisticated computerized system. The organization would first have to establish the ability to understand and manage basic financial procedures before any further enhancements would be possible.

Problem Type

There is a broad spectrum of problems where management looks to automation for a helping hand. On one side, there are decisions where the application of computer support is absurd. At the other extreme, we have problems that are so complex and unstable that the only logical approach is to rely totally on the intuitive insights of the human mind. In the middle ground, however, is a wide band of applications where decision support can be used successfully. Decisions can be partitioned into five classes based on their relative degree of difficulty:

1. *Type 0.* A large percentage of decisions can be solved by a simple "one-two-three" approach. Such simplicity may result from:

- ☐ The mechanistic aspect or nonthought-provoking nature of the problem (reviewing financial transactions, maintaining inventory to predefined levels).
- ☐ The lack of any "acceptable" alternative (comply with federal regulations, economic survival through staff cutbacks).
- ☐ Singularity of the management objectives (accept the lowest cost bid from "equally" qualified vendors).
- ☐ The absence of complications or other influencial factors (terminating an employee who has been selling trade secrets).

The choice may not be easy to swallow but the process leading up to the final decision is a simple one. In such cases, the most logical approach is to use an "Intra Occular Impact" philosophy (the answer is so obvious it hits you between the eyes).

2. *Type A.* One level up from the Type 0 decisions is a set of problems where the major benefit to using automation is to "shine a little light" on a dimly lit area. The procedures for arriving at a decision are still relatively simple but the speed and thoroughness of computers can facilitate the process. The manager is fully capable of analyzing the situation by hand, however, automation helps to improve the efficiency with which an acceptable solution can be reached. (Band 1 of the "DSS Spectrum" in Chapter 2 corresponds to this type of problem). Examples include:

- ☐ Using computer graphics as a visual aid to evaluate the comparative benefits of several alternatives or to pick out trends and tendencies (changes in customer profiles/demands, growth plots, financial trends, cash flow predictions).
- ☐ Sorting through large volumes of data to identify sets that satisfy certain criteria (30 days past due, clients that use selected products in specific regions, accidents that caused damage greater then $500, etc.).
- ☐ Automating the repeated computation of values that represent simple decision points (return on investment period, breakeven point, economic reorder quantities, cash flows, spreadsheets, etc.)

3. *Type B.* The next category of problems requires that a "brute force" technique be used to find the best course of action. The number of objectives *and* possible choices make it difficult to understand which alternative provides the most favorable "all around" outcome. Such problems usually require some form of quantitative procedure to analyze the situation (Chapter 9) and fall into Band 2 of the DSS spectrum (Exhibit 2–1). Consider an academic institution that must decide which staffing policies provide the highest level of student instruction. The decision maker must trade-off between various conflicting objectives, such as:

- ☐ Minimize the budget.
- ☐ Maximize the ratio of instructors to students.
- ☐ Raise salaries to a competitive level that attracts a high calibre of instructors.
- ☐ Maintain a large number of full time instructors to insure program continuity.
- ☐ Use part-time transient instructors where possible to foster a continuing exchange of new techniques from the "real world."

Developing balanced staffing policies without the aid of computer support would be difficult. Management would be hard pressed to evaluate the relative importance of each objective and the cost of each proposed policy without computer assistance.

4. *Type C.* The next level of difficulty deals with decisions where the structural complexity and sheer size of the problem exceed management's abilities to visualize the process in action (Band 3 of Exhibit 2–1). Consider the requirement to establish military recruiting targets that will provide a force of 600,000 people five years in the future for some 300 disciplines. Training programs to create the necessary skill mix range from six months to three years. The problem is analogous to trying to organize an entangled "can of worms." The decision process must have the foresight to plan and schedule replacements so that they are ready to fill slots as other personnel leave (retirement, death, termination, etc.). Only through the use of computerized quantitative procedures can the manager expect to achieve an acceptable solution.

5. *Type D.* At the far end of the spectrum is a group of problems that are so overwhelmingly complex and dynamic that the only reasonable approach is a qualitative "hit and miss" proposition. Consider the subjective tug of war process where legislation passes through the political arena. Imagine a system that could quantitatively evaluate all of the factors and determine how the decision will impact society (economic growth, social repercussions, geographic implications, environmental issues, labor implications, technological progress, etc.). Attempting to model the intricate forces that influence our complex society would be like trying to handle a fire-breathing dragon with a plastic fly swatter. The multitude of influencial factors, extensive uncertainty, and continually changing structure severely limit any attempt to apply decision support in such an environment. Problems of this calibre are best left to the intuitive judgment of human beings.

WHERE IS DECISION SUPPORT USED?

Most literature focuses on a single aspect of the management process where decision support is applicable, namely: financial planning and analysis. Financial analysis deals with determining where expenditures are cost efficient, when an investment is appropriate, examining the financial condition of an organization, performing portfolio analysis, and similiar financial activities. Although financial planning does benefit significantly from DSS applications, decision support has become a valuable asset to virtually every management function at all levels of the decision process. The following survey illustrates several areas of successful application within each plateau of the decision process, specifically: operational, tactical and strategic decisions.

Operational Decisions

Administering the day-to-day affairs of an organization generally requires decisions of an operational nature. Such activities typically deal with coordinating and/or scheduling a complex set of tasks, or choosing the best assignment of limited resources across interrelated requirements. Decision support has been used successfully to support operational decisions in areas such as: logistics and material distribution [4,15,16,19,28]; personnel or task assignments [9]; vehicle dispatching and routing [3,5,11,25]; production scheduling [20,22]; and workload and personnel scheduling [13,30].

Tactical Decisions

Tactical decisions occur when a manager must choose the best tactics and methods for satisfying the near term objectives of the organization. Tactical planning and analysis is used to determine which procedures, policies and resource levels will be the most effective in managing the operational affairs of an organization. Tactical decisions are typically associated with broad managerial or administrative functions that cut across the organization like preparing the budget, setting staffing policies, managing the organization's finances, establishing internal control procedures, setting procurement and inventory policies, and so forth. Decision support has been used to answer tactical questions in areas such as: determining staffing requirements and recruitment policies [8]; projecting the expected workload and resource/budgetary requirements [1,17,21]; and performing financial planning and analysis [12,24,31,32].

Strategic Decisions

Organizations periodically examine alternative strategies for satisfying long range goals. The intention is to investigate avenues for enhancing the overall effectiveness and efficiency of the organization for the "long haul." The major focus of strategic planning is to resolve long term issues (two to five years) that take a significant period of time to take effect or that require an extended lead time for implementation. Examples include: long term investments, major equipment acquisitions, new market entry, corporate reorganizations, and facility shutdown or relocation. DSS have been used successfully to support strategic decisions in such areas as: establishing long-range staffing requirements [6,18,23]; selecting plant locations and layouts [10,19]; evaluating long term capital expenditures [2,14,27]; and evaluating strategic organizational issues [7,26,29].

HOW IS DECISION SUPPORT APPLIED?

How the DSS is applied to the decision process depends upon the problem being solved and the environment it is used in. To understand how a DSS is used we must examine the properties of a decision-support application and how these properties compare across the three levels of decision making (operational, tactical, and strategic).

Properties of Decision Support

Each organization will have its own distinctive "personality." The style of management, personal philosophies, method of operation, market environment, etc., will influence how decisions are reached. Certain characteristics are relevant to all decision-making activities and important to establishing decision-support capabilities, for example:

- ☐ *Type Audience.* The user populace can be classified as technically oriented (individuals with an analytical, scientific or engineering background), technically informed (managers without a technical background but previously exposed to computer applications), and technically naive (no previous experience or contact with automation.)
- ☐ *Dynamics.* The rate at which conditions change will depend upon the functions and activities performed by the organization and, in turn, will affect the longevity of information used to manage the operation. We can classify the dynamic nature of an organization by the rate at which data becomes obsolete, namely: steady (as in a military operation where weapon capabilities and personnel structures are measured in years); relatively steady (as with a manufacturing and distribution operation where material cost, shipping rates, etc., are valid in terms of months); or unsteady (as in an aircraft or vehicle maintenance facility where personnel availability, spare parts, and workloads vary daily).
- ☐ *Time Frame.* Some decisions have a life span of no more than a day (as in dispatching operations where drivers, vehicles, and routes are assigned on a daily basis). Others remain in effect for extensive time periods (as with a decision to establish central warehousing or distribution facilities at new locations).
- ☐ *Precision.* In certain situations a manager may only require a very rough idea of how conditions will affect the outcome of a particular problem (as in estimating the approximate tonnage required to repair all the roadways for a large state). In other cases, a high degree of precision is crucial (like scheduling a production line so that components arrive at the correct station in a precise sequence for assembly of a complex mechanical system).
- ☐ *Accuracy.* Although accuracy and precision are frequently used as synonyms, they have distinctively different requirements. Precision deals with the closeness of a solution, whereas accuracy relates to how reliable or dependable the answer must be. Depending upon the repercussions or loss from the wrong choice, the decision maker may be willing to accept a greater risk at being "inaccurate" (the chance of making the wrong decision).
- ☐ *Stability.* The stability of the underlying structure of a problem will influence how it responds to different conditions. In many situations the basic structure of a problem remains relatively unchanged over time. An example would be an electrical generating facility where failures may shut down parts of the system but the power transmission network remains relatively constant over time. In other cases, the structure may change gradually (as with organizations that periodically revise their structure and operation to adjust to changes in the marketplace) or may change rapidly (like in an intelligence system where force concentrations and movements alter daily).

The features and properties of the DSS must match the characteristics of the problem being analyzed and the needs of the particular decision process in question. This can be the most difficult part of establishing an effective mating between the machine, the human, and the problem. The properties of a DSS can be aligned with the problem characteristics in the following manner.

- ☐ *User Friendliness.* The type of audience that will use the DSS will govern the extent of "user friendliness" that must be programmed into the system, the level of documentation that must accompany the DSS, and the extent of training that must be provided. For example, technically oriented users, believe it or not, are generally more comfortable interacting with a machine that deals in brevity and terminology that is of an analytical nature. Technically naive users require an interface that is totally conversational, resembles the spoken dialogue, and provides self-tutoring features (see Chapter 8).

- ☐ *Currency.* For a DSS to be useful the data used by the system must remain current. The dynamics of the problem in question will determine the revision capabilities that must be provided with the DSS.
- ☐ *Level of Detail.* The more precision that is required, the greater the level of detail that must be incorporated into the design of the DSS. The amount of detail affects the internal sophistication of the system and the continual effort that will be necessary to maintain operational currency.
- ☐ *Frequency of Use.* The decision time frame and data currency will determine how often the DSS is required to support the decision maker.
- ☐ *Reliability.* The decision maker must feel confident that the DSS reflects reality and provides accurate results.
- ☐ *Structural Flexibility.* Ideally we would prefer a problem whose structure never varies and is always stable. In the real world, however, problems are rarely "permanently fixed." The DSS must be capable of allowing the decision maker to make revisions as the setting and environment of the problem changes.
- ☐ *Span of Influence.* The scope of a decision will determine the extent of influence to the organization in terms of: the time horizon for which the decision is applicable, and the extent to which the impact is felt across the organization.

Why should we care about matching DSS properties with a particular application? Why not simply design each system so that it satisfies the upper extreme of each requirement (totally conversational, as detailed as possible, maximum accuracy, total structural flexibility, etc.). The answer is one of economics. Each property tacks on an additional developmental and operational cost. For example, the greater the flexibility, the more design effort is required; and the more user friendly the system, the greater the staff time to develop the package.

Matching Features with the Decision Process

Because of the diverse and dynamic environment affecting each level of the decision process, the support provided must be versatile yet attuned to the specific needs and conditions at each level. The properties and features of a DSS can be equated to each level:

- ☐ *Operational Decisions.* Routine operations are generally managed under such dynamic and fluid conditions that the decision life span and data obsolescence is measured in days, weeks, or a few months. Under such conditions, the system must be capable of quick response and simple to access for frequent use and updating by operational personnel. Another distinguishing property is the "semi-permanent" structure of the problem being analyzed. Demand and resource levels may fluctuate but the kinds of information processed and types of questions being answered remain the same (how

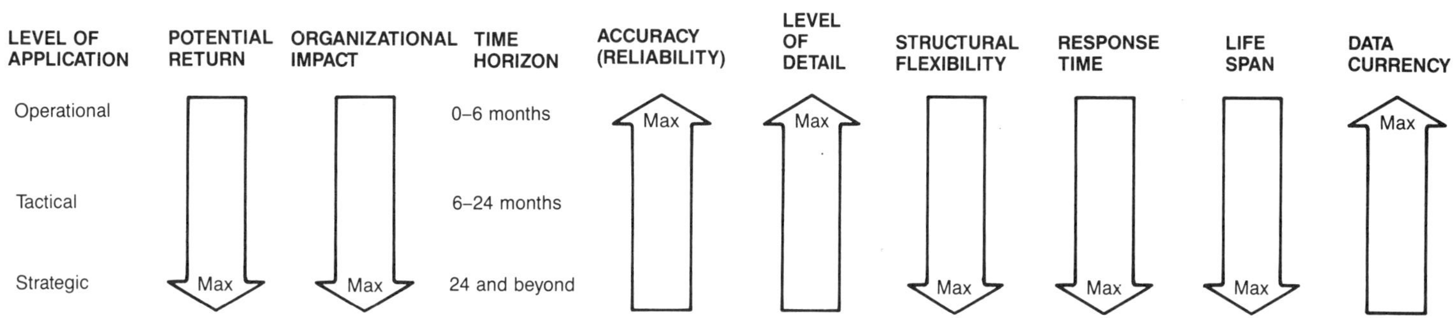

EXHIBIT 4–1 Comparison of DSS Properties.

many workers, which routes to travel, what vehicles should be assigned, etc.). The intricacy of operational problems necessitates that a significant degree of detail and precision be exhibited by the system. Improper directions usually cause a domino effect and disruptive chain reactions throughout the total process (time delays, late charges, overtime, missed sales, etc.).

- *Tactical Decisions.* Tactical decisions influence the policies and procedures that will regulate the organization for a moderate duration (six to 24 months). Such decisions are based on estimated conditions. The currency of the information is not as much of an issue as the capability to deal with uncertainty and to provide robust answers under varying conditions. Similarly, the circumstances being analyzed are broader than those at an operational level. Precision and level of detail are less than in an operational setting. Information is usually measured in averages. Recommended courses of actions are provided as "ballpark" figures. In an operational setting the user would deal with specific requirements, like scheduling person A to work on assignment B in time period C, or delivering product X to customer Y along path Z. In tactical planning, the decision maker is more concerned with general results, like controlling workforce levels and funding expenditures to within four percent of allocations.
- *Strategic Decisions.* Strategic issues offer the greatest opportunity for improvement (and loss) in the overall effectiveness and performance of the organization. The requirement to foresee into the distant future necessitates that strategic analysis rely heavily on the speculative capabilities of management (like trying to drive in a dense fog at night on a mountain top). It also means that the decision maker must accept results that are very coarse, at best. The DSS is typically applied in an environment with significant uncertainty using data that is low in resolution. The intent is to cite large scale differences between the proposed alternatives. Response time is seldom the issue. The crucial factor is to apply as much corporative knowledge and insight as possible.

It should be clear that the influence of a decision (time frame and organizational impact) increases at each higher level of decision making. This has an equivalent effect on the properties and characteristics of the application as we move to higher levels of the decision process (Exhibit 4–1). For example:

- The resulting repercussions extend further across the organization as does the potential savings.
- The precision and required degree of resolution decreases (for example, operational planning identifies the keyhole, tactical support provides guidance to the appropriate doorway, and strategic analysis helps to locate the general neighborhood of the house).
- Longevity and life span of the decision increases.
- Structural flexibility and latitude increases (that is, the amount of special rules and entry restrictions that must be observed by the user decreases).
- The required response time and information currency decreases.

EXERCISES

1. For those systems you classified as decision support applications in Exercise 1 of Chapter 2, identify the following properties that would be associated with that DSS:

a. Estimated longevity (time frame) of the decision (days, weeks, months, etc.).

b. The extent of repercussions from faulty decisions (localized to a particular operation, internal impact across various levels of the organization, severe repercussions to the stabliity and future of the whole organization).

c. Level of the decision process (operational, tactical, strategic).

2. Based on your experiences, identify a real world decision that is at the level of difficulty associated with each class of problems we discussed (Type 0, A, B, C, D). Do not use the examples presented in this chapter.

REFERENCES AND SUGGESTED READING

1. Avramovich, D., T. Cook, G. Langston and F. Sutherland, "A DSS for Fleet Management: A Linear Programming Approach," *INTERFACES,* June, 1982.
2. Balbirer, S. and D. Shaw, "An Application of Linear Programming To Bank Financial Planning," *INTERFACES,* October, 1981.
3. Belardo, S., P. Duchessi and J. Seagle, "Microcomputer Based Decision Support for Vehicle Fleet Routing," *INTERFACES,* November/December, 1985.
4. Bell, W., "Improving the Distribution of Industrial Gases with an On-line Computerized Routing and Scheduling System," *INTERFACES,* November/December, 1983.
5. Brown, G. and G. Graves, "Real-Time Dispatch of Petroleum Tank Trucks," *Management Science,* January, 1981.
6. Collins, R., S. Gass and E. Rosendahl, "The ASCAR Model for Evaluating Military Manpower Policy," *INTERFACES,* June, 1983.
7. David, F., "Computer Assisted Strategic Planning in Small Businesses," *Journal of Systems Management,* July, 1985.
8. Davis, M., "A System for Workforce Level Management and Control Within the Government Sector," *INTERFACES,* June, 1982.
9. Davis, M., "A Resource Assignment System for Event Scheduling in a Flight Training Environment," *INTERFACES,* August, 1980.
10. Farwell, D., "A Model-Based Approach to Decision Support Flexibility," *INTERFACES,* October, 1982.
11. Fisher, M., A. Greenfield, R. Jaikuman and J. Lester, "A Computerized Vehicle Routing Application," *INTERFACES,* August, 1982.
12. Frank, J. and J. Schnabel, "Timing of Borrowing Decisions—A Decision Support System," *Journal of Systems Management,* April, 1983.
13. Gaballa, A. and W. Pearce, "Telephone Sales Manpower Planning at Qantas," *INTERFACES,* May, 1979.
14. Gerding, B. and D. Morrison, "Selecting Business Targets in a Competitive Environment," *INTERFACES,* August, 1980.

15. Glover, F. and D. Klingman, "Network Application in Industry and Government," *AIIE TRANSACTIONS,* December, 1977.

16. Glover, F., D. Klingman, D. Karney and J. Mote, "An Integrated Production, Distribution and Inventory Planning System," *INTERFACES,* 1979.

17. Golabi, K., R. Kulkarni and G. Way, "A Statewide Pavement Management System, *INTERFACES,* December, 1982.

18. Gray, P., "A Faculty Model for Policy Planning," *INTERFACES,* February, 1980.

19. Harrison, H., "A Planning System for Facilities and Resources in Distribution Networks," *INTERFACES,* February, 1979.

20. Hehnen, M., "An Integrated Decision Support and Management Control System," *INTERFACES,* September/October, 1984.

21. Herderson, J. and D. Schilling, "Design and Implementation of Decision Support Systems in the Public Sector," *MIS Quarterly,* June, 1985.

22. Hodson, T. and G. McDonald, "Interactive Scheduling of a Generalized Flowshop," *INTERFACES,* June, 1981.

23. Joiner, C., "Academic Planning Through The Goal Programming Model," *INTERFACES,* August, 1980.

24. Klein, R., "Computer-based Financial Modeling," *Journal of Systems Management,* 33, no. 5, May, 1982.

25. Levary, R. and R. Boykin, "An Interactive DSS for Analyzing Ship Voyage Alternatives," *INTERFACES,* March/April, 1985.

26. Naylor, T., "Effective Use of Strategic Planning, Forecasting and Modeling in the Executive Suite," *Managerial Planning,* January/February, 1982.

27. Naylor, T., *Corporate Planning Models,* Reading, MA: Addison-Wesley Publishing Co., 1979.

28. Prastacos, G. and E. Brodheim, "The Long Island Blood Distribution System . . .," *INTERFACES,* November, 1979.

29. Rector, R., "Decision Support Systems—Strategic Planning Tool," *Managerial Planning,* May/June, 1983.

30. Ritzman, L. and L. Krajewski, "Shift Scheduling in Banking Operations," *INTERFACES,* April, 1980.

31. Smith, B., "A Lease Portfolio Planning Model," *INTERFACES,* December, 1981.

32. Wilkinson, J., "Financial Modeling within Distributed Systems, *Journal of Systems Management,* March, 1984.

5

Special Considerations and Aspects of DSS Applications

At its conception, many envisioned that the concept of decision support applied only in areas where:

- ☐ The decision maker would be permanently linked to a terminal.
- ☐ The system would be totally generic and capable of molding to any scenario or environment.
- ☐ The system would be void of any prescribed operating procedures or rules.

Practitioners found great promise in the concept, but ignored such criteria as too restrictive for most real-world situations, given the executives working environment and the state of the technology. The field of DSS began a natural growth to encompass a broader spectrum of possible applications. Although many debate which came first, decision support has branched into various areas of specialized interest based on where and how the system is used, for what purpose, and the relative scope or domain of the application. This section discusses some of the special aspects and considerations to applying automated support to the decision process.

FUNCTIONAL AND OPERATIONAL FRAMEWORK

The functional framework of a DSS relates to the scope of management activities supported by the system (market forecasting, production scheduling, budget analysis, etc.). Operational framework deals with the breadth and spacial dispersion of the DSS user base. The following examples show how the functional and operational complexity of a decision-support application can vary from being fairly simple to rather broad and comprehensive:

☐ *Specialized Single Site Application.* Exhibit 5-1 illustrates a system designed to support decisions dealing specifically with workforce planning and management (Chapter 12,

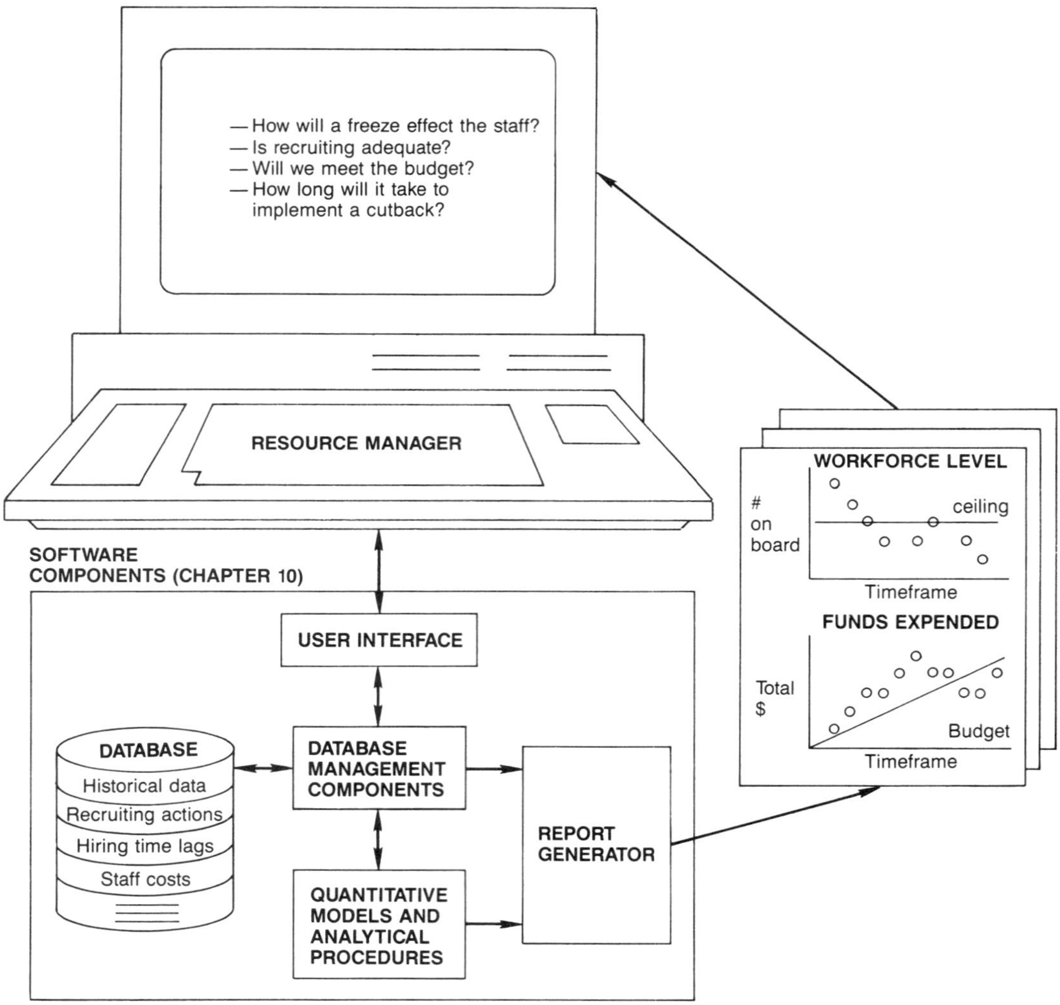

EXHIBIT 5–1 Specialized Single Site Application.

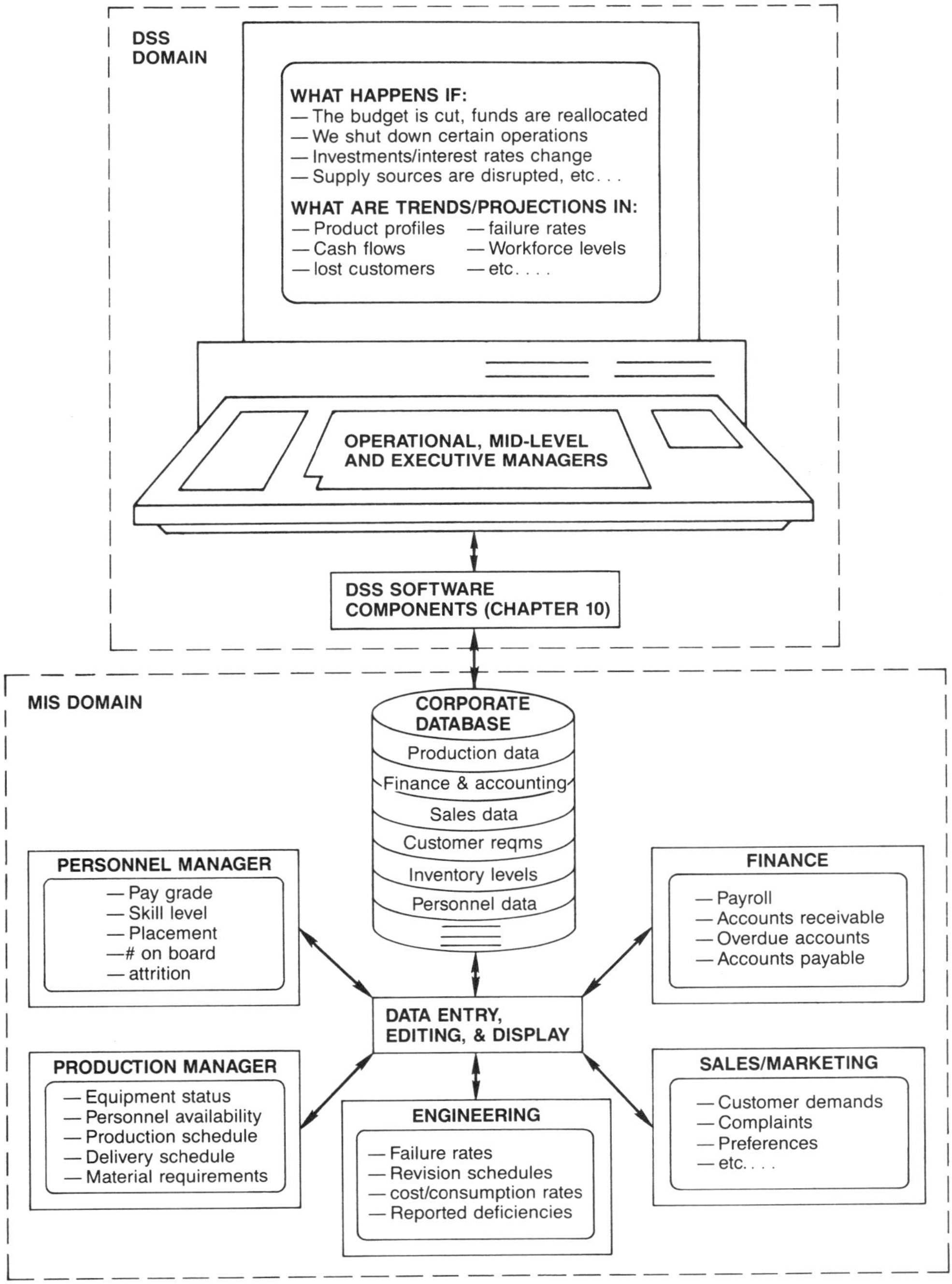

EXHIBIT 5–2 A Multi-Purpose Decision Support Application.

Case 1). Information is entered (recruiting actions, staffing costs, hiring practices, staffing policies, etc.), and decision formulated (freeze policies, staffing ceiling, budget allocations, etc.) from a single site within the organization (i.e., the CEO support staff).

- *Multiple Function/Multiple Site Application.* Exhibit 5–2 demonstrates an application that supports a multitude of management functions (manufacturing control, financial planning, market forecasting, personnel management, etc.) at all three levels of the decision process (operational, tactical, strategic). Case 5 of Chapter 12 represents an actual application where access and use of the system is distributed at various geographic locations.

GROUP DECISION-SUPPORT APPLICATIONS

In Chapter 3 we discussed one form or style of decision making, referred to as the *political model,* where a decision was not the result of a single individual but the "tug of war" process between a group of participants. We noted that, in such cases, the final outcome typically resulted from the persuasive ability and political "clout" of the group members. There are situations, however, where a DSS can help to combine the knowledge and synergy of a group of knowledgeable individuals to help identify the most appropriate or acceptable alternative. In such applications the decision is based primarily on the judgment, experience, and corporate memory of the group. Consider the following situations:

- A group of executives can evaluate a set of potential investments using similar criteria (market stability, capital base, return rates, etc.) and still draw varied conclusions about the favorability of each candidate. The return ratio and likelihood of success is assessed by each participant and combined in a manner that reflects the overall potential for each investment.
- Determining the relative importance and priority of a set of initiatives or projects often requires that a group of managers provide their views as to the comparative merit of each item in terms of experience and organizational perspectives using various rating criteria (cost savings, breakeven period, capital outlays, etc.).
- Establishing the best staffing strategies for an academic institution can require that the corporate insight of administrative executives and department heads be used to evaluate the importance and contribution of various factors (tenure promotion policy, tuition growth rate, staff-to-faculty ratio, salary policy, etc.). The opinions of each participant are taken into account, along with financial constraints, to reflect the near and long-term effects of such policies on the quality and stability of the institution's academic program. After examining the combined effects of their opinions, each participant reassesses their position and the process is repeated until an acceptable course of action is reached.

DSS have been used to help organizations exploit the combined qualitative experience and intuition of a core of technical experts, managers, and executives [1,7,11,12, 14,16,22]. Although the specific objectives and features of each group DSS vary, the general benefit to using the system evolves from its capability to help the group: con-

sider the relative importance of various factors and issues on a host of potential alternatives; evaluate the implications of their combined professional experience; alter their preferences and ratings based on interaction with the group result; and continue until the preferred group alternative is reached.

EXPERT SYSTEMS

Each profession relies heavily on the reservoir of knowledge accumulated by technical experts for that field. Whether it be the doctor diagnosing an illness, a lawyer searching for a legal precedent, or a maintenance crew trying to analyze the cause of a failed system, each decision requires that the expert exercise his accumulated experience and intuitive judgment to solve the problem. A special breed of automated support known as "Expert Systems" helps a user to evaluate specific problems as if he were a "king of all trades." The concept and principles behind Expert Systems is best illustrated by an example.

For the general populace, an assessment of climatic conditions is usually based on a news report or a quick scan of the prevailing weather. If the sky is overcast, an individual might guess that precipitation was expected. If it were cold, it might come in the form of snow. If the temperature was less than 25 degrees, it is likely the snow will stick to the roads and cause traffic problems. In effect, you would be drawing *inference* about the weather at some future time based on your observations of current conditions and your experience about what such conditions mean. The more facts you had about the situation, and the broader your base of experience and knowledge about meteorological factors, the more reliable your assessment (inference) would be. For example, the fact that a cold front was 100 miles Northwest with a SE wind of 20 miles per hour (mph) would also be relevant.

If somehow the experience and expertise of meteorologists could be absorbed and stored, then virtually anyone could examine prevailing conditions and make a better assessment about the weather by using the *knowledge base* from the experts. That is, of course, assuming they knew how to use the information and how to relate it to the observed conditions. One approach would be to provide an automated system that prompts the user for all the known and pertinent factors. For example:

WHAT IS THE AMBIENT TEMPERATURE?
30 degrees

WHAT IS THE BAROMETRIC PRESSURE
29.67

ARE THERE ANY PRECIPITATION FRONTS WITHIN A 400 MILE RADIUS?
Yes

WHERE IS THE CENTER OF THE FRONT?
Chicago

WHAT IS THE SPEED AND DIRECTION?
30 mph SE

The system would then compare these conditions to the *knowledge base* of experience and expertise stored in the computer, analyze the relationships between all relevant factors, and finally draw *inference* about these facts to estimate potential weather trends, such as:

THE GENERAL FORECAST IS CLOUDY SKIES AND PRECIPITATION WITH THE FOLLOWING PROFILE:

Day	*Predicted Condition*	*Likelihood*
Monday	Clear Skies	60%
Tuesday	Overcast, rain at 17:00	50%
Wednesday	Turn to sleet then snow	30%

In essence, this is the underlying principle behind an expert system: to provide the capability for a broad base of users to build upon the accumulative knowledge and experience of a highly specialized core of experts. Expert Systems can be effective in providing support to the following areas:

- ☐ Failure diagnosis (electronic circuits, nuclear facility failure, medical diagnosis, mechanical system troubleshooting, etc.).
- ☐ Trend and data analysis (intelligence/threat analysis, toxic chemical evaluation, petroleum site surveys, etc.).
- ☐ System design (computer configuration, circuitry development, mechanical engineering design, etc.).
- ☐ Management planning and control (plant layout, manufacturing planning, combat mission planning, etc.).

In an Expert System, "Expert" information is retained on a computer in the form of a "Knowledge Base." The reservoir of information consists of logical relationships and deductive rules that affect the likelihood, preference and characteristics of various outcomes under different conditions. For example:

- ☐ *If* the coolant temperature exceeds 200° for more than *five minutes THEN* there is a *good chance* that the *primary pump* is starting to *fail.*
- ☐ There is a *90 percent chance* that *WHEN* the *coolant temperature exceeds 200° BUT* the *temperature* at the *exhaust port* is still *below 120°* that the *primary pump* is still functioning *properly* provided *coolant temperature* does *not exceed 300°.*
- ☐ When *primary and secondary circuits fail* it is *acceptable* for the *core temperature* to *increase* up to 30°.
- ☐ When operating on a *single backup* pump at *full capacity* then the system becomes *unreliable after 48 hours.*

As a result of this IF-THEN structure, Expert Systems are often referred to as "rule based" systems. An Expert System can examine and compare a given situation and its symptoms against the information stored in the knowledge base to help hypothesize: the likely outcome from a given set of circumstances; the cause of a problem; or the best course of action. Exhibit 5–3 illustrates the components of a typical Expert System. Samples of actual expert systems include:

- ☐ XCON. A system designed by Digital Equipment Corporation to help junior engineers verify the configurations of customer orders, identify voids in the order, and to recommend improvements.
- ☐ HELP. A system created by Dr. Homer Warner (and released for general use by Control Data Corporation) to assist physicians in diagnosing a patient's condition.
- ☐ PROSPECTOR. An expert system developed at SRI International that evaluates mineral sites for potential deposits.
- ☐ TACTICIAN. A system designed by Titan Systems Inc. to evaluate alternative scenarios in a military combat operation.
- ☐ DART. The Diagnostic Assistant Reference Tool System (DARTS) helps users analyze equipment failures. DARTS began development in 1980 with the support of IBM and is currently oriented toward problems dealing with computer hardware.

Like other types of DSS, Expert Systems are interactive by nature and aimed at supporting unstructured problems. The difference between Expert Systems and other forms of decision support stems form the underlying procedures that determine how a problem will be analyzed and how the results will evolve. In Chapter 2 we noted that DSS applications frequently rely on quantitative procedures to mathematically

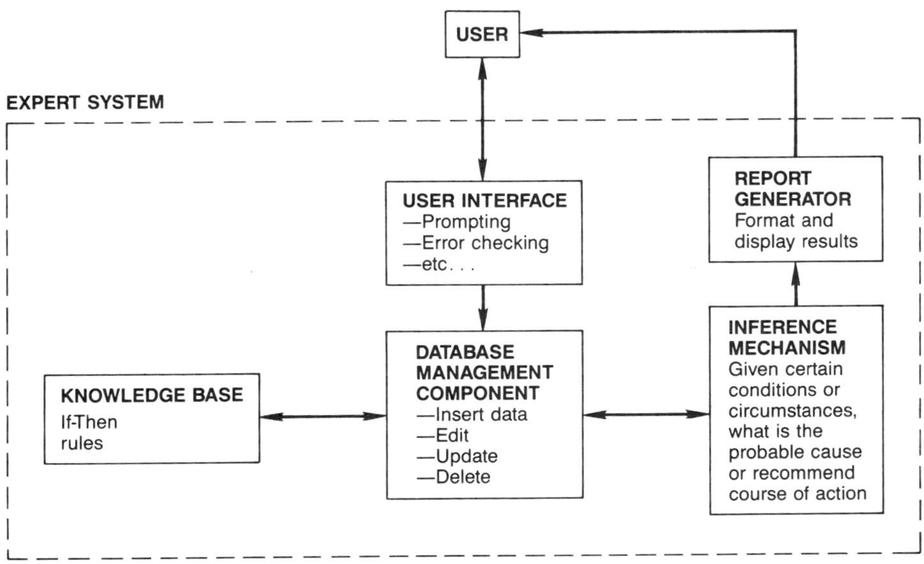

EXHIBIT 5–3 Components of an Expert System.

manipulate large bundles of information. Techniques such as linear programming, statistical analysis, and event simulation (Chapter 9) are examples of analytical methods that are *algorithmic* by nature (e.g., they depend on mathematically oriented procedures) and often used in DSS applications to analyze complex problems. Expert Systems are not founded on mathematical (algorithmic) procedures but on experience and "rules of thumb" (often referred to as heuristics). The Expert System finds its answer by searching through a knowledge base made of heuristic rules. In summary, while other forms of decision support are based on algorithmic procedures, Expert Systems are heuristic by nature.

Although Expert Systems do have the potential for supporting tactical and strategic decision making, most of the current applications deal with operational activities. References [3,8] provide a survey and comparison of a variety of Expert Systems. Readers interested in further discussions on the concept, design and application of Expert Systems can also consult references [2,10,13,15,18].

DECISION AIDES THAT EMULATE THE THOUGHT PROCESS

Imagine sitting at a terminal and typing in:

> "I have to cut the budget by 10 percent. I want you to look at our operations in regions 6 and 7 then tell me which should be shutdown or cutback. Make sure that we can still satisfy the projected customer demands over the next three years."

The computer is being asked to emulate human deductive logic and recommend a course of action, much like the HAL computer in the science fiction fantasy "2001-A Space Odyssey." Although such an application may seem farfetched by current standards, the technology referred to as "Artificial Intelligence" (AI) is moving us in that direction. Decision Aides that go beyond typical DSS applications, and straightforward rule based Expert Systems, to emulate the thought process and help analyze, plan, and solve complex problems are on the horizon [3,8]. Consider the "Le Courtier" system developed by Cognitive Systems Inc. Le Courtier acts as a stockbroker advisory system for a bank wishing to market its brokerage services to a wider audience. In essence, the system emulates the process through which a potential investor and stockbroker interact to arrive at a decision as to the portfolio that best meets the needs of each individual. Exhibit 5-4 illustrates how the system: examines the financial preferences of the user, perceives his goals and objectives, and finally advises the best stocks for that particular individual.

There are three aspects of the Le Courtier system that deserve special consideration as a decision support application. First, the system communicates with the user in a natural language that emulates the spoken tongue of the user. Second, Le Courtier relies on various rule based relationships to reflect the experience and expertise of a stockbroker (similar to the role of an Expert System). Finally, various quantitative procedures (Chapter 9) are hidden within the framework of the system to mathematically evaluate which investments are preferred under each given set of circumstances.

```
> What's the best banking stock?

    The best stock is determined by tne measure of performance called
    alpha. The banking stock with the best alpha is:
           ABC Bancorp     1.2

> Should I buy It?

    ABC  Bancorp  has  excellent  market  performance   (alpha=1.2).
    However,  investing in this would violate your preference that no
    more  than  15%  of your portfolio should  be  in  banking.   You
    presently  have 5,000 shares of XYZ Bank (15% of your  portfolio)
    which you should hold.

> I want to buy 100 shares of ABC anyway.

    I am taking this preference into account and will re-evaluate  my
    recommendations.

> Should I buy GHI Computer?

    GHI  Computer has poor market performance (alpha=4.3).  I do  not
    recommend  investing  in it at this time.  A better stock in  the
    High Technology sector would be LMN Semiconductor (alpha=1.1).

> I want to give you my own definition of the "best" stock in the high
  technology sector.

    Please enter your definition.

>  The lowest alpha among high tech stocks with earnings greater  than
   $1  million, p/e less than 30 and revenues growth>35% in the past year

    Thank  you.  I will take your definition of best high  technology
    stock into account when making future recommendations.

> What is the best high tech stock?

    The best high technology stock is PQR Electronics: Alpha=1.8, '83
    earnings=$3.4M, P/E=23, 82-83 revenue growth=47%

> Should I buy TUV systems?

    I would not recommend purchasing TUV Systems because it  violates
    your  rule  that  P/E<30  and  revenue  growth>35%.
    TUV  Systems: P/E=47, 82-83 revenue growth=25%
```

EXHIBIT 5–4 The "Le Courtier" Stockbroker Advisory System. *Courtesy of Cognitive Systems, Inc.*

The Le Courtier system is one example of a DSS that uses AI techniques to communicate with the user in a natural language. The use of Natural Language Processors (NLP) is one area of AI research that is receiving much attention and is likely to have significant implications on decision-support applications in general. In an NLP system the user communicates with the computer by typing in normal spoken English. The system is virtually free of any command or syntax structure (Chapter 8). Readers interested in further discussions of AI and NLP are referred to Chapter 13 and references [5,17,19,20,21].

THE DOMAIN OF AN APPLICATION

Another aspect of systems designed to support the decision process is the scope or range of applications for which it was intended to operate. The "domain" of a DSS deals with how broad an area the system can be applied to without redesign of the internal mechanism (referred to as the program code). For example:

- *Singular Purpose Applications* are designed to support a particular problem with its own peculiar requirements and specialized structure. The "specialized single site application" depicted in Exhibit 5–1 illustrates a singular purpose DSS. Such applications are frequently referred to as "domain dependent" because they are designed for use in a particular environment to solve a specific type of problem. Examples would include, a flight training management system [6], a system to manage and maintain a fleet of capital intensive vehicles [4], a statewide pavement management system [9], and the Le Courtier system depicted in Exhibit 5–4.
- *Generic Systems* are designed to support a general class of decisions where the underlying structure and characteristics of the problems are similar (resource allocations, flow distribution, ranking and choice problems, etc.). As a result, generic systems are often referred to as being "domain independent." They are not restricted to one specific application but to related types of problems where the decision-making environment (and quantitative procedures) are the same. The following illustrates some of the areas where generic systems are being successfully applied:
  - User-oriented systems that are conversational in nature and used to evaluate and analyze any situation that can be formulated as a flow process (product distribution, fluid transfer, production scheduling, funds transfer, etc.). The user simply employs options provided within the system to reorient the DSS to that particular application (change terminology, alter user prompts, revise display heading. etc.).
  - A conversational optimization (Chapter 9) package that can be directly applied by the busy manager to perform budget analysis, resource allocations, workforce planning, portfolio evaluation, product selection, and similar problems without requiring any reprogramming.
  - Thought Structuring Systems (TSS) that help managers: partition a problem into its fundamental parts; visualize the relationships between those parts; organize thoughts into a well-structured and formulated process; and to assess the objectives, their relative importance and the consistency of his choices. These systems are designed around the human thought process, not the application or problem itself. They help the individual structure and formulate decisions at each step of the decision-making process (Exhibit 3–2). Exhibit 5–5 illustrates a hypothetical application of a commercially available TSS ("Decision-Aide" from Kepner-Tregoe Inc.). In this example, the decision maker must choose which of four alternative approaches should be used to improve the market share for a particular product: increased advertising, special discounts, a contest, or lower prices. The TSS helps the manager to:
    - —Define the factors (Chapter 3) that influence and impact the decision (Exhibit 5–5a).
    - —Identify the various objectives and desired outcomes (Exhibit 5–5b).
    - —Define specific characteristics and properties of each alternative in terms of the various management objectives (Exhibit 5–5c).

TO SELECT METHOD TO IMPROVE MARKET SHARE

Decision Planning	File: MARKET
SITUATION	MAJOR COMPETITIVE PROMOTION IS EXPECTED
CURRENT IMPACT	
ON PEOPLE:	LOW MORALE IF WE DO NOT RESPOND
ON PRODUCTIVITY:	WE NEED SALES TO KEEP UNIT COSTS DOWN
ON CLIENTS:	COULD LOSE CLIENTS TO COMPETITORS
ON ORGANIZATION:	RESPONDING TO THREAT WILL STRAIN US
ON REVENUE:	NEED A RESPONSE THAT MEETS THREAT
ON COSTS:	HAVE LIMITED FUNDS TO FIGHT COMPETITION
LONG-TERM IMPACT	
ON PEOPLE:	MAJOR IMPACT ON HIRING PLANS
ON PRODUCTIVITY:	CANNOT AFFORD TO LOSE MARKET SHARE
ON CLIENTS:	CUSTOMER LOYALTY WILL BE TESTED
ON ORGANIZATION:	OUTCOME TO DECIDE FATE OF HI-GRADE FILM
ON REVENUE:	MUST GROW DESPITE COMPETITION
ON COSTS:	ALL FUNDS MUST BE INTERNALLY GENERATED

EXHIBIT 5–5a Factors Influencing the Decision. ©Kepner-Tregoe, Inc., 1985. *Courtesy of Kepner-Tregoe, Inc.*

TO SELECT METHOD TO IMPROVE MARKET SHARE

List of Objectives File: MARKET

MUST OBJECTIVES

INCREASE PEAK SHARE BY 2%
COST LESS THAN $50,000
IMPLEMENT WITHIN 5 MONTHS

WT.	WANT OBJECTIVES
10	MAXIMIZE PEAK MARKET SHARE
7	ENSURE REPEAT SALES
6	COUNTERACT COMPETITION
4	MAXIMIZE SALES INCREASE
4	MINIMIZE COSTS
3	STRENGTHEN QUALITY IMAGE

EXHIBIT 5–5b Management Objectives to Improving the Market Share. ©Kepner-Tregoe, Inc., 1985. *Courtesy of Kepner-Tregoe, Inc.*

TO SELECT METHOD TO IMPROVE MARKET SHARE

ALTERNATIVE: ADVERTISING File: MARKET

MUST OBJECTIVES	DATA	STATUS
INCREASE PEAK SHARE BY 2%	3.6%	GO
COST LESS THAN $50,000	35,000	GO
IMPLEMENT WITHIN 5 MONTHS	4.5 TO 5 MONTHS	GO

WT.	WANT OBJECTIVES	DATA	SCORE	WT. SCORE
10	MAXIMIZE PEAK MARKET SHARE	3.6% INCREASE	10	100
7	ENSURE REPEAT SALES	SOME FALL-OFF	8	56
6	COUNTERACT COMPETITION	DEALERS WILL LIKE	10	60
4	MAXIMIZE SALES INCREASE	12%	10	40
4	MINIMIZE COSTS	35,000	7	28
3	STRENGTHEN QUALITY IMAGE	WORD AND PICTURE EMPHASIS	10	30
		TOTAL WEIGHTED SCORE		314

EXHIBIT 5–5c Characteristics of the Advertising Alternative. ©Kepner-Tregoe, Inc., 1985. *Courtesy of Kepner-Tregoe, Inc.*

TO SELECT METHOD TO IMPROVE MARKET SHARE

Adverse Consequences File: MARKET

Summary of Adverse Consequences for: ADVERTISING

ADVERSE CONSEQUENCES	PROBABILITY	SERIOUSNESS
AD AGENCY MISSES DEADLINE	MEDIUM	HIGH
TESTIMONIALS BACKFIRE	LOW	HIGH
DEALERS DON'T COOPERATE	LOW	HIGH
CONTINUAL ADS NEEDED	HIGH	MEDIUM
BAD SALES PROJECTIONS	MEDIUM	MEDIUM
PROFESSIONALS RESENT ADS	LOW	MEDIUM
TESTIMONIALS COST TOO MUCH	MEDIUM	LOW

EXHIBIT 5–5d Consequence Associated with the Advertising Alternative. ©Kepner-Tregoe, Inc., 1985. *Courtesy of Kepner-Tregoe, Inc.*

Decision Aide | Make Balanced Choice | by KEPNER-TREGOE

Your decision statement is: TO SELECT METHOD TO IMPROVE MARKET SHARE
Your balanced choice is: ADVERTISING

MUST STATUS: GO
MOST IMPORTANT WANTS

WT	OBJECTIVE/DATA	SCORE
10	MAXIMIZE PEAK SHARE 3.6% INCREASE	10
7	ENSURE REPEAT SALES SOME FALL-OFF	8
6	COUNTERACT-COMPETITOR DEALERS WILL LIKE	10

MOST IMPORTANT RISKS	PROB.	SER
AD AGENCY LATE	MED	HI
TESTIMONIALS BACKFIRE	LO	HI
DEALERS REFUSE	LO	HI
CONTINUAL ADS NEEDED	HI	MED

Please summarize your conclusions about ADVERTISING

INSTRUCT J.T. TO HOLD WEEKLY MEETINGS WITH AD AGENCY TO KEEP THEM ON SCHEDULE

EXHIBIT 5–5e "Best" Choice for the Method to Improve the Market Share. ©Kepner-Tregoe, Inc., 1985. *Courtesy of Kepner-Tregoe, Inc.*

—Examine the consequences associated with each alternative (Exhibit 5–5d).

—Choose the most appropriate ("balanced") alternative (Exhibit 5–5e).

☐ *Generator Systems* are used to help create and build decision-support applications. They are designed to facilitate the construction of a DSS aimed at a particular sphere of application (financial planning, ad hoc information query, Expert Systems, etc.). The attractiveness of generator systems stems from the significant reduction in both developmental time and cost. When designed from scratch (see Chapter 10), the time required for creating the system can range from several months to a year or more with an associated cost exceeding $200,000. When a generator system can be used to build the DSS, the task of designing the software (Chapter 10) is essentially complete. The individual responsible for implementing the DSS simply uses features and commands within the generator to construct a system that satisfies the requirements for the particular application. Appendix A lists several DSS generators and Chapter 10 provides further discussion of generator systems.

EXERCISES

1. With the capabilities and features of a Thought Structuring System (TSS) in mind, hypothesize a decision applicable to this type of support and, within the context of

Exhibits 5–5a through 5–5e, depict the influential factors, the objectives and desired outcomes, the characteristics and consequences associated with each alternative.

2. For each application in Exercise 1 of Chapter 2 that you classified as a DSS, identify some of the "questions" that could be answered or "what if" drills that could be run with the system (see Exhibits 5–1 and 5–2).

3. A major international organization relies on a large scale information system to help forecast, acquire and manage their broad base of personnel resources. Like many personnel intensive operations (sales operations, commercial aircraft maintenance facilities, military forces, etc.), personnel are the prime contributors to the final product and a major concern for the success and stability of the organization. The system in question functions as follows:

   - ☐ Accounting of authorized personnel positions, skill levels, and recruiting status is decentralized (for example, entered and maintained by field units into a corporate database located at headquarters).
   - ☐ One component of the system (referred to as "*staff builder*") allows management to consider field inputs, long term staffing goals, funding restraints, etc., and arrive quantitatively at balanced staffing policies and targets.
   - ☐ Many of the staffing policies must conform to inherent organizational practices and periodic guidance from executive leadership in a group interaction forum.
   - ☐ There is a large number of "rules of thumb" that must be considered and accounted for in establishing the most acceptable staffing policies (that is, IF a freeze is in effect THEN a 4 to 1 ratio of skill X to skill Y is recommended, etc.). The system queries the staffing experts before each session for new rules and recommends possible courses of action to achieve specified goals.

   Based on the topics discussed in the last two chapters, scratch a diagram that identifies:

   - ☐ What types of decision support are we dealing with?
   - ☐ The relationship (flows) between each major component of the overall system (Exhibits 2–2 and 5–2 provide examples).
   - ☐ At each level of the system show what level of the decision process we are dealing with.

REFERENCES AND SUGGESTED READING

1. Adelmam, L., "Real-Time Computer Support for Decision Analysis in Group Settings," *INTERFACES,* March/April, 1984.

2. *An Overview of Expert Systems,* National Bureau of Standards, NBS Publication NBSIR 82–2525.

3. Andriole, S., "The Promise of Artificial Intelligence," *Journal of Systems Management,* July, 1985.

4. Avramovich, D., T. Cook, G. Langston and F. Sutherland, "A DSS for Fleet Management: A Linear Programming Approach," *INTERFACES,* June, 1982.

5. Barr, A. and E. Feigenbaum, *The Handbook Of Artificial Intelligence,* Los Altos, CA.: William Kaufman Publishing, 1982.

6. Davis, M., "A Resource Assignment System for Event Scheduling in a Flight Training Environment," *INTERFACES,* August, 1980.

7. Foreman, E., "Decision Support Systems for Executive Decision Makers," *Information Strategy: The Executive Journal,* Summer, 1985.

8. Gevarter, W., *Artificial Intelligence, Expert Systems, Computer Vision, and Natural Language Processing,* Park Ridge, N.J.: Noyes Publishing, 1984.

9. Golabi, K., R. Kulkarni and G. Way, "A Statewide Pavement Management System," *INTERFACES,* December, 1982.

10. Harmon, P. and D. King, *Expert Systems: Artificial Intelligence in Business,* New York, N.Y.: Wiley & Sons, 1985.

11. Huber, G., "Issues in the Design of Group Decision Support Systems," *MIS Quarterly,* September, 1984.

12. Jophins, D., "Computer Models Employed in University Administration," *INTERFACES,* February, 1979.

13. Konopasek, M. and S. Jayaraman, "Expert Systems for Personal Computers," *Byte,* May, 1984.

14. Kull, D., "Group Decisions: Can Computers Help?" *Computer Decisions,* May, 1982.

15. Michaelsen, R. and D. Michie, "Expert Systems in Business," *Datamation,* November, 1983.

16. Rathwell, M. and A. Burns, "Information Systems Support for Group Planning and Decision-Making Activities," *MIS Quarterly,* September, 1985.

17. Rauch-Hindin, W., "Artificial Intelligence: Coming of Age," *Systems and Software,* August, 1984.

18. Roberts, S., "Computers Simulate Human Experts," *Mini-Micro Systems,* September, 1983.

19. Roberts, S., "Artificial Intelligence," *Mini-Micro Systems,* December, 1983.

20. Simon, H., *The Science of Artificial Intelligence,* Cambridge, MA: MIT Press, 1981.

21. Spoerl, J., "AI Environment Speeds Software Development," *Systems and Software,* August, 1984.

22. Thomas, R. and A. Burns, "The Case for Distributed Decision Making Systems," *MIS Quarterly,* September, 1985.

6

Composition of A DSS

We have taken the liberty of referring to a DSS as a "black box" or media through which managers gain insight into the complex and mystical realm of today's messy decisions. In practice, a successful DSS application is composed of more than just a computerized system. Decision support requires the existence and cooperative interaction of four basic elements (Exhibit 6–1):

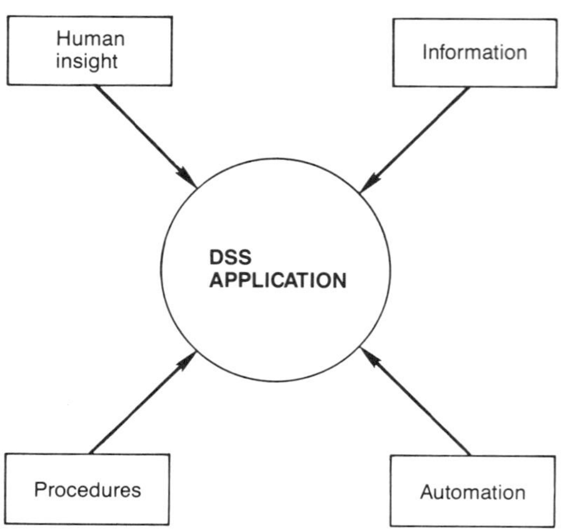

EXHIBIT 6–1 Elements of a DSS Application.

- ☐ Human insight.
- ☐ The information describing the problem.
- ☐ Procedures for operating the system within the organization.
- ☐ The automated facility itself (the computer).

The "automation" segment of a DSS is comprised of two parts: the computer hardware and the software. Within this framework the DSS is structured into five major components (Exhibit 6–2): the database, data base management facilities, quantitative

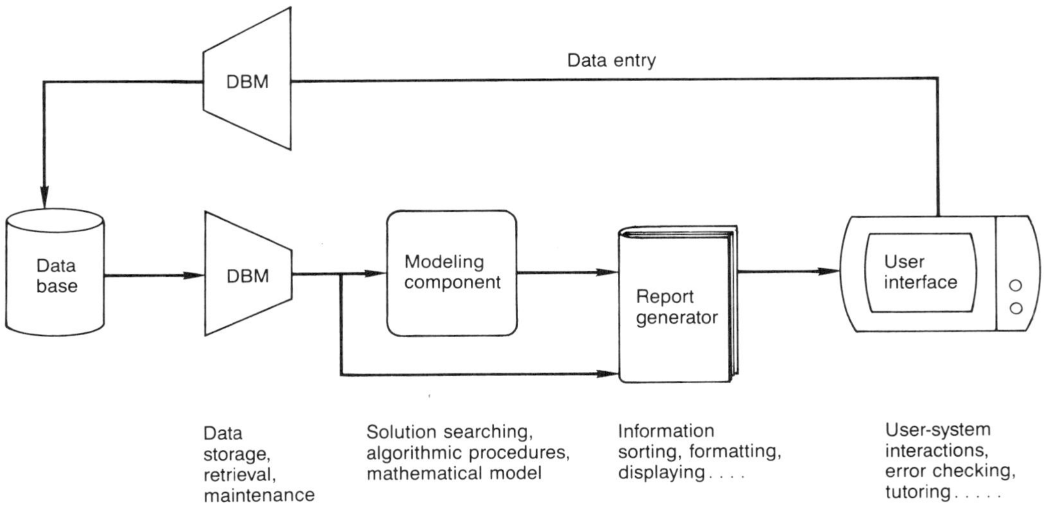

EXHIBIT 6–2 Components of the DSS.

modeling component, report generator, and the human interface. Generally speaking, a DSS is composed of essentially the same parts as other types of information processing systems. The distinction between the internal workings of a DSS and other systems stems from four major factors:

- ☐ The methods used to interface with the user (Chapter 8).
- ☐ The existence of a quantitative component (Chapter 9).
- ☐ The structure and characteristics of the software (Chapter 10).
- ☐ The fact that, except for the user interface component, the user is "blind" to the intricate internal operation of the system.

This chapter provides an overview of the five major parts of a DSS. Chapters 7 through 10 discuss the specific aspects of each DSS component.

THE DATABASE AND HOW IT IS MANAGED

The database contains the reservoir of information that describes all of the pertinent conditions and characteristics of the problem in question. The typical database might contain usage rates (cost per unit processed, material consumption, staff requirements), functional relationships (organizational structure, physical layout, workload demands), capacities (inventory, allocated funds, available staff), management policies (production targets, deadlines, hiring/freeze policies), and much more.

The type and volume of data necessary to support the decision process will depend upon the operation itself, the level of use, and the degree of management involvement. Consider, for example, two systems designed for assisting in workforce management. The first supports operational decisions and is used directly in the scheduling and assignment of staff. The database is made up of very detailed and specific information such as: personnel availability, qualifications, current assignments, workshifts, pay rates, task skill requirements, durations, priorities, due dates, prerequisite activities, and so forth. The second DSS is used by management to establish "passive" policies and controls that indirectly maintain the workforce level and funding expenditures within tolerable limits. In this case, the database is relatively small consisting primarily of aggregate quantities such as budgetary and ceiling limits, total number of personnel on board, average attrition rates, recruiting actions in process, and freeze policies.

Databases can be stored on a variety of different media, depending on the type of computer being used and the amount of data required for the application. Whether the information is maintained on a magnetic tape, hard disk pack or a flexible disk unit, the data is organized into a series of files. Each file contains up to several thousand related records that define various bits of information about a specific entity (a person, a job, a warehouse, a production line, etc.).

Take, for example, the large database required for mangement, control, and planning of a nationwide manufacturing and product distribution process. Assume that 10 different products are manufactured at 20 different plants. These products are shipped to any of 200 centralized warehousing and distributor facilities located around the country. Each warehouse satisfies customer demands for a defined region. Each region contains approximately 5,000 outlets (customers). For this application the data is stored in three separate files.

The first file contains all information pertaining to the production facilities (plants). Each record in the file defines all of the characteristics pertaining to a particular plant such as: its name, the geographic location, products manufactured at that facility, inventory capacities, and production rates. The second file defines all of the facts about the warehousing and distribution facilities. Each record depicts the warehouse name, location, storage capacity, products handled, and customers serviced from that facility. The third file deals with the means of transportation between plants, warehouse and clients. Each record pertains to one specific route and contains information such as: where the route starts (plant 1, plant 2, warehouse 1. . .etc.); where the route ends (a warehouse or particular customer); method of transportation (air, rail, freight . . .); distance; shipment cost along that route; rate of loss or spoilage; and so forth.

The type of computer facility needed to process the data will depend upon the required storage capacity and how the information is entered into the computer. Although most DSS applications are suitable to the total spectrum of computer hardware (main, mini, micro), there are exceptions. To illustrate, consider how much space would be necessary to retain the database for our manufacturing example. The space required for the first and second file would be minimal, roughly one million bytes (called a megabyte). However, the file containing transportation data would be massive. There would be approximately 20 million records for all the possible routes and means of transportation between plant, warehouse and client. Many of the routes would be impractical and could be eliminated. Assume that only five million paths are logical. Each record will take about 100 characters (bytes) of data to store all of the pertinent facts about each route (starting point, destination, cost, etc.). The total database would require roughly 500 million bytes of storage exceeding the capacity of today's microcomputers. Similarly, such a large scale operation would require a distributed processing computer system to permit multiple users at all the various sites to access and use the database. Thus, for such a large application, a mini- or mainframe computer would be required (by today's standards).

A portion of the DSS must be dedicated to the function of actually storing, retrieving and formating information to and from the database. This segment of an information processing system is typically referred to as the Data Base Management (DBM) facility or, when considered as an independent component, a Data Base Management System (DBMS). The DBM component can be included as an integral part of the DSS software or can be provided by a separate "off the shelf" DBMS package designed to interface with other systems. The advantages and disadvantages of electing to use an existing DBMS package or to code DBM capacities directly within the DSS are discussed in Chapter 10. A more in-depth discussion of the DBM component and the role it plays in a DSS are provided in Chapter 7.

THE QUANTITATIVE COMPONENT

The quantitative component of a DSS is the most difficult to both understand and implement. The quantitative model provides a mathematical representation of the complex structure and relationship between the various parts of the problem. Quantitative models are necessary in order that a physical system can be depicted and analyzed by a computer. The mathematical formulation embedded within the model provides a descriptive mechanism through which information can be manipulated repeatedly and the decision maker can emulate what will actually take place. Just how involved and elaborate the quantitative component must be to realistically model the real world depends directly on the degree of difficulty (Chapter 3) of the problem. The quantitative segment of an application can be partitioned into four parts (Exhibit 6–3):

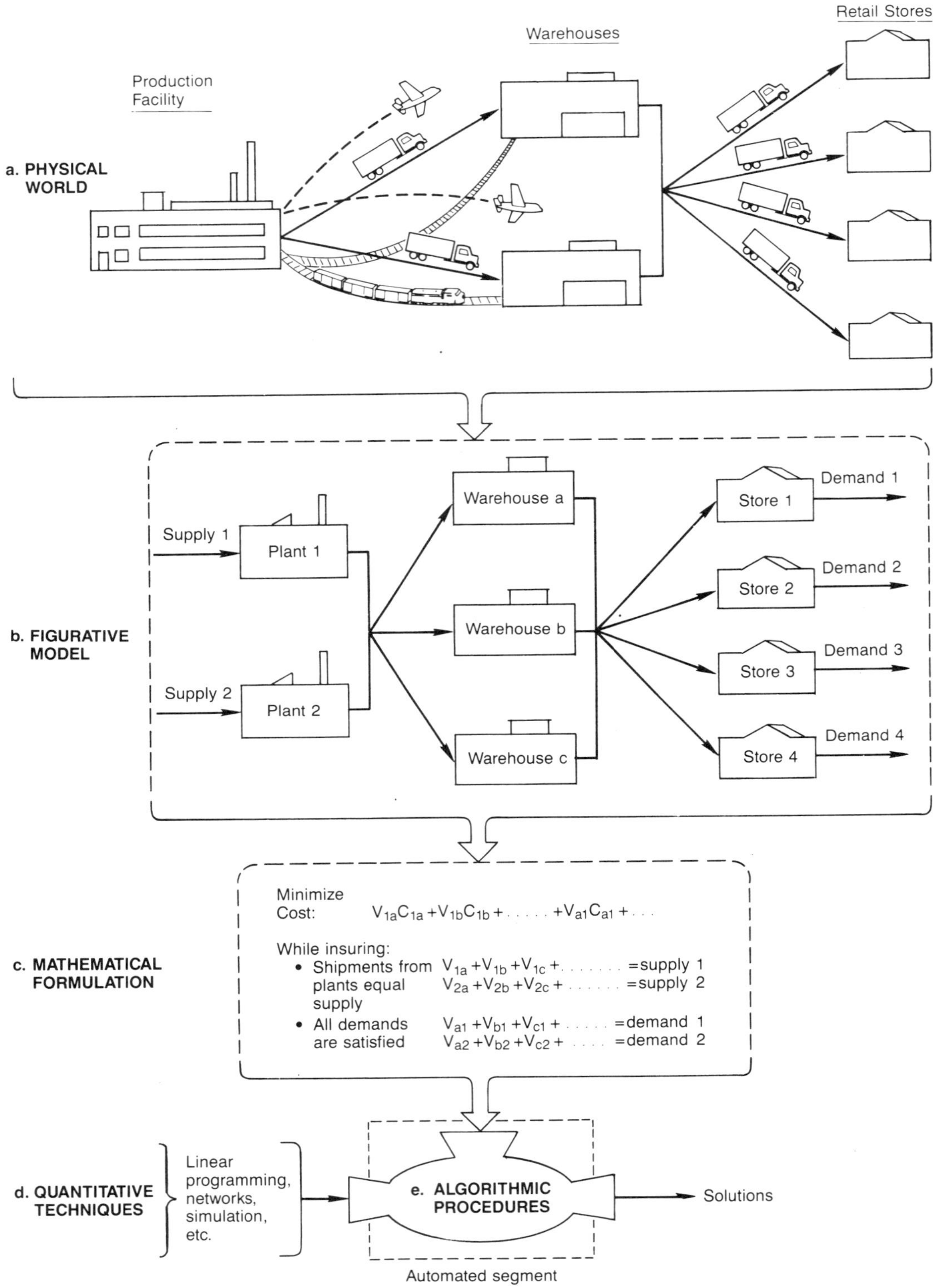

EXHIBIT 6–3 Quantitative Steps to a Decision Support Application.

- ☐ *The Figurative Model.* The first step is to translate the physical world (6–3a) into a diagrammatic or graphic form that depicts the structure of the problem and the relationship between its respective parts (6–3b). The figurative model acts as a pictorial or verbal statement about the problem. Although graphic representation may not be crucial in the simpler cases, it is essential to the more complicated and large scale applications.
- ☐ *Mathematical Formulation.* The figurative model must then be expressed in mathematical terms. The mathematical formulation "stitches" the elements of the problem together and depicts how the various parts depend and react to conditions in other parts of the problem (6–3c).
- ☐ *The Quantitative Technique.* Over the years, analysts have developed a large repertoire of quantitative "tools" that can be used to mathematically model complex situations (6–3d). Chapter 9 summarizes some of the more common techniques and illustrates how they are used (linear programming, simulation, networks, etc.). Each quantitative procedure is designed to analyze specific types of problems (production scheduling, material distribution, risk analysis, resource allocation, etc.).
- ☐ *Algorithmic Procedures.* The mathematical formulation is then transformed into a step-by-step procedure that can be used to solve the problem (6–3e). The specific algorithmic procedure that is selected will depend upon a multitude of factors (size of the problem, the chosen quantitative technique, the developer's background and experience, available software packages, etc.).

Sample of the Modeling Process

To better understand how the process works, consider a "simplification" of a very comprehensive DSS application: Nationwide distribution of products for a large scale manufacturing operation (Exhibit 6–3).

- ☐ The physical problem consists of a series of production plants, warehouse facilities and customer sites (6–3a). Products are shipped from the plant for temporary storage and distribution at the warehouses. Depending on customer locations and stock levels, products are eventually shipped out to the customer. Based on vehicles available, shippng cost, and so on, the decision maker must decide which plants should ship to which warehouses; which warehouse facilities service which customers; and where storage facilities should be geographically located.
- ☐ The complex physical layout and structure of the problem can be modeled as a series of circular figures to represent each plant, warehouse and customer, connecting paths to represent which plant ships to which warehouse, and which customers are serviced by which warehouse (Exhibit 6–3b). Associated with each path will be the volume of material it carries and the cost of shipping one unit along that route.
- ☐ The decision maker's objective is to minimize the cost of distributing products from production to the customer. The DSS will help the manager find the most inexpensive method of satisfying customer demands while conforming to the various constraints of the problem (supply at each plant, warehouse capacities, vehicle availability, etc.). The graphic and verbal interpretation of the problem must be formulated into numerous mathematical expressions to analyze the operation. For purposes of convenience let

us assume that only the following requirements need to be defined in a mathematical form:

- Minimize the total cost to ship the required products along all possible routes.
- Insure that the demands of each customer are satisfied. (The sum of all products shipped from each warehouse to a particular customer equals his demand.)
- The quantity shipped by each plant must balance with its production capacity. (The amount sent to all warehouses from a particular plant must equal the number of units produced at that plant.)

Based on the structure of the problem, a quantitative technique is chosen (Exhibit 6–3d). This particular problem is well-suited to solution by network optimization (discussed in Chapter 9). Step-by-step automated procedures (Exhibit 6–3e) are developed or an "off the shelf" package is used to manipulate the data in searching for an acceptable solution.

Obviously this particular example is quite extensive. Many decision support applications do not require such an elaborate scheme for quantitatively modeling and analyzing the problem. The procedure in Exhibit 6–3 does, however, reflect the general steps and scope of effort necessary to establish quantitative capabilities in a decision-support framework.

REPORT GENERATOR

The power of decision support comes not only from its quantitative abilities but also from the freedom provided to the manager to quickly review and access large quantities of information in a condensed form. The function of the report generator is to consolidate, arrange, sort, and display data in a concise and easily understandable format. The effective report generator allows each user to prescribe what range of information is to be examined and how it will be displayed. For example, in addition to determining the best distribution of products for a specific set of circumstances, the manager might also wish to know:

- ☐ What customers have a demand in excess of some specific amount?
- ☐ Which routes or modes of transportation (rail, air, etc.) have a shipping cost within a specified range?
- ☐ What is the total demand placed on each warehouse by all clients within a specified distance?
- ☐ How much of a particular set of products will be shipped through a specified region by a certain mode of transportation?

In a properly designed system the report generator gives the user the ability to query information in any conceivable fashion. Software packages are available that can provide report generator capability without the need for designing it directly into the DSS code. Often DBMS packages can also perform the functions of a report generator.

However, depending upon the computer hardware and user needs, many applications mandate that the report generating features be included in the DSS software.

USER INTERFACE

At the front end of any successful DSS application is an effective interface with the user. The user interface component is responsible for providing all interaction and communication between the computer and the manager. In the "ideal" DSS the interface component hides the technical complexities and internal mechanism necessary to automate the process. This places a significant burden on DSS developers. The user interface must function as an "understanding" interpreter and arbitrator between two foreign parties communicating in totally dissimiliar languages: the spoken tongue of the user and the strange rambling of computer terminology. To accomplish such a feat, the designer must insure that the user interface performs the following functions:

- ☐ Translate user inputs into the appropriate directions for the computer.
- ☐ Provide instructions and guidance that holds the hand of the newcomer without burdening the experienced veteran.
- ☐ Check the validity and logic of all user inputs (logical dates, inconsistent demands, etc.).
- ☐ Provide "self-teaching" features for the novice.
- ☐ Generate appropriate and informative responses that explain the results, recommend possible corrective actions, or suggest new directions to be evaluated.

Recall that the primary purpose of a DSS is to assist the decision maker directly. This requires a user interface attuned specifically to an audience that is unaccustomed to the typical "computereze" that technical personnel are comfortable with. Users must be able to communicate with the system on their terms. One of the unfortunate consequences of our fast-paced economy is the tendency to misinterpret or exploit a new concept. The major cause of dissatisfaction among managers wishing to apply decision support has been the absence of truly "user-friendly" features. Many of the systems referred to as DSS lack the user interface necessary to allow the busy manager and executive to apply the system directly.

Why then do so many systems fall short of a "human oriented" interface? One major reason is the time and effort required to design software so that it is tolerant and forgiving of the user, and can be understood without a lengthy and involved learning process. Depending upon the application, roughly 30 to 60 percent of development goes into creating an effective user interface. The second major cause stems from software designers. The background and technical training required to develop sophisticated computer systems often leads the designer to accept the premise that what is "good for the goose is good for the gander." Many analysts and programmers frequently ignore the reluctance of nontechnical users to accept the complexities of computer jargon.

In Chapter 4 we discussed three basic types of audiences: technically oriented, technically informed, and technically naive. There are situations where a "semi-technical" interface can be tolerated. Such conditions arise when the technical staff is responsible for operating the system, inputting the various scenarios proposed by management, translating the results to the decision maker, and repeating the process until the preferred course of action is found. Such a procedure may be feasible for some of the more exotic and large scale applications (intelligence analysis, military tactical analysis and strategic evaluations, facility location studies, etc.). However, the primary candidates and merit for applying DSS are in those areas where a conversational, English-oriented dialogue with the user is essential.

EXERCISE

To appreciate how a quantitative model is developed, consider a simplified problem. The movement of personnel in and out of an organization can often be modeled as a container of fluid. The level of the fluid represents the level of the workforce (call it "W"). At the bottom of the container is a hole where fluid leaks out at a rate proportionate to the level of the workforce. This leakage represents people leaving the system (referred to as "attrition"). Assuming that this rate of annual attrition (call it "a") is constant, then the flow of people out of the organization will equal the attrition rate times the level of the workforce ("aW"). The flow of people into the organization can be viewed as another container where the fluid level represents the level of personnel recruiting (call it "R"). At the bottom of this reservoir is a hole where fluid leaks out at a rate proportionate to the recruiting level (referred to as the annual rate of hiring "h"). The flow out of this container (and into the organization) would be the product of the level of recruiting and the rate of hiring ("hR"). Draw the figurative model for this situation. To insure that the level of the workforce remains constant in the organization, what condition or relationship must hold true between the various parts of this problem?

7

Database Management Capabilities

The field of Database Management (DBM) is very broad and the central topic of many texts. Although the functional aspects of DBM are important to the system designer, they are beyond the scope and intent of this text. However, a basic understanding as to what DBM does and how it does it will provide an appreciation for the role DBM plays in the overall DSS application. We will discuss a few key concepts and fundamentals about DBM. Readers interested in a more in-depth discussion of DBM technology can consult the references at the end of this chapter [3,4,6,7,8,10,13,14].

FUNCTIONAL ASPECTS

The DBM component is that portion of the system responsible for getting information to and from the database. When the DBM capabilities are included as an integral part of the system, the DBM program is tied specifically to that application. The program statements that access and manipulate information from the database are actually integrated directly into the programming code of the system (Exhibit 7–1). When a DBMS is used, the DBM capabilities are provided as a separate independent system. In most cases, this means that many applications can be served concurrently from the same DBM program and can access mutual databases more readily. A DBMS can be generalized into four major components (Exhibit 7–1):

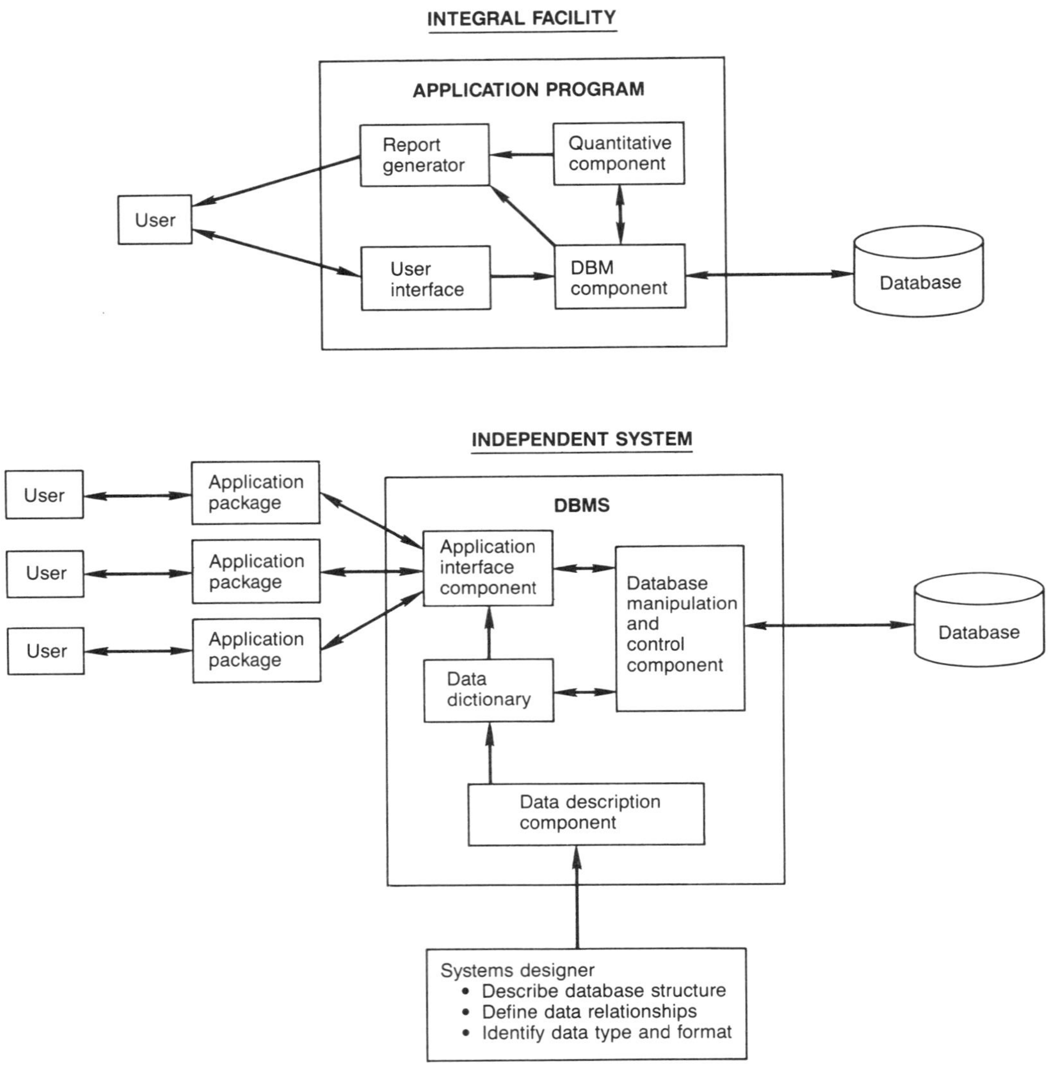

EXHIBIT 7–1 How the DBM Component Functions.

- ☐ The data description component (used by the developer to create and structure the database).
- ☐ The data dictionary (identifies what is stored in the database).
- ☐ The database manipulation and control component (provides access, data insertion, deletion, file maintenance, and data updates).
- ☐ That portion of the DBMS that interacts with the various applications.

DBM capabilities are a central function to any information system. The DBM component acts as both a conductor and controller in directing and funneling the flow of information between the database and other parts of the system. In terms of a DSS, the relationship between the DBM components and other parts of the system can be summarized as follows:

- ☐ *Database Maintenance.* DBM provides data maintenance and "housekeeping" capabilities. This includes updating, inserting, deleting, retrieving, sorting, and general "clean-up" (archiving, data compression, etc.) of information stored in the database.
- ☐ *Quantitative Component.* When the application requires the use of quantitative procedures (Chapter 9), the DBM unit provides the historical and parametric data (resource levels, consumption rates, costing factors, workload estimates, etc.) needed in the computations. The DBM component can also retain a track record of the various scenarios (that is, "what if" drills) that have been evaluated. This is especially important in the more sophisticated applications where the manager can quickly become overwhelmed by where he has been (all the possible alternatives evaluated) and where he needs to go next (what he has learned from his previous solutions). By viewing trends in the solutions (changes in cost, productivity, etc.), the decision maker has a progressive record that can provide insight as to which new alternatives need to be evaluated (increase resources in division A, decrease investments in option B, etc.).
- ☐ *Report Generator.* Based on the instructions and commands issued by the user, the report generator retrieves information from the database via the DBM facility, sorts and organizes the data into the prescribed report format, and displays the information back to the user.

DATA DICTIONARY

The data dictionary provides a running inventory of each data element, where it is located, what it is used for, what type of information it is (date, written text, numeric, etc.), and what application uses it. This is especially important in the more sophisticated multi-user systems where a variety of applications rely on the same DBMS. Data dictionaries can be used by the software itself (to keep track of information) or by the organization. In the latter case, the dictionary can help users (and applications developers) insure the consistency and currency of information maintained at different sites by various users.

ORGANIZATIONAL METHODOLOGY

In the previous chapter we discussed the contents of a datafile. It is also important to understand how information is stored and organized in the datafile because it affects the programming complexity and revision flexibility. A variety of methods are used by DBM facilities to organize and structure the datafile. We will examine three of the more prevalent approaches: relational, hierarchical and rule based systems ([16,19] provide a survey of some of the commercially available systems).

- ☐ *Relational.* Relational systems store information in the form of a table (Exhibit 7–2). Each row represents one record of information about some entity (a person, vehicle, organization, etc.) and each column represents one attribute about that entity (name, location, identification number, etc.). Relational databases are intuitively appealing because of their tabular layout. They are also easier to deal with and develop.

- ☐ *Hierarchical.* Information in a hierarchical system is structured in the pattern of an upside down tree. Each field in a record can be related or tied to other records by pointers (Exhibit 7–2). The operational aspects required for the DBM to keep track of and access information structured in such a manner can be quite complex and may result in complicated programming procedures for the developer.

- ☐ *Rule Based.* We mentioned in Chapter 5 that many applications require the corporate memory and experience of an organization (or group of experts) be used to identify the probable cause for an event, or the recommended course of action for a specific set of circumstances. DSS used to support such decisions were referred to as Expert Systems. For such applications, the information is stored in the database in the form of "IF-THEN" rules that reflect the relationship between observed conditions and the likely reason for the conditions. The database storing such *cause and effect* relationships is commonly referred to as a knowledge base. In a rule-oriented database, information is organized and structured in an "IF-THEN" pattern, for example:
  - IF outlet.pressure < 120 AND inlet.temperature < 600 THEN RESULT = flow.regulatory OR fuel.injector OR bleed.port
  - IF signal.ratio < .4 AND input.voltage > 1.2 THEN circuit 3 CONDITION = normal
  - IF salary > 3000, liability < 15000, assets > 10000 THEN loan.ceiling = 40000.

In terms of relational and hierarchical systems, there are proponents of both methods. The use of hierarchical systems is the more traditional approach (historically speaking) to structuring data. Many of the established DBMS have been built upon a hierarchical philosophy. Systems designers "weaned" on such DBM facilities are often reluctant to change. However, because of their simplicity and productivity improvements, relational systems are gaining increased interest.

In most situations it is a matter of judgment. If the DBM will be an integral part of the application program and a tabular form will suffice, then a relational structure should be used because of programming simplicity and the flexibility for structural changes in the event revisions are required. If the structure among the records is totally predictable and unchanging (as in a manufacturing control system), and the data fosters a complex tree structure (Exhibit 7–2), then a hierarchical system would be appropriate.

RELATIONAL (TABULAR)

VEHICLE TYPE	NUMBER	CAPACITY	LOCATION OR DESTINATION	SCHEDULED PREVENTIVE MAINTENANCE	STATUS
Tanker	AX104	2000 gallons	Warehouse 4	May 87	In route
Haul	K6B12	100 ton	Dock 2	Sept 86	Loading
Freight	J94D3	1500 cu. ft.	Shop 4	March 87	Down for repair
⋮	⋮	⋮	⋮	⋮	⋮
⋮	⋮	⋮	⋮	⋮	⋮

HIERARCHICAL (TREE)

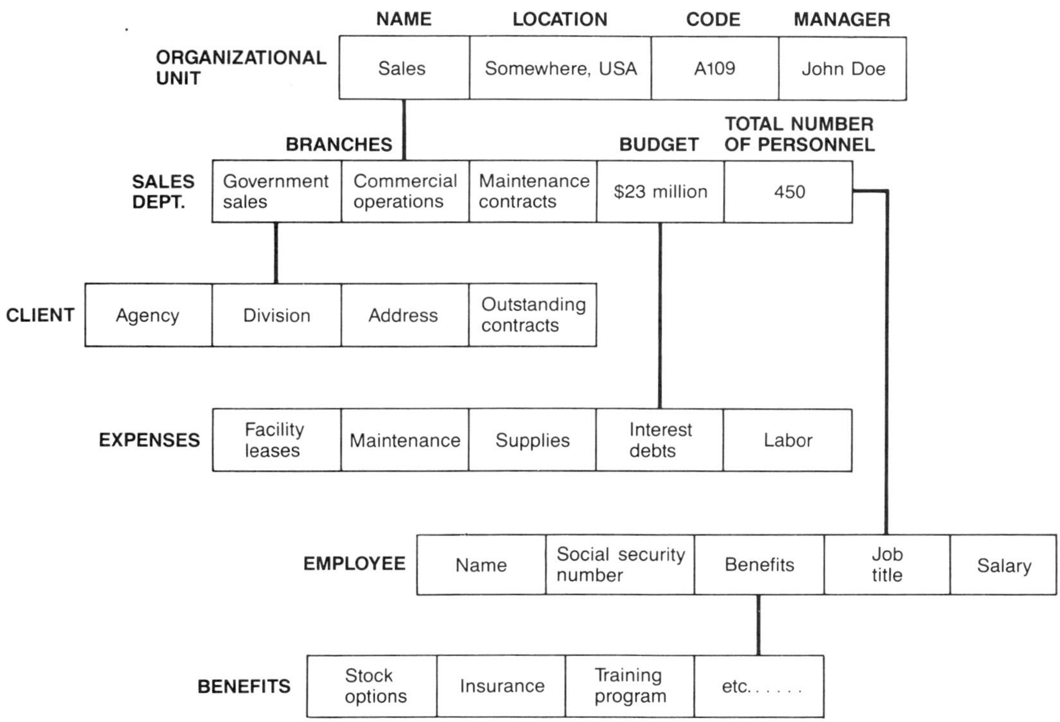

EXHIBIT 7–2 DBM Organizational Methodologies.

DISTRIBUTED SYSTEMS

In a large scale broad-based application, information must frequently be positioned, accessed, and maintained from geographically dispersed sites. Examples would include: inventory tracking and control for a large retail organization, dispersing operations for a nationwide product distribution network, financial transactions for a major banking institution, and the requirement to command and control a continental multi-force military operation. Attempting to maintain information disjointly under such conditions would be impractical. Distributed systems allow an organization to combine and exchange its information resources in a controlled and responsive fashion [1,5,9,11,12,15,20].

In addition to the components depicted in Exhbit 7–1, a distributed system requires a communication media (network) to exchange the data, and information processors to control the routing and sharing of information. The architecture (or layout) of a distributed system can vary extensively depending on where the database(s) is located, where the information is processed, and the interconnectivity of the communication network that links the system together. Exhibit 7–3 demonstrates several sample architectures for distributed systems.

One of the factors that influence a distributed system's architecture is how the application evolves. If the system is implemented from "ground zero" (the organization is void of existing computer hardware), then a controlled and phased implementation plan is possible. In such cases, compatible computer hardware and communication equipment is installed incrementally at each level of the organization. In many situations, however, a baseline of existing hardware, information systems and segmented

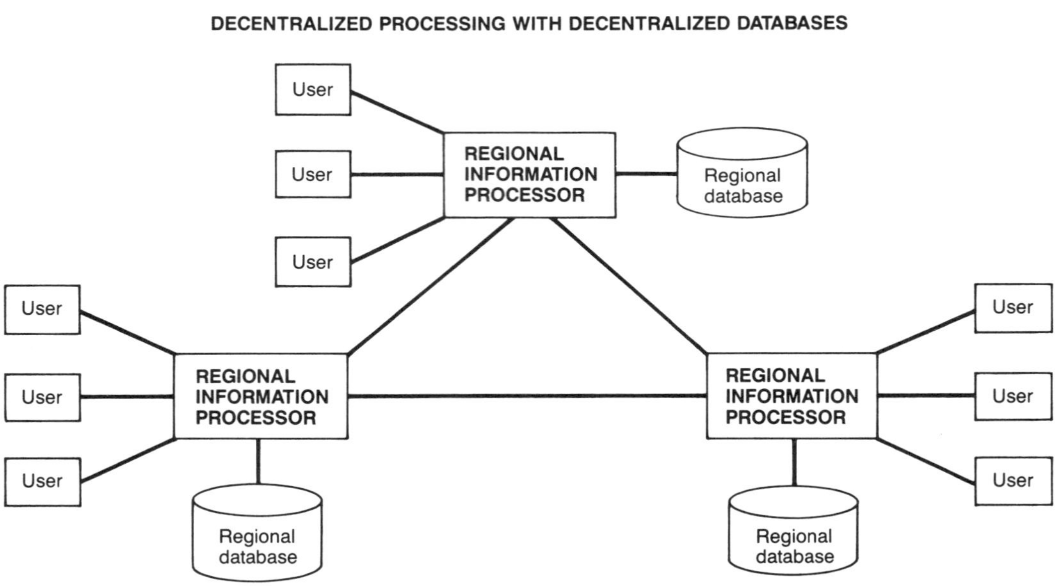

EXHIBIT 7–3 Sample Architectures for Distributed DBM Facilities.

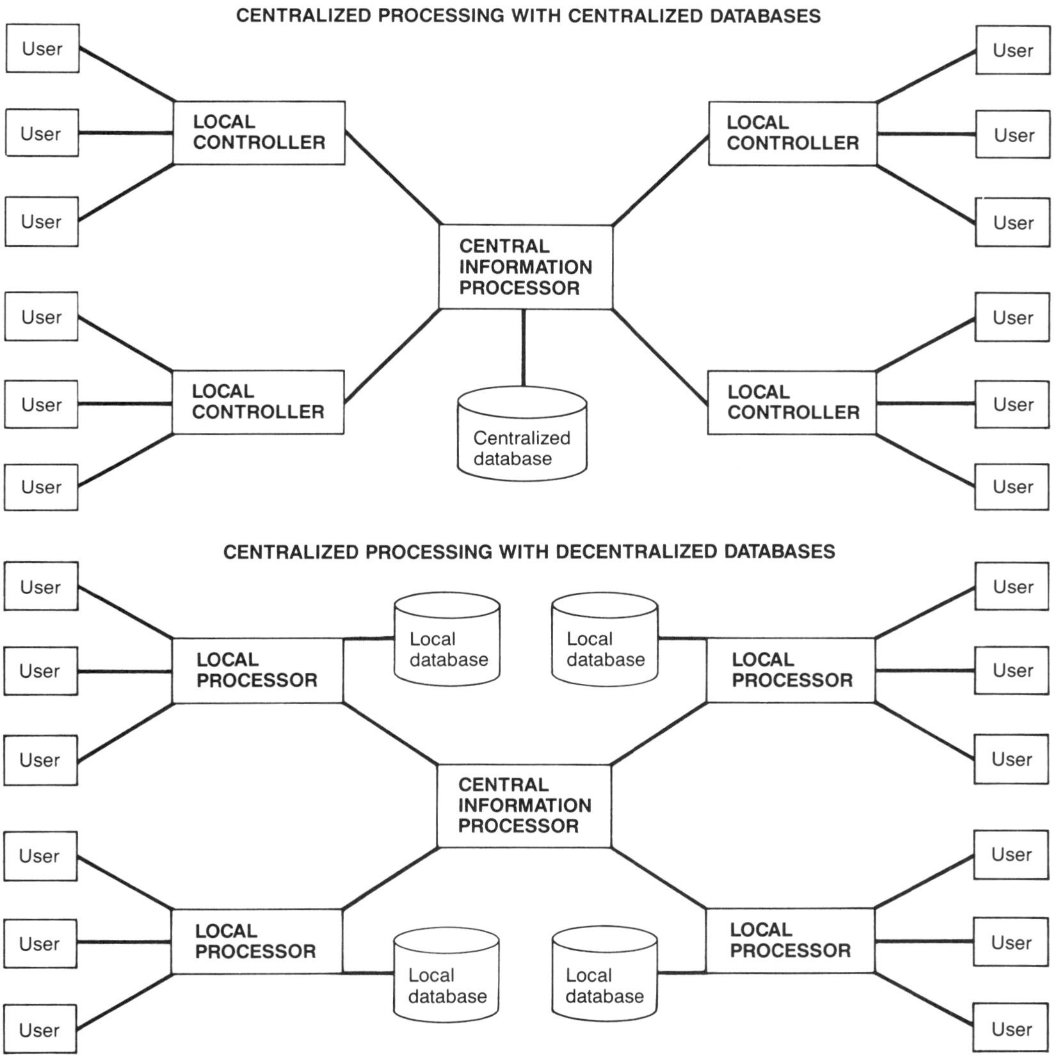

EXHIBIT 7–3 (Continued)

databases is inherited. Creating a distributed system from such fragmented (and often incompatible) hardware/software components is a difficult process, requiring special considerations [2] far beyond those of a system developed from scratch.

Distributed DBM is an important facet of large scale decision-support applications because it allows for common and responsive access to the corporate knowledge of an organization. Managers can make difficult decisions with a broader understanding of their implications across the total organization and with greater assurance that the information reflects the most current conditions. On the positive side, distributed systems allow more complete decisions, provide more reliable information, result in less data redundancy, and are more responsive. On the negative side, they require a significantly greater resource commitment for both implementation and operation, necessitate more complex administrative procedures, and are more difficult to insure security.

EVALUATION CRITERIA

When an independent DBMS is used to provide the necessary DBM capabilities, several factors must be evaluated to insure the system selected best satisfies the requirement [8,17,18], specifically:

- *Performance.* Obviously, the performance of a DBMS is important to the user. Speed, however, can be a crucial factor for applications requiring large databases and/or many concurrent user operations. Under such conditions the manager should obtain an estimate of the average time required for the DBMS to retrieve information for a typical report or computational exercise and assess whether or not such a time factor is acceptable.
- *Flexibility.* We mentioned earlier that certain DBM organizational methodologies (like relational systems) are more flexible to change. Although the structural stability of a problem should be considered in selecting a DBMS, keep in mind that an increase in flexibility is frequently obtained at the cost of reduced performance. In applications where the structure is susceptible to change, the manager must trade off operational performance with the increased productivity provided to application developers by the more flexible systems.
- *Modular Interface.* In the development of the more sophisticated decision-support applications (Bands 2 and 3 of Exhibit 2–1), the ability of a DBMS to interface with other DSS components can be an important consideration. The more elementary systems do not permit file access from other programs and are designed primarily to support ad hoc inquiries or batch-oriented reporting from large databases. Other DBMS allow access of databases by outside programs but requires that the DBMS and other programs be executed independently by the user. The more comprehensive packages have the capability of linking, in an integral fashion, with other programs that were developed using procedural languages (FORTRAN, COBOL, etc.). This means that, from a user's perspective, there is no apparent distinction or separation between the DBMS and the other DSS components (for example, the application is seen as an integral system). The modular adaptability of a DBMS should be considered if it is likely that the package will be required to interface with other programs.
- *Economics.* There is significant variation between the cost of commercially available DBMS. A comparison of the features and capabilities of each system should be stacked up against the price to insure the most cost effective package is acquired.

DATA ADMINISTRATION

When an application relies heavily on a continually changing pool of data, it is essential that the information be administered and maintained in a dedicated and consistent fashion. This means that for each element of information stored in the database, an appropriate unit within the organization is assigned the responsibility for insuring its accuracy and currency. If well-defined and prescribed policies are not institutionalized within the organization, the database can gradually become outdated, inaccurate and unreliable.

EXERCISES

1. Create a relational database (pictorially) for tracking the status of vehicles in a car rental company. Show the records and fields necessary for tracking vehicle characteristics, their location, and customer attributes (pick up date, name, form of payment, etc.).

2. Show the organization and relationship for a hierarchical database used to track projects. Assume each project is made up of several tasks and each task requires various types of resources (funds, staff years, etc.). Be sure to define the characteristics of the records at each level of the hierarchy (projects include a title, a manager, and a description; tasks have a name, a duration, a start/stop date, etc.; and resources include type, source, and amount).

3. Identify a problem where an individual must diagnose the reason for a particular situation based on known conditions (that is, a doctor diagnosing an illness, a car mechanic analyzing the reason why a vehicle will not start, an investigation team trying to assess the cause of an airplane crash, etc.). Create four or five of the "cause and effect" (IF-THEN) relationships in a rule based database.

4. Consider again the application described in Exercise 3 of Chapter 5. Assume that the following conditions apply to the DBM facility for that system:
   - ☐ There are four regional centers. Each center connects all field units in that region. Each region has its own database. Field units do not have a local database but instead store their information at the regional center.
   - ☐ All four regions are interconnected so that any regional database can be accessed by any field unit in any region.
   - ☐ All four regions are connected to a central database located at headquarters. Information is periodically transferred (through the network) from the regional centers to insure the headquarters database remains current.

   Draw a diagram that represents the distributed system for this application. Show where both the databases and information processors are located, and the connections between them.

REFERENCES AND SUGGESTED READING

1. Booth, G., *The Distributed Systems Environment,* New York, N.Y.: McGraw-Hill, 1981.
2. Booth, G., "Distributed Databases on Unlike Computers," in Hannan, J. (ed.), *Database Management,* New York, N.Y.: Auerbach Publishing, 1982.
3. Curtis, R. and W. Casey, "Database: What's in Store?" *Datamation,* December 1, 1985.
4. Date, C., *An Introduction to Database Systems,* Reading, MA: Addison-Wesley, 1981.
5. Delobel, C. and W. Litmin, *Distributed Databases,* New York, N.Y.: North-Holland, 1980.
6. Frost, R., *Database Management Systems,* New York, N.Y.: McGraw-Hill Co., 1984.
7. Hannan, J. (ed.), *A Practical Guide to Database Management,* New York, N.Y.: Auerbach Publishing, 1982.
8. Inmon, W., *Effective Database Design,* Englewood Cliffs, N.J.: Prentice-Hall, 1981.
9. Katzan, H., *Distributed Information Systems,* Princeton, N.J.: Petrocelli Books, 1979.
10. Larson, J., *Database Management System Antonomy,* San Diego, CA: Lexington Books, 1982.
11. Lientz, B., *An Introduction to Distributed Systems,* Reading, MA: Addison-Wesley Publishing, 1981.
12. Lorin, H., *Aspects of Distributed Computer Systems,* New York, N.Y.: Wiley & Sons, 1982.
13. Martin, J., *Computer Database Organization,* Englewood Cliffs, N.J.: Prentice-Hall, 1977.
14. Martin, J., *An End User's Guide to Databases,* Englewood Cliffs, N.J.: Prentice-Hall, 1981.
15. Mohan, C., "Future Trends in Distributed Database Management, in Ariav, G. and J. Clifford (eds.), *New Directions in Database Systems,* Norwood, N.J.: Ablex Publishing, 1986.
16. Perry, R., "Relational DBMS Takeoff," *Computer Decisions,* February 12, 1985.
17. Ross, R., *Database Systems: Design, Implementation and Management,* New York, N.Y.: AMACOM, 1978.
18. Sibley, E., "How to Select and Evaluate a DBMS," *Journal of Information Systems Management,* Spring, 1985.
19. Sweet, F., "What, if Anything, is a Relational Database?" *Datamation,* July 15, 1984.
20. Tashenberg, B., *Design and Implementation of Distributed Processing,* New York, N.Y.: AMACOM, 1984.

8

The User Interface

The promise of versatile and conversational systems has not been fulfilled to the extent purported by many vendors and developers. The disconnect between what decision makers need and what is available can be attributed to two major factors. First, establishing a truly user-friendly interface is not a cost-free proposition. "Ease of use" does not infer ease of programming by any means. Second, most developers are technical by trade and comfortable with analytical terminology and "computerese." They have difficulty understanding the busy world of the decision maker.

The successful DSS must insure that the human side takes top priority over all other considerations. This can only be accomplished if the designer understands that the user interface is the prime motivation for the system and not an afterthought. Technical "wizards" must appreciate that a true decision-support environment does not result from:

- ☐ Using complex jargon and a technical syntax.
- ☐ Relying on a two foot stack of manuals to explain the system.
- ☐ Using training to bring the user in line with the "needs of the system."

THE OBJECTIVE

The ideal DSS establishes a conversational exchange with the user by communicating in simple everyday English. The prime objective must be to bring the computer up to a level that the user is comfortable with and not the reverse. There are four major traps that cause many systems to fall short of the true objectives of decision support: ignoring the user's world, depending on user training to make up for a technical interface, not considering the breadth of the user populace, and not providing sufficient flexibility to the user.

The User's World

Requiring the user to learn new unfamiliar terminology is not only inefficient but causes apprehension on the part of the busy manager. For example, the prompt:

INPUT FILE SPEC

is oriented toward the computer specialist. A more effective query would be:

ENTER THE NAME OF YOUR PROBLEM

The DSS must conform to the user's environment. Terms such as:

INPUT, INTERFACE, ATTRIBUTE, PARAMETER, PROTOCOL, and so forth

are examples of phrases that cause confusion and uncertainty in the majority of normal users. To avoid "terminology traps," the potential user audience should always be consulted for an unassisted interpretation of questions and instructions provided by the system. If a prompt has to be explained, it should be rewritten.

Special Training

One of the greatest fallacies in developing a DSS is to assume that training is a valid substitute for a true user-friendly environment. This is not to infer that training has no value to a successful application. Personnel with no prior experience in using computers can profit from indoctrination sessions. The system should not, however, rely on an extensive training program to compensate for the absence of a well-designed user interface, nor should the user be required to wade through volumes of documentation. Chapter 11 provides a further discussion of user training and system documentation.

Scope Of User Populace

It is much easier to design a DSS for a single group of users to perform specialized operations (such as the automotive industry, medical institutions, banking organizations, petroleum industry), than to create a system that will be used across a broad spectrum of markets and areas of application. If the system will always be used in a specialized market, a terminology peculiar to the particular operation is permissible. Consider the DSS designed to help schedule student pilots for various flight training events (Case Study 2 in Chapter 12). The terms syllabus, currency, brief time, and so forth, have a special concise meaning to the user and are essential to that particular operating environment. If, on the other hand, the DSS will be used by various audiences with different backgrounds, then care must be exercised to select terms that are generic enough to be understood by all, yet convey the correct idea (not an easy task). For example, the term EOD (Estimated Onboard Date) in a workforce planning system may be quite informative to one group of users but can also leave a large number of applicants wondering as to its real meaning.

User Flexibility

A DSS should be designed to grow with the needs of the organization. Rarely in the modern business world do conditions remain stagnant. As the operation changes the user should have the capability to tailor the system to new requirements. The designer should try and visualize future needs and incorporate into the system the flexibility of altering the features of the DSS without having to resort to reprogramming. Although it is impossible to account for all alterations, there are ways to provide the user with a significant amount of freedom in adjusting to new requirements.

THE METHODS

Odds are that a survey of most of the so called "user-friendly" systems would result in a less than favorable response. Why is it so difficult for system developers to respect the real needs of managers and the busy executive? Are there not some standard rules that can be applied to help create a truly conversational environment? The only true requirement to make an interactive system communicate on a human level is to exercise *common sense.* Why this is such a difficult feat is unclear. This section summarizes some of the "common sense" techniques that should be used in constructing a DSS. The noted features should also be considered by managers performing a comparative evaluation of several prepackaged systems or preparing contract specifications for development of a unique application.

Murphy Proofing

Humans, by nature, are error prone. The DSS must be designed to catch practically every mistake that the user can conceivably make. The user should never worry that any of his actions can cause the system to "bomb." The DSS must also verify that all entries are logical and reasonable. For example:

- ☐ Numeric entries are valid (such as all numeric characters, only one decimal, integers where necessary).
- ☐ Values are logical (number of personnel is positive, percentages are less than 100 percent, and so forth).
- ☐ When mistakes are made, the user is informed of his possible correction actions.

Consistency

Whichever methods are used to establish the proper user interface, procedures and practices should be consistent throughout the system. The user should only be required to adapt to one set of rules. Examples include:

- ☐ If the word END is used in one part of the system to terminate an option then "switch hitting" with STOP, QUIT or FINISHED somewhere else is ineffective.
- ☐ Formats should remain constant (that is, if dates are entered as 9/10/85 in one place, changing to 10 SEPT 85 is inconsistent).
- ☐ The order of data entry should stay the same (that is, if items are displayed in a report as NAME, DIVISION, and COST then the system should prompt the user to enter NAME, DIVISION, and COST in the same order).

Stereotypes

The field of human engineering has long established that conforming to normal stereotypes results in less errors and confusion. Human stereotypes deal with the order and groupings that people typically "infer" when responding to a prompt. For example:

- ☐ Questions should almost always be asked in a positive sense (WANT TO DELETE THE RECORD? is preferred to WANT TO CANCEL THE DELETE?).
- ☐ Common everyday responses should be used (the logical response to WANT TO CONTINUE? is YES or NO, not a special ACCEPT or REJECT key).
- ☐ Entries should be requested in an ascending order (ENTER START AND STOP DATES is better than the reverse).

On-line Assistance

Few users have the time or inclination to weed through stacks of manuals. Providing on-line assistance is much more convenient and allows the user to learn as he goes at his own pace. There are a variety of techniques that can be used to facilitate the learning process:

- ☐ TUTOR packages can be included with the DSS to provide an interactive instruction device that demonstrates the system in action.
- ☐ HELP options should be available at each level of the system to inform the user what is expected, what is possible, and how it is done.

- ☐ ALTERNATIVE COURSES OF ACTION can often be provided to help a user determine possible choices and recommended directions.

Help the Novice Without Burdening the Veteran

The effectively designed DSS reaches a proper balance between "assistance" and "nuisance." The system should be able to lead the newcomer by the hand without burdening the experienced user. Some of the methods that allow a DSS to help the novice without slowing down the veteran include:

- ☐ *Selective listing of menus.* Menus are only listed when a question mark is entered.
- ☐ *Multiple level instructions.* Long instructions are provided with each prompt until the user becomes experienced. The user can then select an option that changes instructions to a condensed form.
- ☐ *Result interpretations.* Extensive explanations of solutions are provided until the user becomes a veteran.
- ☐ *Aliases.* The user is allowed to create a set of alternative names or aliases for identifying entries once experience has been gained (that is, the user can either type in ESTIMATED TIME OF ARRIVAL or the selected abbreviation ETA).

Command Structure

There are two basic methods for selecting the different functions and capabilities within a DSS: menu trees and single entry commands. Menu trees are structured like the roots of a tree. At each level (or branch) the user is provided with a list of related options such as: updating different types of data, listing various parts of the problem, identifying selected parameters to be used in the solution, and so forth. Each time an option is selected a new menu of additional options pertaining to that particular function (like updating data) is provided. The user continues selecting options (within options) until the lowest part of a branch is reached (entering data, listing resources, etc.). When the user is finished with one option he returns back up the root (to the next higher branch) by entering END, STOP, QUIT or some similar command. Exhibit 8-1 provides an example of a menu driven system.

Single entry commands permit the user to choose any function or option by just entering one line. This is accomplished by selecting from a long "laundry" list of distinctly different commands. Although single entry commands are faster, they do require the user to recall a multitude of possible choices. For simple systems with only a few functions (options) single entry commands provide an efficient approach. However, in a large scale application (like that of Exhibit 8-1), such techniques place an unacceptable burden on the user.

Menu trees are the most user-friendly approach of allowing the user to define which part of the system he wishes to use. They are a helpful device for the periodic user who does not wish to memorize a set or sequence of special commands. They also require more time than single entry commands since several entries may be required to reach a particular level. To combine the best of both worlds, some of the truly sophisticated systems allow the user to apply both techniques. The newcomer can use the menu trees until he becomes familiar with the system. Then, by entering on one line all the desired options, the user is taken directly to the desired level. For example, the experienced user might choose to enter UPDATE INSTRUCTOR FLIGHTS on the same line and go directly to entering instructor flight records (Exhibit 8–1) instead of stepping from menu to menu. Whichever method is used, the choice of available options should correspond to names or phrases that are naturally associated with the function being executed. For example, a common approach is to number options (0,1 2,3, ...) since this simplifies programming efforts. The more logical and user-friendly method is to use distinctively different words that the user can become more readily accustomed to such as UPDATE, LIST, SEARCH, and so forth.

Data Entry

Regardless of the application, the user will eventually be required to enter data that defines the characteristics and properties of the problem (available resources, physical conditions, desired policies, etc.). There are two important considerations to take into account when selecting the appropriate method for entering information: How will the user be prompted, and how will the data be entered into the system.

There are two basic ways that a user can be asked to enter data. The first approach is to allow the user to select which elements of information are to be defined. The alternative is for the system to sequentially prompt the user for specific items that are necessary to carry out a certain set of tasks.

The next factor to consider is how the information will be entered by the user. There are three fundamental schemes for identifying data: single value, multiple line, and screen patterned entries. The complexity of the problem and type of information will determine which approach is most appropriate. Before examining the pros and cons of each method, a few examples are in order.

In Exhibit 8–2 the user decides which task is to be performed on the files used to store the problem by choosing from a menu of possible options. Once the desired option has been selected, the user is then asked to enter a singular value (the name of the problem to be deleted). Note that the purpose here was very simple and only a single value (the name) was necessary to indicate the user's intent.

Complex managerial problems typically require many parameters to be identified before a solution can be reached. Exhibit 8–3 illustrates a case where the user selects which parameters are to apply in a particular situation and then enters them on multiple lines without further prompting. Deciding which values should be used for a specific setting requires a sophisticated audience with sufficient experience to visualize the total decision environment (Chapter 3). In such cases it is often more effective for the user to be sequentially queried for all the necessary bits of information that are required to solve the problem under given conditions (Exhibits 8–4 and 8–5).

Often the user will be required to enter a large number of characteristics and values for each element of the problem. Consider scheduling the maintenance activities of

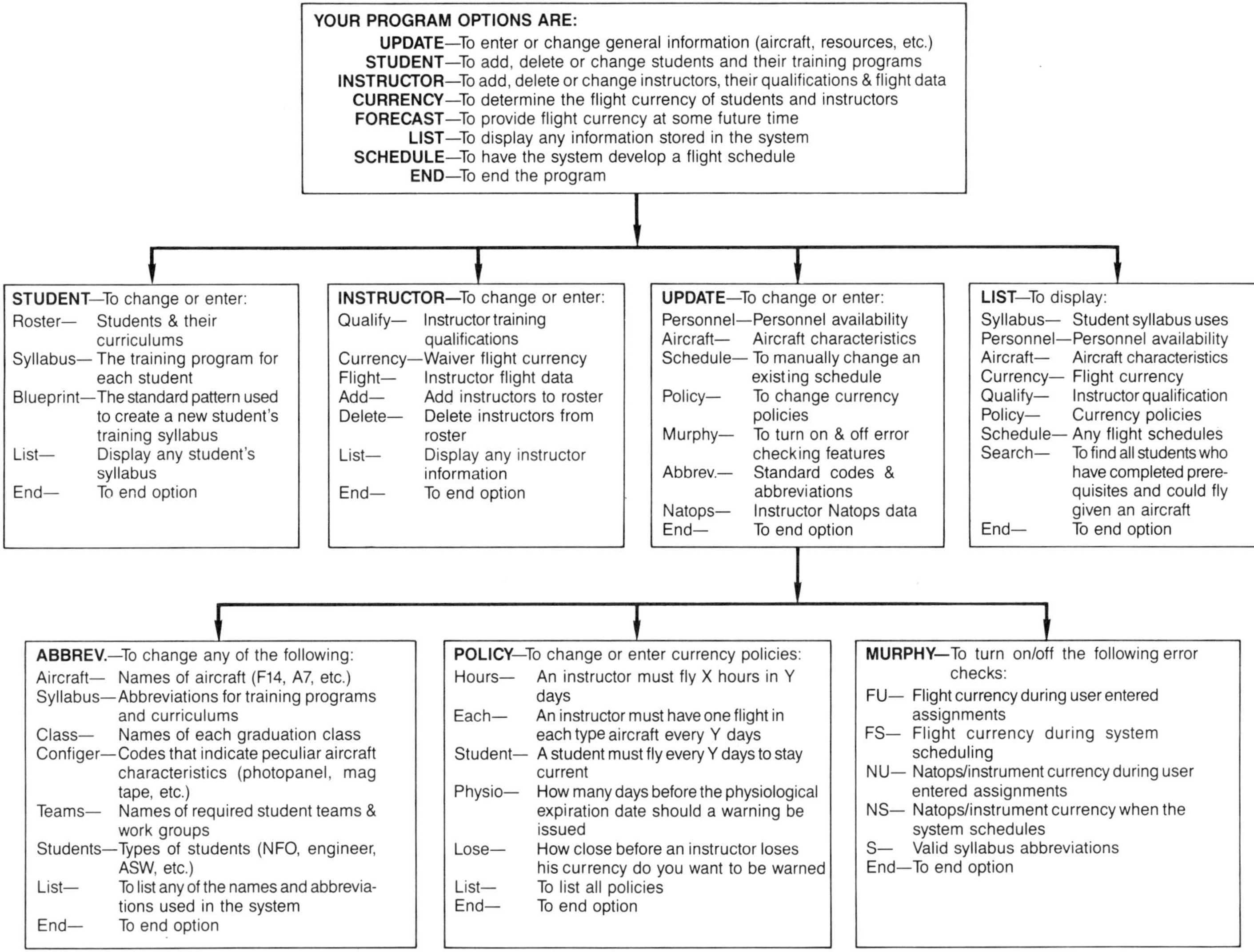

EXHIBIT 8–1 Road Map for a Menu Driven System.

```
     ENTER:

          SAVE -    To save your current problem

          LOAD -    To work on a different problem

          DELETE -  To delete a problem

          NAMES  -  To see the names and titles of existing
                    problems

          END -     To end this option

>DELETE

          ENTER NAME OF PROBLEM TO BE DELETED:

>BUDGET85
```

EXHIBIT 8–2 Selective Entry of Single Values

```
     TO DEFINE WHAT SET OF STUDENTS ARE TO BE SCHEDULED YOU MAY
     ENTER:

          GRADUATE -      and up to five graduation dates

          CURRICULUM -    and up to five study curriculums

          PREREQUISATES -and up to ten prerequisate courses that
                          must have been completed

          QUANTITY -      and the lower and upper limit on class
                          size

          ROOM -          and up to ten rooms that can be
                          considered

          SCHEDULE -      When you are ready to generate the
                          schedule

     NOW ENTER YOUR CHOICES -

>CURRICULUM   MATH  PHYSICS  ENGINEER
>GRADUATE  FALL85   SPRING85
>QUANTITY 2Ø 25
>ROOM MAIN1Ø5 MAIN1ØØ SOUTH3Ø2
>SCHEDULE
```

EXHIBIT 8–3 Selective Entry of Multiple Values.

```
ENTER THE AUTHORIZED STAFFING:  650

     ENTER PROJECTED RATE OF ATTRITION:  2%

     WILL A HIRING FREEZE BE IN EFFECT DURING THE  PROJECTED
     TIMEFRAME:  no

     HOW MANY RECRUIT ACTIONS ARE CURRENTLY IN PROCESS:  43

     ESTIMATED COST PER STAFF YEAR:  50,000

THE AVAILABLE GRAPHICS PER TIME PERIOD ARE:

     FUNDS -    STAFFING COST

     NOB -      NUMBER ON BOARD

     AVERAGE-   MOVING AVERAGE OF NUMBER ON BOARD

     MONITOR -  MONITORING ENVELOPES TO CONTROL RECRUITING

     NONE -     TO RECEIVE JUST TABLES AND NO GRAPHICS

ENTER DESIRED GRAPHICS:

> funds nob monitor
```

EXHIBIT 8–4 Sequential Prompting.

```
     What is the title of your problem?

> Evaluating Production Cutbacks

     What do you what to do?

> Minimize operating costs

     What is the equation that describes your operating costs?

> 500000 PLANT1 +  220000 PLANT2 + 360000 PLANT3 + 320000 PLANT4 +
>  240000 WAREHOUSE1 + 200000 WAREHOUSE2 + 170000 WAREHOUSE3

     What are your constraints?

> PRODUCTION.AT 1800PLANT1 + 1200PLANT2 + 900PLANT3 + 800PLANT4 > 3500
> STORAGE.AT 2500WAREHOUSE1 + 2000WAREHOUSE2 + 1600WAREHOUSE3  >3500
> OPERATE.AT.LEAST2 PLANT1 + PLANT2 + PLANT3 + PLANT4 > 2
> MAINTAIN.AT.LEAST2 WAREHOUSE1 + WAREHOUSE2 + WAREHOUSE3 > 2
```

EXHIBIT 8–5 Sequential Prompting for Complex Relationships.

a vehicle servicing facility. Each job requires entry of up to 18 conditions that pertain to that particular vehicle. A screen patterned entry of information is well suited to such situations (Exhibit 8–6). The user can easily visualize, enter, verify, and change data elements by moving up, down, and across the screen. Once all the information has been entered and viewed for one vehicle, the user continues to the next job.

The decision as to which approach best fits a particular situation will depend on the circumstances of each application. Choosing the most appropriate procedure for prompting and entering data should be based on the advantages of each method in a particular setting as summarized by the following criteria:

1. Single value entry is only appropriate for simple operations to identify two or three values such as:

ENTER START DATE

and

NOW ENTER COMPLETION DATE

2. Multiple line entries are most useful when the values pertain to the same type of information. An example would be a project scheduling application where the user had to identify the acceptable names of staff members (that is, M.DAVIS, K. DAVIS,

```
                 REQUIRED CORRECTIVE MAINTENANCE

JOB NUMBER:__________          DATE:__/__/__

VEHICLE MAKE:________________  YEAR:__

PARKING BAY:_________________  LICENSE NUMBER:_________________

CUSTOMER NAME:______________________________  PHONE:___________

COST ESTIMATE:_______________  SERVICE TIME:____________

SYMPTOMS:_________________________________________________________

         _________________________________________________________

         _________________________________________________________

         _________________________________________________________

SKILLS REQUIRED:__________________________________________________

                 DESIRED PREVENTIVE MAINTENANCE

LUBRICATION:______             TUNE-UP:_______

TIRE ROTATION:______           INSPECTION:_______

COST ESTIMATE:______________   SERVICE TIME:______
```

EXHIBIT 8–6 Screen Patterned Entry.

THOMAS, JOHNSON, MYERS). Multiple line entries can also be used when each value represents a different type of data provided the number of values entered on each line is moderate (say seven or eight). For example, if the user were to identify the characteristics for a fleet of shipping vehicles (type, registration number, capacity, and travel range) then using multiple line entries would be reasonable.

3. If the field (positions) of each value represent a different data element (name, class, qualifications, etc.) and more than seven or eight values must be entered for each record, then multiple line entries become confusing, error prone and inappropriate. In such cases it is more effective to use a screen patterned format as in Exhibit 8–6 (assuming screen facilities are available to the user).

4. Sequential prompting is most helpful in dealing with complex problems that require a large number or parameters and policies to be specified for each decision or in situations where the order of user entry is important. The "technically naive" or "technically informed" user (Chapter 4) is rarely trained in analytical methods and can easily become overwhelmed by the assortment of factors that must be defined in large scale problems. Sequential prompting helps to ensure that all necessary information is identified and validated in the correct order.

5. When the user is technically proficient or the number of required entries is small, then sequential prompting can be inefficient or result in overkill. If the type audience is uncertain, then the truly sophisticated DSS provides the user with the freedom to pick which method is preferred.

Flexibility

Often a system that is used heavily during its infancy will gradually fade away as the organization changes and grows. To prevent early obsolescence, a DSS must be designed with sufficient flexibility to allow the user to tailor system characteristics and capabilities to new requirements. Developing pliable features into a computerized package demands significant insight on the part of the designer. Obviously all future requirements cannot be envisioned and major structural changes are difficult to account for after the program has been designed. There are several features that can be incorporated into a DSS in order to provide a significant degree of freedom to the user. For example:

- ☐ *Nomenclature and terminology* change frequently in most organizations. The user should have the ability to modify what the data elements are called by simply using options available within the system. Names used in format headings, prompts to the user, report columns, and so forth, should also be accessible for revision without having to resort to reprogramming. Consider a manufacturing operation, where instead of distributing products by state, the new policy is to consolidate warehouses by region. The user should be able to have the "state" automatically changed to "region" in headings, prompts and reports by just selecting an option provided within the system.

- *Policy parameters* should not be fixed as permanent constants within the software. The user should have the freedom to revise policies as they change in the organization. For example, if the current policy in a flight training operation requires each pilot to complete at least one flight every 30 days, the supporting DSS must be capable of changing such policies without reprogramming.
- *User created commands* provide an innovative method to allow each user to tailor an application to their particular requirements. As previously noted, it is virtually impossible to preconceive all the intricacies of managing a complex operation. By using clever techniques for remembering a series of user entries and associated prompts, a DSS can be designed so that a user can easily create his own commands and options without going through an elaborate and confusing process. To illustrate, assume that a commercial DSS package is being used to manage and schedule customer deliveries of heating oil or natural gas. At a specific organization there is a particular requirement to determine: which customers are projected to need deliveries today, what deliveries were scheduled yesterday, and which were unsatisfied. Unfulfilled customers are then prioritized and scheduled for tomorrow's deliveries. The DSS is designed so that the user normally performs each of these tasks separately using different options. The user can select a "USER COMMAND" option that will create a new option called "DAILY." The user then tells the system which options and data entries are to be executed when the DAILY option is selected. Thereafter, the system will automatically perform each task in the proper sequence whenever the user created option DAILY is chosen. This feature allows each user to establish their own set of individualized capabilities just by using simple options available within the system.
- *External datafiles,* in a truly versatile DSS, will permit the user to interactively adjust formats so that data created elsewhere can be loaded into the system. Most systems require reprogramming to change the format used for reading information stored in a file. Such requirements occur when information is assembled from physically detached sites or when a database already exists at the time of system implementation.
- *Functional relationships* are often necessary to predict parameter values used in the DSS (cost, customer demands, consumption rates, task duration, and so forth). The user should have the capability of changing the relationships without having to modify the software itself. For example, if customer consumption of heating oil changes from a linear to an exponential function dependent on the average daily temperature, options should be available that permit the user to easily alter the relationship and, in turn, automatically recompute all affected values. Another example would be an application where the cost to ship items from one location to another might be a function of what mode of shipment was being considered (freight, rail, air) and the travel distance between the two points. The user would simply identify the mode of transportation, the start and destination cities, and the system would calculate the shipping cost based on computed distances and rate tables (Exhibit 8–7).
- *Simplifying user entries* is often crucial in large scale applications. The DSS must automate the process through which large quantities of information are entered into the system. For example, to identify possible shipping routes between two cities in Maryland and 30 in Virginia, each with its own characteristics (charge, capacity, travel time, etc.), would require 60 routes to be entered by the user manually. In a well-designed system (Exhibit 8–8), the computer automatically generates the routes and their char-

```
    What characteristics should be assigned to each route?

> ?

    The amount that will be shipped along each route can be affected
    by several factors, such as:

    COST        to ship one unit along that route
    MINIMUM     you will allow to be shipped
    MAXIMUM     shipping capacity
    TYPE        of route (1st class, air, rail, etc)
    END         when you are done

    You  can  either  assign a fixed cost for each route  or  I  will
    assign the cost based on properties of that route.  For  example,
    entering the following for cost will have the noted affect:

    COST   DISTANCE  predicts cost based on the "crow  fly"  distance
                     between two cities.
    COST   REGION    estimates cost based on a charge (rate)  table
                     between two regions.
    COST   LENGTH    uses the travel length of the route to calculate
                     transportation costs.
    COST   1.20      means that it costs $1.20 to ship one unit along
                     that route.

    What characteristics should be assigned to each route?

> cost distance
> min 10000
> max 30000
> type freight
> end
```

EXHIBIT 8–7 Use of Functional Relationships to Assign Values.

acteristics, once the user identifies the starting and destination cities (for example, two lines versus 60 would be entered).

Solution Interpretation

In the more sophisticated applications, the user can quickly become overwhelmed by the complexities of the problem. Because of the complicated relationships between factors that influence the decision, or the sheer size of the problem, the user often needs assistance in interpreting the solution or guidance as to the probable cause for an abnormal outcome. For example, the decision maker may benefit from the DSS suggesting where there are unused resources and where the most profitable area is to reapportion them in a resource allocation problem (for example, the solution insights

```
    What information do you wish to update?

> routes

    How would you like to update your routes?

> ?

    You may update shipping routes between two or more cities by any
    of the following methods:

    ADD       - To add individual routes to your system
    DELETE    - To delete routes
    GENERATE  - To automately generate routes between two areas
    CHARACTER - To change the characteristics of routes (cost,
                capacity, etc)
    END       - To end this option

    How would you like to update your routes?

> generate

    Enter where each route(s) is to start from (cities, regions, etc)?

> Baltimore Landover

    Now indicate the distination points for routes leaving those
    cities?

> ?

    You may specify individual cities, cities within a specific
    region, or cities within an X mile radius from some point (i.e,
    200 Washington)

    Now indicate the distination points for routes leaving those
    cities?

> Region4   Richmond   Williamsburg

    60 routes will be established between these start and
    distination points.
```

EXHIBIT 8–8 Simplifying User Entries for Large Scale Applications.

provided at the bottom of Exhibit 2–9). In another situation, the DSS may inform the user as to possible causes for an unexpected result. For example, in planning for a production distribution operation, the organization may not have sufficient production or storage capacity at selected sites (Exhibit 8–9). In such applications it is essential that the DSS provide the user with suggestions as to his possible course of action.

Approaches to User Interaction

The framework and context for establishing interaction between the system and the user varies extensively across the spectrum of DSS applications. Some of the systems

```
     Enter the desired program option:

> solve the problem

     ***  Sorry but in trying to set up your problem I determined some
          resource shortfalls that prevent me from finding a  feasible
          solution:

            -  The  total amount of products that would be shipped  to
               warehouse6  in order to satisfy your minimum acceptable
               shipments  exceeded its capacity by 50000  pounds.  You
               will have to reduce the minimum acceptable shipments on
               each route entering warehouse6 or increase its capacity.

            -  Production at site2 is inadequate by 36000 pounds.

          Correct these shortfalls then try again.


     Enter the desired program option:
```

EXHIBIT 8–9 Providing Insight As to Solution Shortfalls.

communicate with the user in a rigid command format while others create an interactive environment that closely mirrors the dialogue between two people. There are three general approaches (or levels) to achieving user/system interaction:

- ☐ *Functional Command Orientation.* One approach is to force the user to state his requirements using functionally structured commands. Systems that use this approach rely on rather rigid syntax oriented functional commands, such as:

  REPORT REGION=SW; SALES>100000
  GRAPH X=SALES(1000); Y=DATE(MONTHS)

  This form of user interaction is designed for simplicity in developing the system and for operational efficiency (requirements are stated in a brief and direct format with minimal dialogue between the user and the system). It allows the well-trained user, who will be operating the system frequently, to communicate his needs quickly and with significant functional latitude (the range of capabilities and extent to which the system can be adapted to changing needs).
- ☐ *Conversational Dialogue.* Command structured input necessitates significant user training and continued operation by the user to maintain familiarity. Most DSS applications requires direct intervention and involvement by the decision maker. As a result, a more conversational style is necessary if the system is likely to succeed in supporting real-world decisions. Systems designed with a conversational dialogue communicate with the user in an English-oriented fashion. All instructions and prompts are stated in clear everyday terms that are familiar to the user. The system does not mandate a rigid syntax but allows moderate freedom to the user in stating his requirements. Exhibits 8–7, 8–8 and 8–9 illustrate the dialogue between the user and a DSS designed with a conversational interface.
- ☐ *Natural Language Interaction.* In Chapter 5 we first introduced the concept of a DSS that deals with the user in a form that mimicks the spoken language of the individual.

There is no predefined structure to the user's inputs. The user types in his requirements as if he were communicating with another individual. Natural language systems are the simplest to operate, understand and apply by users at all levels. Exhibit 5–4 depicts a natural language application. Chapter 13 explores the progress in areas associated with establishing a natural language interface.

Exhibit 8–10 provides a general comparison of the three approaches to user interaction in terms of developmental effort, training requirements, state of technology and audience requirements. In summary:

- ☐ Natural language systems represent the highest caliber of user interaction in a computer application. They are on the "leading edge" of technology and just beginninig to appear commercially. They also are the most difficult to develop, some requiring four to six years to create a marketable product.
- ☐ Conversational systems are appropriate for a wide range of applications where the system will be used on an infrequent basis and extensive dedicated training is unacceptable. They establish a high degree of user acceptance and comfort for the technically naive and technically informed audiences (Chapter 4). The technically oriented user, however, often views such systems as too talkative and prefers the more brief and succinct form of communication provided by functional command systems.
- ☐ Command structured systems provide the most expeditious approach to creating a DSS application where development speed and operational productivity are the primary concern. They also, however, require significant organizational commitment in training and in dedicating staff time to their operation. They are typically inappropriate for higher levels of the decision process. Although many "hard line" traditionalists are satisfied with this form of interaction, the general trend in user acceptance and market potential is toward the higher caliber forms of user interaction.
- ☐ When used in the context of a specifically targeted audience, each approach has merit. For example, functional command systems are highly productive for the well-trained individual and provide significant freedom to create an application tailored to a specific need. On the other hand, the higher forms of interaction are ideally suited to the occasional or untrained user. To accommodate the requirements of each audience the

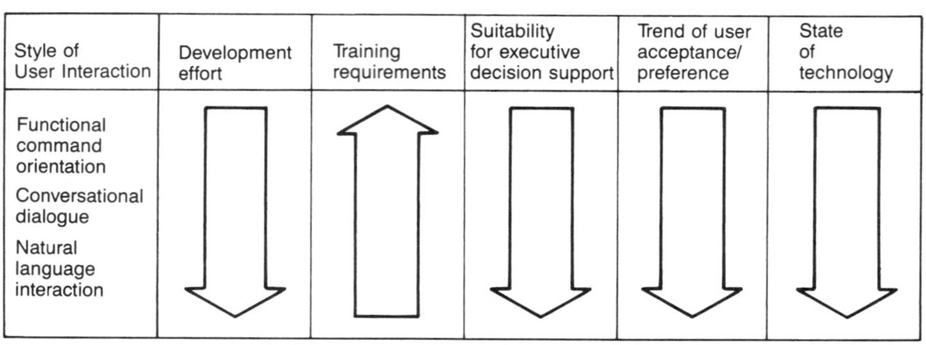

EXHIBIT 8–10 Comparison of Approaches for User Interaction.

more progressive systems allow the user to select which method of interaction they prefer. For example, RAMIS II, a Fourth Generation Language product (Chapter 10) by Martin Marietta Data Systems, can be operated using any of the three approaches.

THE PRICE

Establishing a versatile and truly user-friendly system increases both the time and cost to develop a DSS. The more tolerant and flexible the system, the more complex and involved the programming effort becomes. Depending on which of the previously discussed features are incorporated, the effort and cost to design the system can increase significantly. When the software is built from scratch (Chapter 10) creating a user-friendly environment can affect the development effort to the following extent:

- ☐ Providing self-tutoring facilities and help options is simple from a programming perspective. However, ensuring that the narrative and examples are clear and easy to understand is more difficult. Tutoring and help functions add roughly 10 to 20 percent to the cost of the system depending on the size of the application.
- ☐ Establishing a conversational dialogue requires insight on the part of the developer and significantly increases the coding effort. Tack on the need for foolproofing and the total effort will experience a 40 to 60 percent increment in cost.
- ☐ Allowing the user to create his own commands requires sophisticated and intricate programming techniques but has a relatively small impact on the design cost (approximately five to 10 percent).
- ☐ Providing the ability to automatically alter the nomenclature and terminology used in the DSS is an involved process. It requires that variable names and character strings be used in a logical and consistent fashion throughout the total package. Such an effort can add between 15 and 30 percent to the cost of the system.

EXERCISES

1. Review some of the current literature on information systems (references in Chapters 2 and 4 provide a starting point). Select several systems that are promoted as "user friendly." Examine those systems in light of the criteria and features discussed in this chapter. Note where there is conformity or disparity, and state whether you would classify those systems as being user oriented (from a manager's perspective). Also note what audience they were designed to support (technically naive, technically informed, or technically proficient) as described in Chapter 4.

2. Consider the following comment:

> "The apparent disfavor many users have voiced over the lack of truly user-friendly features is not really an indication that systems must move toward a more user-oriented interface. Instead, the problem stems from the lack of managers undergoing comprehensive training programs."

State whether you agree or disagree with this comment and why.

3. Many vendors and system's developers are reluctant to commit the resources necessary to establish a totally conversational or user-oriented interface. What are the potential benefits to both the developer and the user, and the impacts to the development process, that result from establishing a totally user-friendly and tolerant environment?
4. We noted that the term "user friendliness" is often misused in the promotion of systems. Part of the problem stems from the nebulus context of the phrase. Part results from the need to survive in a highly competitive market. Provide a list of what features and characteristics a system must exhibit to qualify as being legitimately referred to as a user-friendly system (in your eyes).
5. Review some of the current literature on information systems and select one or two examples for each style of user interaction (functional command orientation, conversational dialogue, and natural language interaction). Note how the systems were promoted (user-oriented, conversational, natural language dialogue, etc.) and state whether you feel the "labels" used to promote the system truly reflect the nature of the user interaction.
6. Select one of the systems depicted in the exhibits of Chapters 2, 5, 8 or 9 that illustrate a DSS in action. State which of the three approaches to user interaction was used, then show what that session might look like using the other two styles of user interaction.

REFERENCES AND SUGGESTED READING

1. Badre, A. and B. Shneiderman, *Directions in Human Computer Interaction,* Norwood, N.J.: Ablex Publishing Co., 1982.
2. Chapanis, A., "Computers and the Common Man," in Kasschan, A. (ed.), *Information Technology and Psychology,* Westport, CT: Praeger, 1982.
3. London, K., *The People Side Of Systems,* New York, N.Y.: McGraw-Hill, 1976.
4. Martin, J., *Design of Man-Computer Dialogues,* Englewood Cliffs, N.J.: Prentice-Hall, 1982.
5. Meyer, K. and M. Harper, "User Friendliness," *MIS Quarterly,* March, 1984.
6. Meads, J., "Friendly or Frivolous," *Datamation,* April 1, 1985.
7. Morland, D., "Friendliness," *Datamation,* February, 1982.
8. Palme, J., "Interactive Software for Humans," in Shackel, B. (ed.), *Man-Computer Interactions: Human Factors Aspects of Computers & People,* NATO Advanced Study Institutes, no. 44, 1981.
9. Rubinstein, R. and H. Hersh, *Designing Computer Systems for People,* Chapter 8 & Chapter 9, *Digital Press,* 1984.
10. Shneiderman, B., *Designing the User Interface: Strategies for Effective Human-Computer Interaction,* Reading, MA: Addison-Wesley, 1987.
11. Thimbleby, H., "User Interface Design," in Monk, A. (ed.), *Fundamentals of Human-Computer Interactions,* Academic Press, 1984.
12. Tomeski, E. and H. Lazarus, *People-Oriented Computer Systems,* Van Nostrand Reinhold Co., 1975.

9

Quantitative Models and Their Applications

Recall that a DSS provides more than just the speed of automation (Chapter 2). It allows the manager to reach decisions that would normally exceed the human ability to manipulate, analyze, and evalute the effects of a multitude of complex factors. The quantitative power of a DSS results from the use of sophisticated mathematical procedures and analytical techniques. Although the analytical methods are typically complex, the properly designed DSS provides a "shell of protection" to the manager. The basic premise and philosophy behind decision support is to make a quantitative user out of the nonquantitatively trained individual.

Chapter 6 partitioned the quantitative aspects of the DSS into four primary segments or steps (Exhibit 9–1). The first step provides a pictorial representation of the physical world to help visualize and model the parts of the problem along with their structure and relationships. This figurative model is then translated into a mathematical form that ties together the various parts so that the total problem can be manipulated and solved analytically. Various quantitative techniques (or tools) have evolved over the years to help analyze different types of problems (resource allocations, material distribution, production scheduling, etc.). Once the appropriate quantitative technique is selected, an analytical procedure (commonly referred to as an "algorithm") is used to actually solve the problem.

Creating the pictorial model and selecting the appropriate quantitative technique for a particular problem is not a clear-cut process. To a great extent, the skill to model

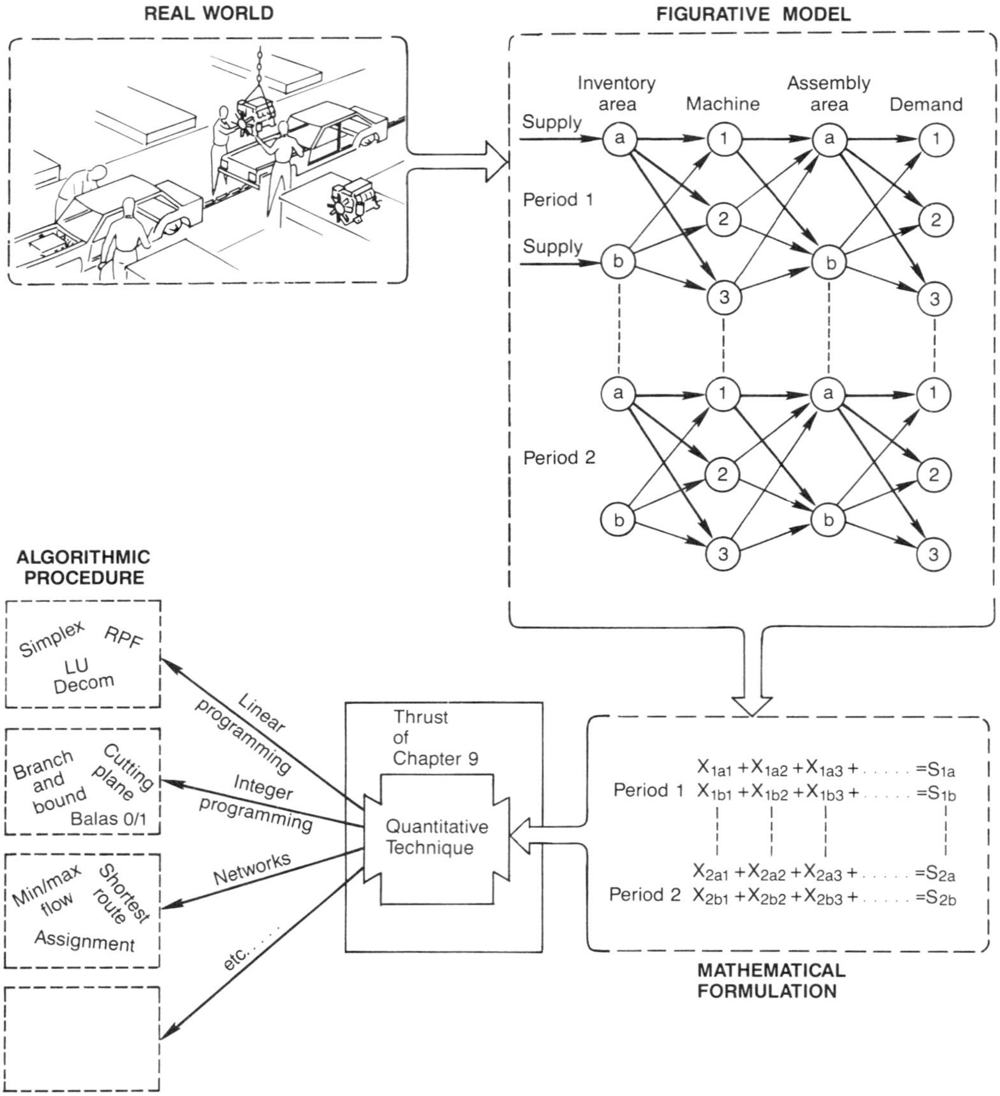

EXHIBIT 9–1 Steps to Quantifying a Problem.

a real-world situation and to create its mathematical equivalent is part training, part intuition, and part inherent ability. The training results from a variety of mathematically oriented disciplines (engineering, management science, statistics, physics, operations research, etc.). The intuition comes from years of accumulative experience in dealing with similar problems. The inherent ability to visualize complex problems and translate them into a mathematical form is usually a personal attribute of the individual.

The algorithmic procedures are far beyond the scope and intent of this text (sources for the various procedures are referenced throughout this chapter). The mathematical formulation is a natural outgrowth of the way the problem is modeled and the quantitative technique that is chosen. This chapter will focus on the general classes of problems and the quantitative techniques that are often used to support the decision process. This is not to infer that all decision-support applications require involved quantitative procedures. Some of the more elementary applications can suffice using relatively simple procedures (Band 1 of the DSS spectrum discussed in Chapter 2). For the more comprehensive applications, however, quantitative methods become essential.

Becoming proficient in the application of quantitative methods cannot be accomplished by reviewing one chapter in a text whose primary objective is to examine the total breadth of decision support. Nor is the knowledge of what goes on inside the model (the mechanics) essential to applying a DSS. A basic understanding of some of the more frequently used quantitative tools will, however, help the reader to appreciate the role of the quantitative model in DSS applications. By the end of the chapter the reader should be better able to understand the total decision-support environment in terms of the decision requirements (such as, demand forecasting, resource assignment, and activity scheduling); the functioning process (an organization, a manufacturing process, military operations, and so forth); the supporting models; the helpful quantitative techniques; and how each part fits into an integrated framework (Exhibit 9–2).

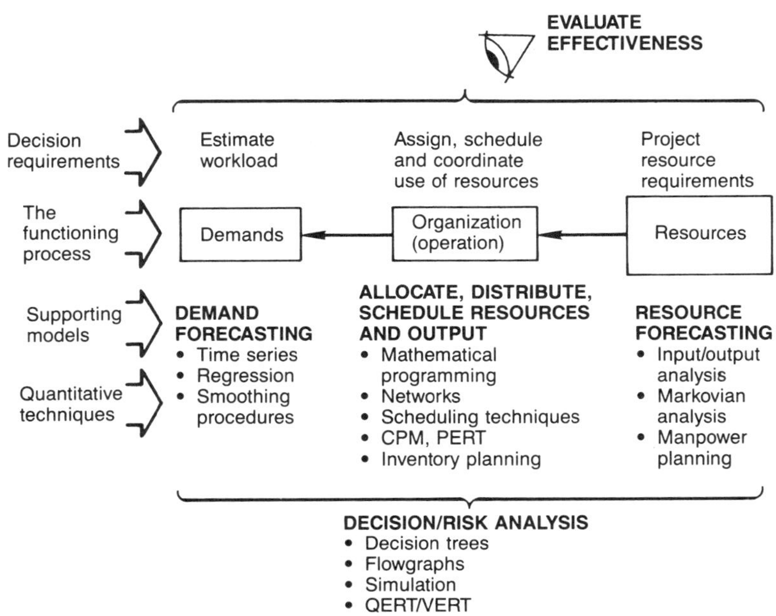

EXHIBIT 9–2 Quantitative Management—How It Fits Together.

TYPES OF MODELS AND PROBLEMS

Chapter 2 divided the basic functions and activities of management into four areas: operations planning and management, resource allocation and acquisition, workload and demand forecasting, and process evaluation and analysis. In a similar fashion, the problems that a decision maker faces can be grouped into various categories based on their structural similarities. Exhibit 9-3 illustrates the general classes of quantitative models and the types of problems to which they are typically associated.

Allocation Models

One of the more frequent problems that a decision maker must deal with is how to spread scarce resources across various programs. Allocation models can help the manager trade off between competing alternatives in order to arrive at the best overall balance across all programs, goals, and objectives. Allocation decisions are required in budgetary planning, staff assignments, financial analysis, manpower allocations, petroleum exploration, and similar problems where personnel, funds, material, equipment, and facilities must be allotted to many investment alternatives, projects or product lines.

Distribution Problems

There are many situations where an organization must determine the best way to move items from one location to another. Such requirements arise in military operations, banking institutions, and commercial activities where funds, materials, products, and the like must be transported through a complex maze of channels and paths. Distribution models are used to support decisions dealing with cash management, logistic systems, inventory planning, vehicle routing and dispatching, electric power distribution, manufacturing processes, fuel distribution, and so on.

Activity Scheduling

Scheduling a sequence of interrelated activities can be a formidable task. The decision maker must determine the order and schedule for a complex set of events that will result in the optimum use of resources, maximum output levels, provide the least costly method for satisfying workload demands, etc. Scheduling problems occur in production operations, project scheduling, workshift planning, equipment maintenance, flight operations and similar types of activities.

Decision/Risk Analysis

The manager often has to decide which course of action will result in the minimal risk (or maximum gain) in terms of hazards, profits, lost opportunity, time delays, and so forth. What makes such problems difficult is the uncertainty with which the possible events will occur. Decision/risk analysis is frequently required in areas such as weapon system analysis, portfolio evaluation, venture analysis, hazard evaluation (nuclear plants, toxic chemicals), and vehicle safety analysis.

Demand/Resource Forecasting

The prerequisite to all management activities is to estimate what demand (workload) will be placed on the organization. Once the expected workload has been projected, the next step is to predict the amount of resources that are required to satisfy the demand. Some of the typical areas where demand/resource forecasting is necessary include: manpower planning, training predictions, market forecasting, combat attrition analysis, budget projections, and predicting maintenance requirements.

Process Management and Control

The complex nature and interdependence of many large operations or programs can cause significant loss and delays without proper planning and oversight. The manager must be able to monitor, coordinate and control the assignment, schedule, sequence and progress of personnel, raw materials, and equipment through the total process. Examples where effective process management and control is essential include: manufacturing operations (inventory, production, distribution); military operations at a theater level (command, control and communication); project management of a multimillion dollar contract (planning, scheduling, funding, tracking); and disaster and response programs (evacuation, medical attention, shelter, restoration).

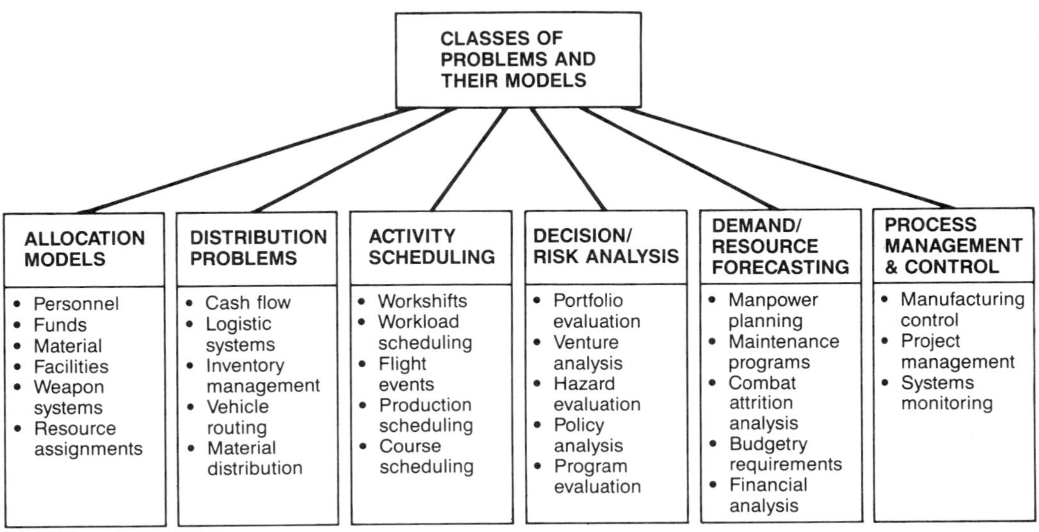

EXHIBIT 9–3 Quantitative Models.

QUANTITATIVE TECHNIQUES

An array of quantitative tools has evolved over the years for analyzing complex problems. Each technique is designed and structured to handle selected types of problems. This section introduces some of the more commonly used methods. Exhibit 9–4 provides a general comparison of the tools and the areas where they are most applicable. References 1 through 6 provide broader coverage of the various techniques and their associated solution procedures.

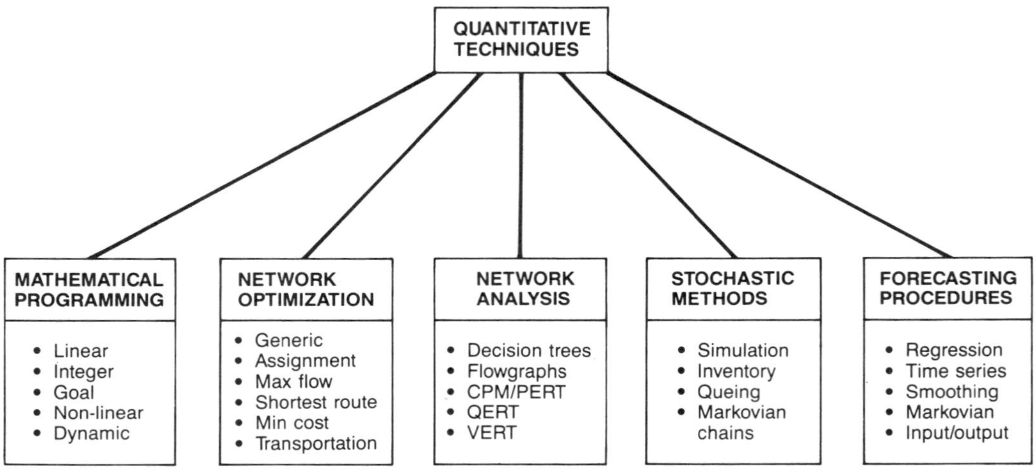

EXHIBIT 9–4 Tools for Quantitative Support.

Mathematical Programming

Many decisions require that the manager find the optimum course of action while conforming to a multitude of resource limitations and policy restrictions. When the management objectives (minimize cost, maximize output, reduce production time, etc.) and the constraining factors (available resources, complete at least 10 projects, shutdown no more than three facilities, etc.) can be expressed as a set of equations, mathematical programming techniques are normally applicable. Consider the general problem of the investor who must select the best combination of investments over a specified period of time. The goal is to obtain the greatest possible profit given the available funds, tax breaks, minimum investment durations, and so on.

A somewhat simplified example would be the corporate executive planning which government contracts, product research, and new market development efforts the organization should commit resources to over the next three years. Assume (for convenience) that if an effort is undertaken, there is a 100 percent chance that the initiative will succeed and the economic gain to the organization is known. Each effort will require different portions of the organization's pool of resources (funds, personnel, facilities). The decision maker must determine which combination of initiatives will provide the greatest return with the available resources. Because of uncertainty, the executive also wishes to initiate at least four of the seven possible projects.

Using estimates of the resources required for each initiative, their expected profit, and the amount of each resource that is available (Exhibit 9–5a), the problem can be represented as a set of equations (Exhibit 9–5b). The variables (PRODUCT1, PRODUCT2,. . .) can take on a value of either one or zero depending on whether or not the manager should invest in that product. The last constraint is to insure that at least four out of seven projects are undertaken. Mathematical programming techniques allow the decision maker to analyze such problems. In this case the best mix of investments (products) is obtained by investing in products 2, 3, 4, 6, and 7 for an expected return of approximately $11.2 million.

(A) RELEVANT DATA

	REQUIRED STAFF-YEARS	FUNDING (MILLIONS)	PROFIT (MILLIONS)
PRODUCT1	120	15.0	8.0
PRODUCT2	25	5.0	2.0
PRODUCT3	15	6.0	1.0
PRODUCT4	60	10.0	4.0
PRODUCT5	8	3.2	0.5
PRODUCT6	12	4.0	1.2
PRODUCT7	20	12.0	3.0

RESOURCES AVAILABLE: 155 STAFF-YEARS 40 MILLION DOLLARS

(B) MATHEMATICAL FORMULATION

MAXIMIZE PROFIT OF: $8P_1 + 2P_2 + 1P_3 + 4P_4 + .5P_5 + 1.2P_6 + 3P_7$

WHILE CONFORMING WITH THESE LIMITATIONS:

$$120P_1 + 25P_2 + 15P_3 + 60P_4 + 8P_5 + 12P_6 + 20P_7 \leq 155 \text{ STAFF-YEARS}$$

$$15P_1 + 5P_2 + 6P_3 + 10P_4 + 3.2P_5 + 4P_6 + 12P_7 \leq 40 \text{ MILLION}$$

$$P_1 + P_2 + P_3 + P_4 + P_5 + P_6 + P_7 \geq 4 \text{ PROJECTS}$$

EXHIBIT 9–5 Picking the Best Mix of Projects.

Depending on the structure and characteristics of the problem, there are several special types of mathematical programming procedures:

LINEAR MODELS

When all the objectives and constraints can be expressed with linear relationships (cost of project A plus cost of project B plus. . . .) then the simplest and most frequently used technique is referred to as "linear programming" [8,14,23,29].

INTEGER MODELS

If any of the results must have integer values (12 projects, 72 aircraft, five factories, and so on) then integer programming techniques are required [13,16,18]. The solution for the previous project selection example required integer programming and was obtained using a commercially available microcomputer package (Appendix A) designed specifically for managers and busy executives.

MULTIPLE OBJECTIVES

There are many situations where management objectives are not simple and straightforward (like maximizing profit). The decision maker may wish to satisfy several competing objectives and target goals (maximize profit, reduce layoffs, expand the customer base, new equipment purchases should be close to 25 percent of the capital base, roughly 15 percent of the current vehicle fleet should be renovated, etc.). Decisions with multiple objectives require that the manager trade off between goals with different scales of comparison (dollars, number of people, customers, units of equipment, etc.) much like trying to combine apples and oranges into a common denominator. Goal programming and multicriteria techniques are often used to analyze problems with multiple objectives [9,17,19,20,22,24,25,26,27,28].

There are several additional techniques that are used less frequently to solve mathematical programming problems with very unique structures. Examples include dynamic [10,11], nonlinear [7,21], quadratic and geometric [12] programming methods.

Network Optimization

Mathematical programming methods are well-suited to a variety of resource allocations, scheduling, and distribution decisions. There are, however, various situations where mathematical programming procedures require an excessive amount of time to solve. Many large-scale problems can be formulated and expressed in a special "network" representation that can be exploited and solved very quickly. Network models are formulated as a set of junction points that are commonly referred to as "nodes" (such as, cities, facilities, machines, time periods, and people) and interconnecting paths known as "arcs" (roadways, routes, investments, work assignments, and so forth). Logistics systems, vehicle routing, manufacturing operations, product distributions, funds management, inventory planning, and workload scheduling problems usually possess the special structure that allows network optimization techniques to be used.

Exhibit 9–6 illustrates a simplified network optimization problem. The decision

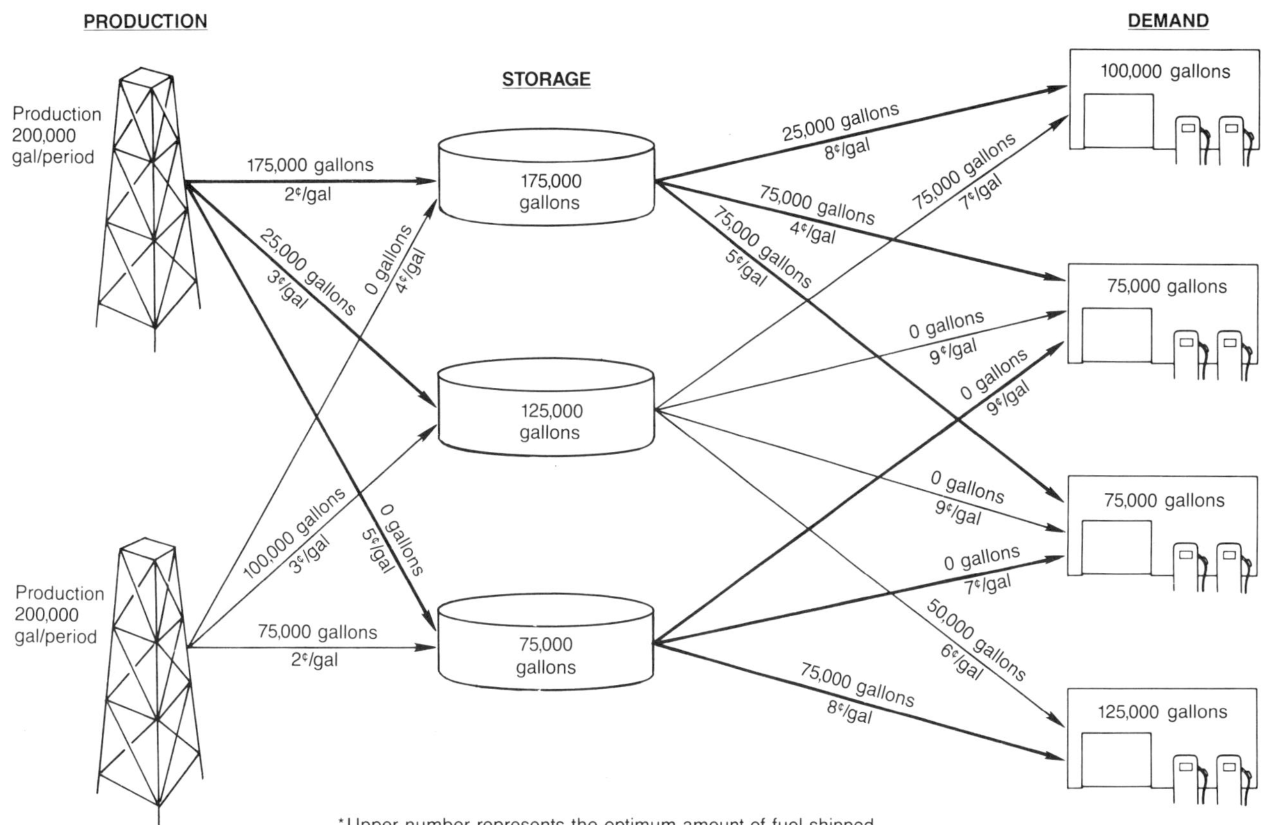

*Upper number represents the optimum amount of fuel shipped between those points.
Lower number indicates the cost to ship one gallon of fuel along that route.

EXHIBIT 9–6 Sample Fuel Distribution Problem.

maker must choose which storage facilities are supplied by which pumping stations, and which customers are serviced by each storage facility. the objective is to satisfy all customer demands at minimum shipping and storage costs. Note that the solution shown meets the production capacity of each station, the storage capacity of each tank, and the demands of all customers at minimum cost. The size of this particular problem allowed the "best" solution to be obtained visually. Practical sized applications can have hundreds of thousands of possible paths and require computer assistance to reach the optimum solution.

Until recently, network models and their solution procedures were tuned and grouped into specific classes: such as, resource assignment, shortest route, maximum flow, minimum cost, and transportation problems [30,31,33,34]. In the late 1970s several computation advances were made that allow virtually all network optimization problems to be handled by one generic (and extremely efficient) solution procedure [32]. The procedures are so efficient that problems requiring hours to solve with traditional mathematical programming methods can now be solved in a matter of minutes.

Network Analysis

Often there is a significant degree of uncertainty associated with the various factors that influence the outcome and the alternative courses of action that can be taken. If parts of the problem (such as, events, activities, tasks, and decisions) can be represented in a network format, then there are several quantitative techniques that can help the manager analyze likely outcomes, potential bottlenecks, risky alternatives, probable repercussions, and so forth. Network analysis methods can be used to evaluate ventures, examine capital investments, plan and manage large-scale projects, assess the impact of organizational policies, perform safety analysis, and an assortment of similar requirements. The following identifies the more prevalent network analysis techniques.

DECISION TREES

When a manager has to make a complex set of choices, each dependent on a previous chain of events, then decision trees provide an effective device for laying out and analyzing alternative outcomes. Some of the choices may be more risky than others but they can also result in a greater gain should they succeed. If the chance that a particular event will take place is known, and the gain or loss from taking that path can be estimated, decision trees [35,37,40,41] can be used to determine the expected likelihood and cost/profit associated with the various alternatives. Exhibit 9–7 provides an example of what a decision tree would look like. Exhibit 9–8 illustrates a commercial package (Confidence Factor by Simple Software) being used to solve a decision tree problem dealing with the release and testing of a new product.

FLOW ANALYSIS

Decision trees are helpful for straightforward problems where the primary purpose is to enumerate all the possible outcomes, their risk, and cost/profit. There are many situa-

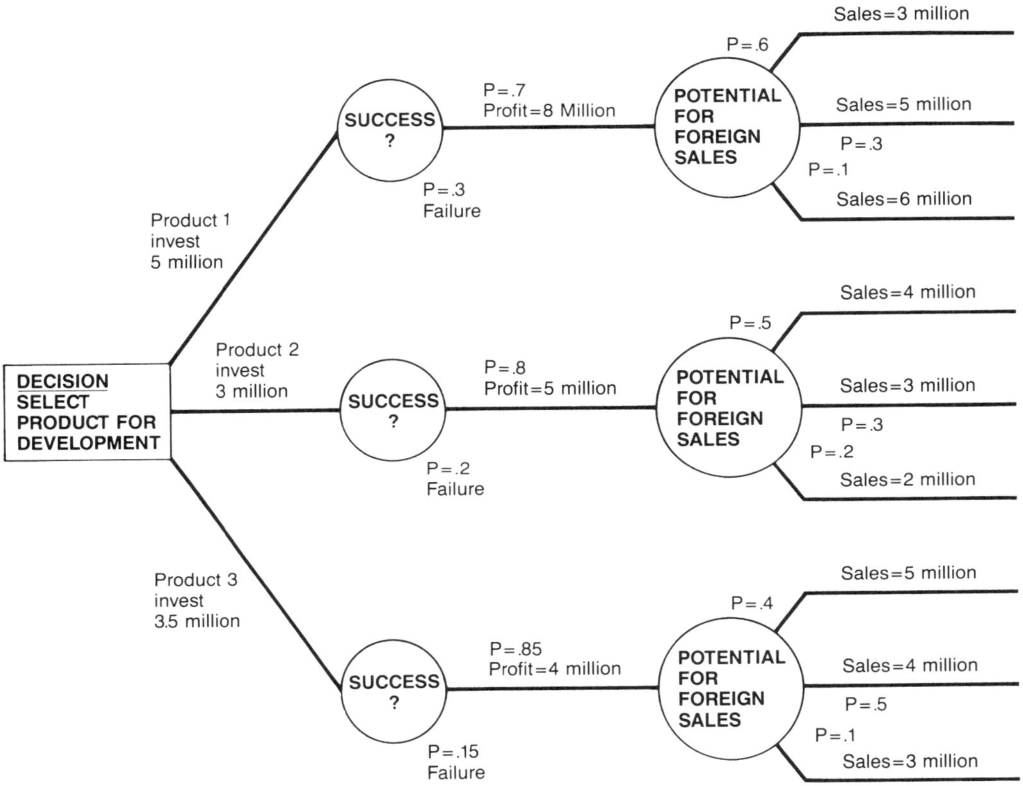

EXHIBIT 9–7 Decision Tree for Selecting Product Investments.

tions where the relationships between the various events and activities are too complex to analyze using decision trees. The occurrence of one event (or decision) may cause part of the process to be repeated. Consider a personnel recruiting process that has been simplified into five steps (Exhibit 9–9): A vacancy occurs, the hiring process is started; the process either succeeds or fails (faulty paperwork, field of competition too small, etc.); if it fails, the process is repeated; if it succeeds, a candidate is selected and accepts; after so many days, the candidate reports on board. Each event has an associated chance of occurring and corresponding duration if it does take place. In this problem, we might estimate the likelihood that a successful hire will occur and the average time it will take to bring someone on board. The fact that we can cycle around an unknown number of times, each adding to the duration, requires a different type of quantitative procedure. Flowgraph techniques [42] allow the problem to be reduced to a relatively simple mathematical expression that can be used to analyze the situation and determine the effects of different conditions (average length of time to complete parts of the process, the likelihood of success to complete some phase, the effect of different policies, etc.).

CONFIDENCE FACTOR—DECISION TREE PAGE 1

	NODE			SUCCESSOR NODE INFORMATION						
No.	TYPE	DESCRIPTION	VALUE	#. . .%	#. . .%	#. . .%	#. . .%	#. . .%	#. . .%	#. . .%
1	Decision	Should we Test?	2,720	2		3	≥===			
2	Decision	Should we Release?	2,700	4	≥==	5				
3	Chance	Test Results	2,720	6	60	7	40			
4	Chance	Release Results	2,700	8	60	9	40			
5	End	Do not Release	2,000							
6	Decision	Release After +Test	3,200	10	≥==	5				
7	Decision	Release After +Test	2,000	11		5	≥===			
8	End	Good Sales	3,500							
9	End	Bad Sales	1,500							
10	Chance	After +Test	3,200	8	85	9	15			
11	Chance	After −Test	1,800	8	15	9	85			

The added value of a Market Test is ONLY $20,000
If it costs more than $20,000 to conduct the test—Don't!

The classic example for the use of Decision Tree Involves the release of a new product and the value of product testing. ABC Company is presently achieving annual profits of $2Million, they have developed a new product with profit potential of $1.5 Million and the cost of releasing the new product is estimated to be $500,000, the chance of success is estimated to be 60%. Should we release the new product?

EXHIBIT 9–8 Solution of a Decision Tree Using a Commercial Package. *Courtesy of* Simple Software, Inc.

GERT

Flowgraph procedures are helpful for small problems, however, the method becomes extremely laborous as size increases. GERT (Graphical Evaluation and Review Technique) is a computerized approach to performing network analysis. The GERT approach [38,39] is built on flowgraph principles but expands the capability by permitting the various parts of a process to be tied together through mathematical relationships.

VERT

Both flowgraphs and GERT are used in situations where events and their relationships occur in a mathematically predictable form. For example, in the recruiting process of Exhibit 9–9, the likelihood of taking any path is constant and the length of time for that activity to take place is an average number. The activities and events are also independent (that is, the time to advertise the position is independent of the time for the candidate to accept an offer), and only one characteristic (time or cost) can be considered. There are decisions, however, where these restrictions limit the usefulness of techniques, such as GERT and flowgraph analysis. The Venture Evaluation and Review Technique (VERT) provides a viable alternative for analysis of more complex and elaborate problems. VERT allows complicated situations, within a network structure,

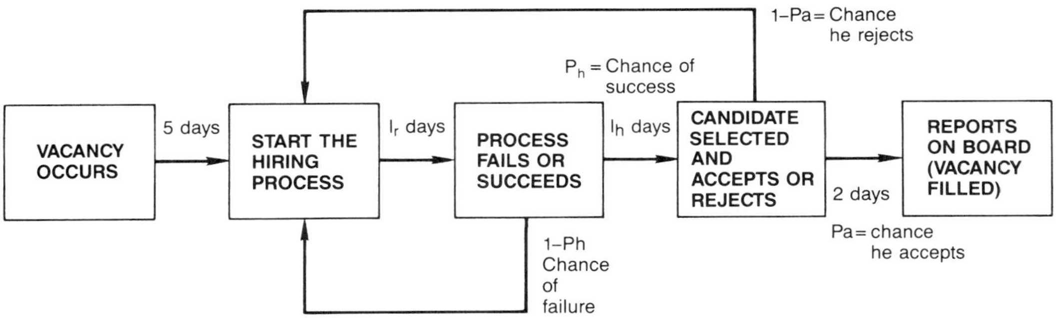

EXHIBIT 9–9 Personnel Hiring Process.

to be modeled with greater flexibility [36] by providing the following additional capabilities:

- ☐ VERT allows cost, time, performance, and risk to be analyzed simultaneously.
- ☐ The chance that an event occurs can be random or depend on other events and outcomes in the process.
- ☐ The cost, time, or performance of one event or activity can be tied to the results or outcome from other parts of the process.

To illustrate the additional power available through VERT, consider two comprehensive applications. In a hazard analysis of a nuclear facility, the failure of one component can increase the workload on the primary backup and thus its probability of backup failure. In the design and development of a military aircraft: Cost will be dependent on the required performance and uncertain inflation; overruns result from increased development time because of research problems; the availability of technological advances will depend on successes in related fields of science; and so forth. In both situations, VERT can be used to model and evaluate the possible cost, time, risk, and performance that can result from a network of complex and interdependent activities.

PROGRAM MANAGEMENT

Managing large-scale programs is a formidable effort. It requires the planning, scheduling, and coordination of a multitude of interrelated tasks, all of which compete and battle for a limited pool of resources (funds, manpower, equipment). To construct a dam, design a high performance military aircraft, build a submarine, and so on, would be unmanageable without the use of quantitative procedures. A variety of techniques have been developed to help managers more effectively plan, analyze, and control large-scale projects. Examples range from the simple Gantt chart, to the more comprehensive Critical Path Methods (CPM), and encompass the rather involved procedures associated with Program Evaluation and Review Techniques (PERT) [43,44]. Exhibit 9–10 illustrates how a commercial package (Project Master by Simple Software Inc.) can be used to manage and plan a project. Once the activities and their duration/cost have been identified (Exhibit 9–10a), the system schedules the project (Exhibit 9–10b) and then informs the manager of the likelihood that the project will be completed by a specified date (Exhibit 9–10c).

Stochastic Methods

A few of the methods discussed so far are designed to help managers deal with uncertainty (decision trees, flowgraphs, etc.). To handle problems that respond in a more "unpredictable" fashion, analysts have developed various techniques that estimate the random behavior of a system (organization, personnel structure, operation, etc.). The following summarizes a few of the quantitative procedures that are used to analyze problems with an underlying stochastic (random) nature.

INVENTORY MODELS

Establishing the appropriate replenishment policy is important in controlling inventory cost and response time. Whether it be a logistic system, a manufacturing operation,

ProjectMaster (tm) PAGE 1
JOB DESCRIPTIONS

JOB TITLE	DURATION LIKELY	BEST	WORST	DIRECT COST	EARLY START	ACTUAL FINISH
1 PREPARE SITE	5	4	7		/ /	/ /
2 DIG FOUNDATION	6	4	9		/ /	/ /
3 ROUGH ELECTRIC	4	2	5		7/11/84	/ /
4 ROUGH PLUMBING	4	3	6		/ /	/ /
5 POUR FOUNDATION	5	4	6		/ /	/ /
6 SECOND POUR	4	3	6		/ /	/ /
7 INSPECTION	1	1	1		/ /	/ /
8 FRAMING	20	18	25		/ /	/ /
9 ROOF	10	9	23	6000	/ /	/ /
10 PLUMBING	6	5	8	3000	/ /	/ /
11 HEATING AND A.C.	4	3	5	7000	/ /	/ /
12 SHEET METAL	5	4	7	2000	/ /	/ /
13 ELECTRIC	5	4	8	2000	/ /	/ /
14 SECOND INSPECTION	3	2	5		/ /	/ /
15 LATH	5	4	7		/ /	/ /

Press ESCape when completely finished with all JOB DESCRIPTIONS

EXHIBIT 9–10a Identifying the Project Activities, Their Cost, and Duration. *Courtesy of* Simple Software, Inc.

```
               Week            Month    9     9     9     9    10    10    10    10    10    11    1984
               Beginning       Day      3    10    17    24     1     8    15    22    29     5
               Job                   ________________________________________________________________
             9 ROOF                 |CCCCCCCCCCC
            10 PLUMBING             |XXXXXffffff
            11 HEATING AND A.C.     |XXXffffffff
            12 SHEET METAL          |XXXXffffff
            13 ELECTRIC             |XXXXffffff
            14 SECOND INSPECTION    |           CCC
            15 LATH                 |              CCCCC
            16 HANG DRY WALL        |              Xsssssssssss
            17 STUCCO               |                   CCCCCCCC
            18 PAINT OUTSIDE TRIM   |                          CCCCC
            19 PAINT OUTSIDE        |                              CCCC
            20 OUTSIDE CLEAN-UP     |                                  CCCC
            21 CABINET              |                XXXXXX fsssssssssss
            22 PAINT INTERIOR       |                XXXXXXXsssssssssss
            23 PLUMBING FIXTURES    |                XXXXfffsssssssssss
            24 ELECTRIC FIXTURES    |                XXXXXffsssssssssss
            25 INTERIOR CLEAN-UP    |                      XXXXffffffffffss
            26 WALK THRU            |                                  XXff

               Press ESCape when ready to review Reports
               To view around a Focus Center, enter Job Number  18   and Date  10/10/84
```

EXHIBIT 9–10b Computed Schedule of Project Activities. *Courtesy of* Simple Software, Inc.

To Estimate Schedule
Completion Probability,
Mark Box with ENTER Key
& Enter Desired End Date.
[ ] 10/21/84

To Estimate Schedule End
Date, Mark Box With ENTER
Key & Enter % For Desired
Completion Probability.
[ ] 75

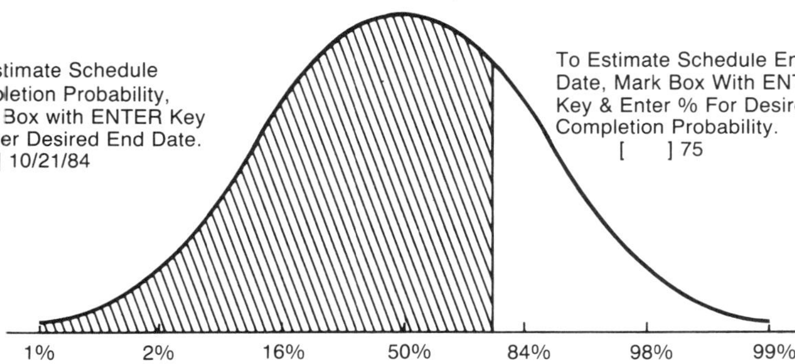

MEAN END DATE 10/26/84   STANDARD DEVIATION 3.14 WORKDAYS

For the Desired Probability of 75% the Estimated Date of Successful Completion is 10/30/84

[ ] ANALYZE [ ] PRINT REPORT [ ] NEXT REPORT [ ] RETURN TO MENU

The report shows the estimated date on which the project would complete for a given level of probability.

EXHIBIT 9–10c Likelihood That the Project Will Finish By a Specific Date. *Courtesy of* Simple Software, Inc.

or a retail store: The decision maker must evaluate a variety of factors that determine what level of inventory is most effective (consumption rate, item shelf life, restock lead time, warehousing cost, etc.). Consider a software distributor outlet. Purchase price is based on the number of units bought. If too many units are purchased at one time, the company will be forced to "eat" leftover stock when a new version is released. Stocking too few items can mean lost sales. The trick is to establish reorder points that balance the lost sales, overstock, and economic lot sizing to come up with the best strategy. Inventory models provide a valuable quantitative tool to support inventory decisions [50,55].

QUEUING MODELS

Facilities that provide one or more different types of services must create the proper trade-off between customer waiting time and the idle time that can result from too many servers. Fast food restaurants, airport flight patterns, maintenance operations, freight loading docks, and bank teller operations are all situations where the manager must decide how to provide acceptable service at minimum cost. Too many servers (repair stations, loading areas, cashiers, etc.) and the organization will be paying for "free time." Too few servers and the customer will spend excessive time waiting in line. The random nature of waiting line (or queuing) problems stems from uncertainty in the rate of arriving customers and the rate at which they can be serviced. A variety of analytical procedures have been developed to analyze queuing problems [45,52,56].

MARKOVIAN MODELS

There are many situations where knowledge about the condition of a process at some future point in time is important to the decision maker. What will the staffing level be in each skill series in three years? How will an air traffic control system respond under different aircraft stacking conditions? How will an enemy move and behave to different threats in various battle scenarios? In each case, something (a person, thing, policy, organization) progresses from one state of existence (one job, a grid location, etc.) to another (leave the organization, move to new coordinates, and so forth). Markovian chains can be used to answer such questions provided we know the chance of advancing from one condition to another. An analogy would be when a teenager first comes home from school. There is an 80 percent chance the first stop will be the refrigerator, 15 percent they will go immediately to their room, and five percent that their books will be dropped on the floor as they immediately return outside. Given they are in their room, there is a one percent chance of putting away their books and quietly doing homework, 75 percent they will proceed to the refrigerator, and 24 percent they return outside. At the refrigerator, the probability is 30 percent that they will stay there until the next period, 10 percent they move to their room, and 60 percent they rush outside. Markovian chains could be used to estimate the average number of trips to the refrigerator each hour or how long the parents will be blessed by the presence of their offspring. Although Markovian chains are indeed stochastic models, they are typically applied to forecasting decisions [48,51].

To ensure that staffing levels satisfy organizational goals and workload projections, personnel systems are often formulated in terms of a Markovian model [49]. Markovian models have been used to support workforce planning and analysis decisions in such areas as: establishing a military force structure; student and instructor flows through academic institutions; staffing of financial positions in banking organizations; and maintaining a workforce structure in federal institutions. Exhibit 9–11 illustrates what a simplified Markovian model would look like. Using the rates at which personnel move from one class to another, Markovian techniques can be used to answer questions like:

- ☐ How many individuals will be in each class at some future time (say five years) given current staffing and promotion policies?
- ☐ On the average, how long will an individual stay in each class?
- ☐ What recruiting and promotional policies can be used to eliminate near- and long-term shortages?

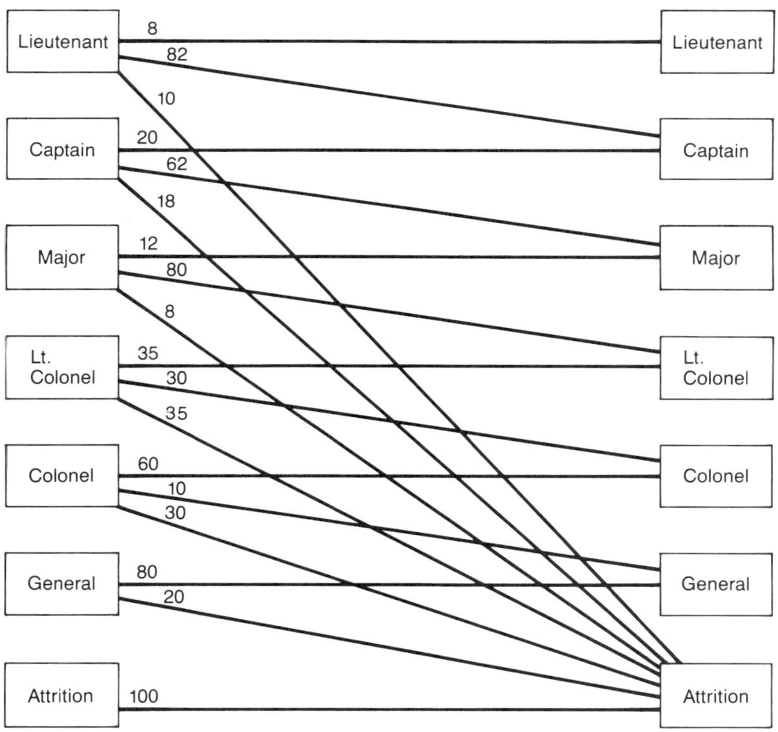

EXHIBIT 9–11 Progression of Officers. The (hypothetical) numbers on the three paths leaving each officer rank represent the chance that a person (for example, a captain) will remain in grade (as a captain) will advance (for example, to a major) or terminate (for example through attrition).

☐ How will cutbacks in recruitment and training of certain disciplines influence the availability of qualified personnel for management positions?

SIMULATION

Whenever possible, a quantitative procedure should be selected that provides a "closed form" solution. Closed form infers that the same answers can always be computed directly from the mathematical expression describing the problem (that is, For $x=2$ then $y=x^2$ will always produce 4). Real-world problems do not always result in precise answers. The inputs and conditions often vary to such an extent that the only recourse is to simulate how the problem will behave under various scenarios. Consider the requirement to establish the level of medical staffing, supplies, and bedding facilities in a large hospital during a 24-hour period under emergency conditions (earthquake, large scale fires, etc.). The rate at which patients arrive will fluctuate over time, starting off gradually, building to peak demand, then decaying to normal operations. The type of injuries and medical services will also vary randomly. The response time to divert blood supplies and emergency vehicles from other facilities will depend on road conditions (damage, rush hour, available vehicles during the crisis, etc.). Analyzing such a complex situation in a closed form is virtually impossible. Simulation techniques are used as a last resort to evalute such complicated operations [46,47,53,54,57,58]. Exhibit 9–12

CONFIDENCE FACTOR—RISK SIMULATION PAGE NO.1

NO.	TASK DESCRIPTION	SUCCESSOR TASK INFORMATION #...%	#...%	#...%	#...%	MOST LIKELY	BEST CASE	WORST CASE
1	INTERVIEW USERS	2 100				10	7	14
2	ANALYZE INTERVIEWS	3 20	4 80			3	2	5
3	RE-INTERVIEW AS REQ.	4 95	2 5			1	1	2
4	ACTION PLAN OPTIONS	6 70	12 30			2	1	3
5	MAKE IN-HOUSE							
6	DESIGN PHASES	6 15	7 85			18	14	21
7	DEVELOPMENT STEPS	7 20	8 80			11	9	15
8	DEBUG/TEST/VALIDATE	9 70	8 30			20	17	24
9	PROVIDE TRAINING	10 100				8	4	10
10	INSTALL FINAL SYSTEM					3	2	4
11	BUY OUTSIDE							
12	PURCHASE PRODUCTS	13 100				5	3	7
13	CONFIGURE & ADAPT	9 90	13 10			10	5	14

ESTABLISHMENT OF DSS CAPABILITY WITHIN AN ORGANIZATION

EXHIBIT 9–12a Simulating the Development and Implementation of a Simple DSS. *Courtesy of* Simple Software, Inc.

CONFIDENCE FACTOR—RISK SIMULATION PAGE NO. 2

NUMBER OF SAMPLES =	40
MEAN =	74.2445
STANDARD DEVIATION =	25.2363
2% PROBABILITY =	23.7719
24% PROBABILITY =	56.5791
50% PROBABILITY =	74.2445
76% PROBABILITY =	91.9099
98% PROBABILITY =	124.7170

ESTABLISHMENT OF DSS CAPABILITY WITHIN AN ORGANIZATION

EXHIBIT 9–12b Results of the Simulation (Duration of Effort). *Courtesy of* Simple Software, Inc.

provides an example simulation intended to estimate the time required to develop and implement a hypothetical DSS (Chapter 11). The simulation was performed using "Confidence Factor" from Simple Software Inc. In Exhibit 9–12a the problem is entered and in Exhibit 9–12b the results of the simulation are provided.

Forecasting Techniques

In practically all business activities, the manager has to predict the attributes of an organization, operation, or system that are functionally related to a set of characteristics. Examples include: estimating next year's budget requirements given current production rates and the expected workload; projecting customer demands based on marketing strategies and historical records of seasonal demands; predicting the cost of a new aircraft given its range, speed, weight, and mission; and predicting spare part requirements based on the characteristics of a fleet of vehicles (type vehicles, average annual mileage, etc.). A wide assortment of forecasting procedures is available ranging from simple statistical regression to more comprehensive procedures like time series analysis.

STATISTICAL REGRESSION

Usually there is a relationship between the attributes of a system and the characteristics that are of interest to the decision maker (such as, cost, performance, and reliability).

Unfortunately, the expression that describes that relationship is rarely known. The manager must rely on historical data to estimate the relationship. Because the real world is impure, however, the actual relationship can only be approximated.

Consider the intuitive relationship between the weight of a vehicle and its mileage. As the weight increases more energy is required to accelerate the vehicle and to counter ground friction. Weight, however, is not the only variable affecting gas mileage. Aerodynamic drag, driving habits, engine design and size, tire inflation, climate, and many other conditions also influence a vehicle's gas mileage. The manager rarely possesses knowledge about all of the factors that can influence how the system will behave. Statistical regression techniques are used to account for these "unknown" factors and to relate attributes of a system or process to other conditions [63,64,65]. Exhibit 9–13 illustrates a relatively simple and user-tolerant commercial product (STATVIEW by Brainpower Inc.) that helps the user perform statistical analysis. In the situation depicted, correlating two stock market indices, the user begins by entering the data line-by-line (Exhibit 9–13a) until the information has been entered for all indices (Exhibit 9–13b). The user tells the system what analysis is to be done by selecting an option from a menu (Exhibit 9–13c) at which point the computer displays the resulting regression graphically (Exhibit 9–13d).

TIME SERIES

Many phenomenon respond in a cyclic fashion. Customer demands for swimsuits, forest fires, the use of snow tires, the growing trend in venereal diseases, and the number of

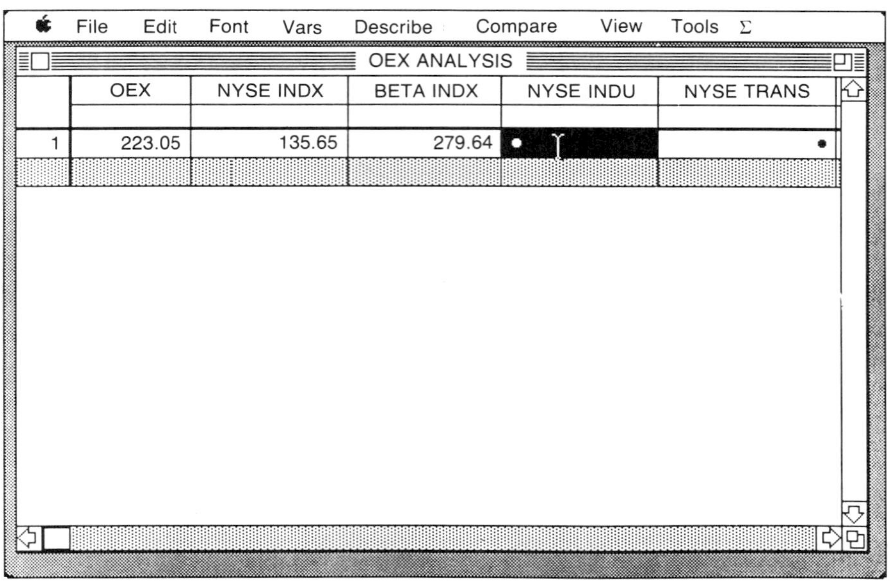

EXHIBIT 9–13a The User Begins By Entering Values for Each Stock Index. *Courtesy of* Brain Power, Inc.

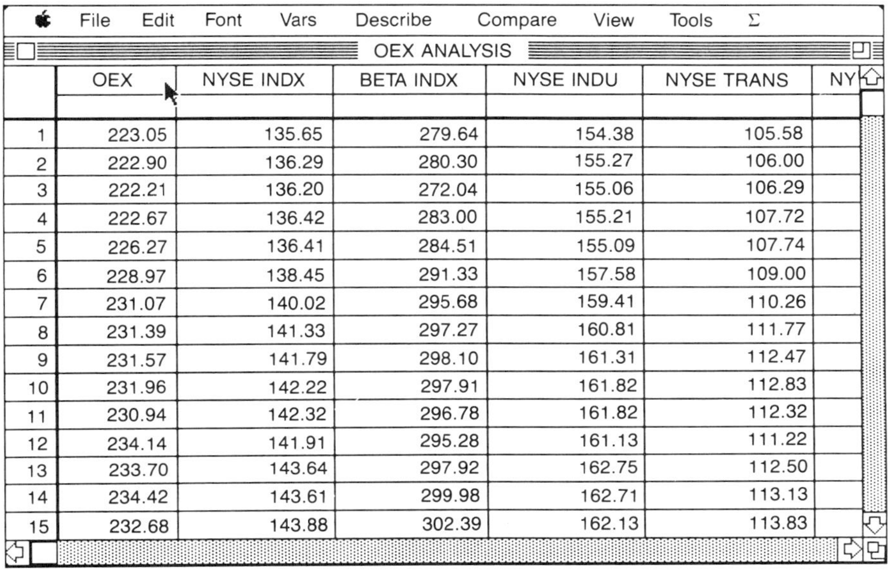

	OEX	NYSE INDX	BETA INDX	NYSE INDU	NYSE TRANS	NY
1	223.05	135.65	279.64	154.38	105.58	
2	222.90	136.29	280.30	155.27	106.00	
3	222.21	136.20	272.04	155.06	106.29	
4	222.67	136.42	283.00	155.21	107.72	
5	226.27	136.41	284.51	155.09	107.74	
6	228.97	138.45	291.33	157.58	109.00	
7	231.07	140.02	295.68	159.41	110.26	
8	231.39	141.33	297.27	160.81	111.77	
9	231.57	141.79	298.10	161.31	112.47	
10	231.96	142.22	297.91	161.82	112.83	
11	230.94	142.32	296.78	161.82	112.32	
12	234.14	141.91	295.28	161.13	111.22	
13	233.70	143.64	297.92	162.75	112.50	
14	234.42	143.61	299.98	162.71	113.13	
15	232.68	143.88	302.39	162.13	113.83	

EXHIBIT 9–13b Values for All Indices Have Been Entered. *Courtesy of* Brain Power, Inc.

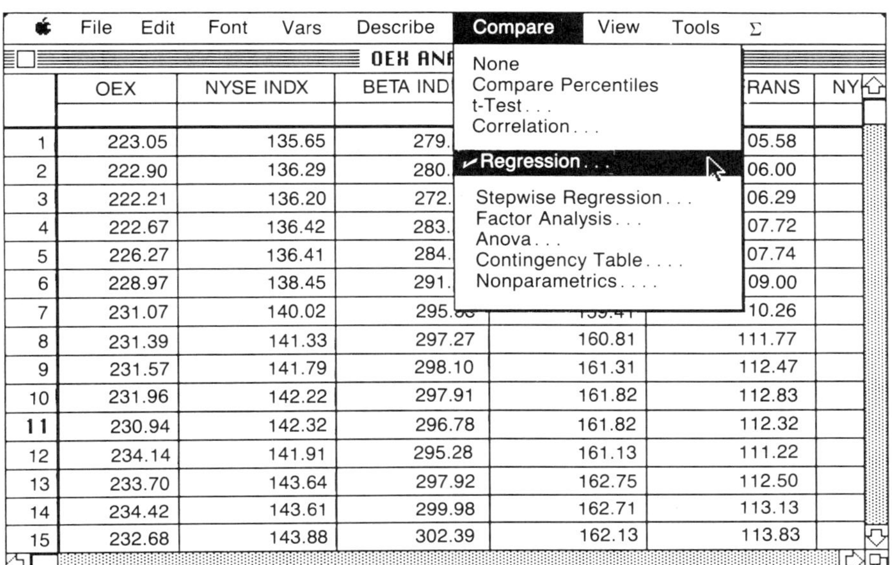

	OEX	NYSE INDX	BETA IND		RANS	NY
1	223.05	135.65	279.		05.58	
2	222.90	136.29	280.		06.00	
3	222.21	136.20	272.		06.29	
4	222.67	136.42	283.		07.72	
5	226.27	136.41	284.		07.74	
6	228.97	138.45	291.		09.00	
7	231.07	140.02	295.		10.26	
8	231.39	141.33	297.27	160.81	111.77	
9	231.57	141.79	298.10	161.31	112.47	
10	231.96	142.22	297.91	161.82	112.83	
11	230.94	142.32	296.78	161.82	112.32	
12	234.14	141.91	295.28	161.13	111.22	
13	233.70	143.64	297.92	162.75	112.50	
14	234.42	143.61	299.98	162.71	113.13	
15	232.68	143.88	302.39	162.13	113.83	

EXHIBIT 9–13c The User Selects What Type of Analysis Will Be Performed. *Courtesy of* Brain Power, Inc.

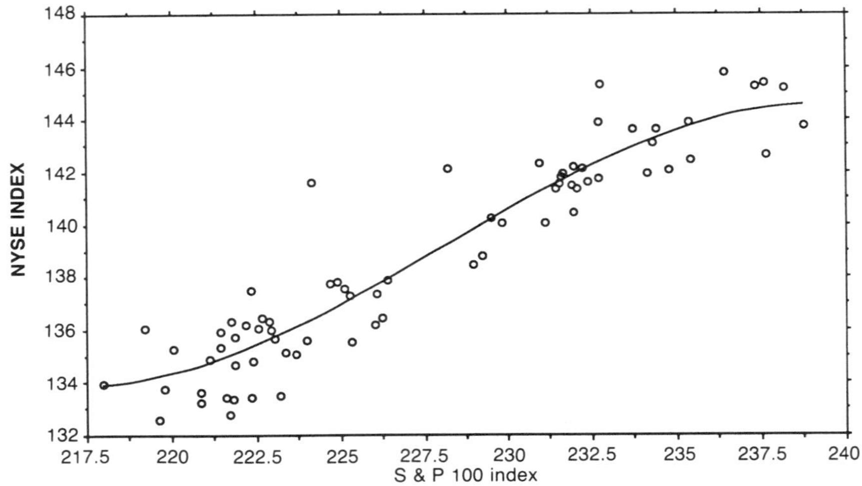

EXHIBIT 9–13d Results of the Analysis—Regression of the NYSE Index vs. S&P 100 Index. *Courtesy of* Brain Power, Inc.

single parents are examples of conditions whose performance can be functionally related to the passage of time. Time series techniques provide a sophisticated and extremely complex method for analyzing time related problems [59,60,61,62]. Exhibit 9–14 portrays the cyclic behavior of a hypothetical process where historical information is used to predict future market demands.

SMOOTHING TECHNIQUES

Because of the erratic nature of most time dependent phenomenon, smoothing techniques are frequently used to help make sense out of the "scatter" pattern of data. Unlike time series methods, which attempt to emulate the total "peaks and valleys" of a behavioral pattern, smoothing techniques try to predict the "trend" of the data. Exponential smoothing and running averages are two examples of smoothing techniques [66] that allows the manager to visualize the general trend of a process (customer demands, stock prices, etc.). Exhibit 9–15 illustrates how moving averages can be used to smooth out the behavior of stock market prices for a particular item. The open circles indicate the daily closing price, while the solid black circles represent the three day (top figure) and ten day (bottom) moving average. Note that although the ten day average provides a smoother curve, the three day average more closely approximates (mimics) the actual behavior.

INPUT/OUTPUT ANALYSIS

Periodically organizations have to project the resources necessary to satisfy the predicted workloads. As the name infers, input/output analysis allows a decision maker to look either forward or backward to answer questions such as:

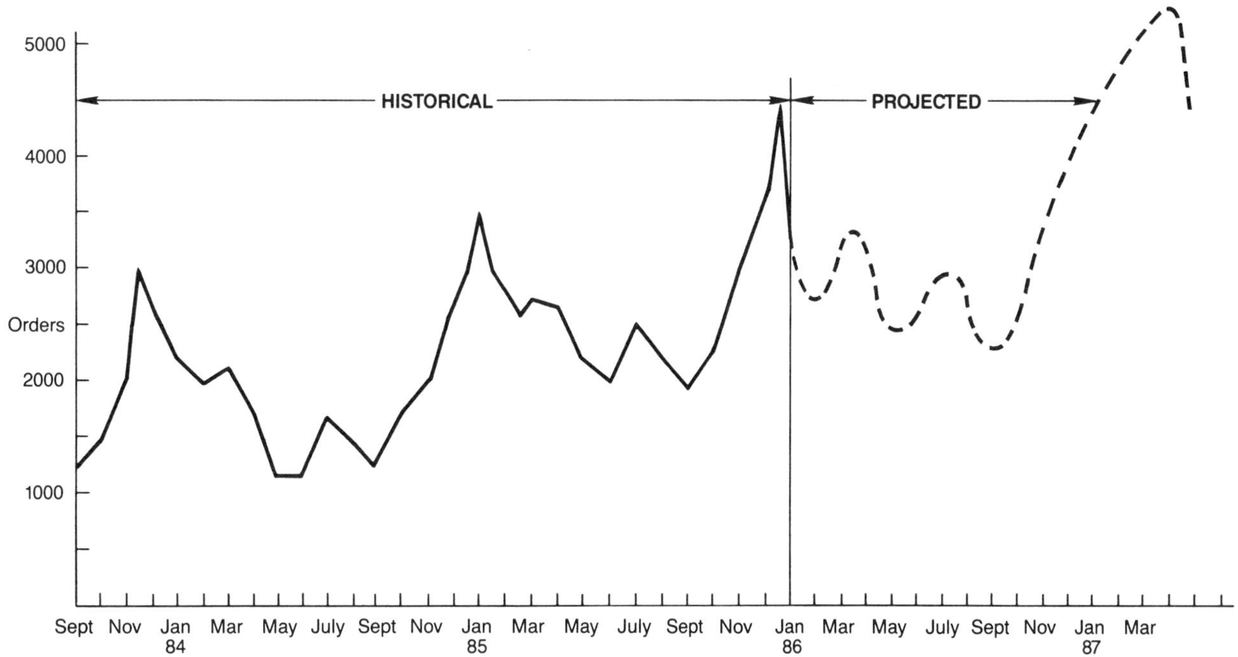

EXHIBIT 9–14 Projecting Customer Orders Using Time Series Models.

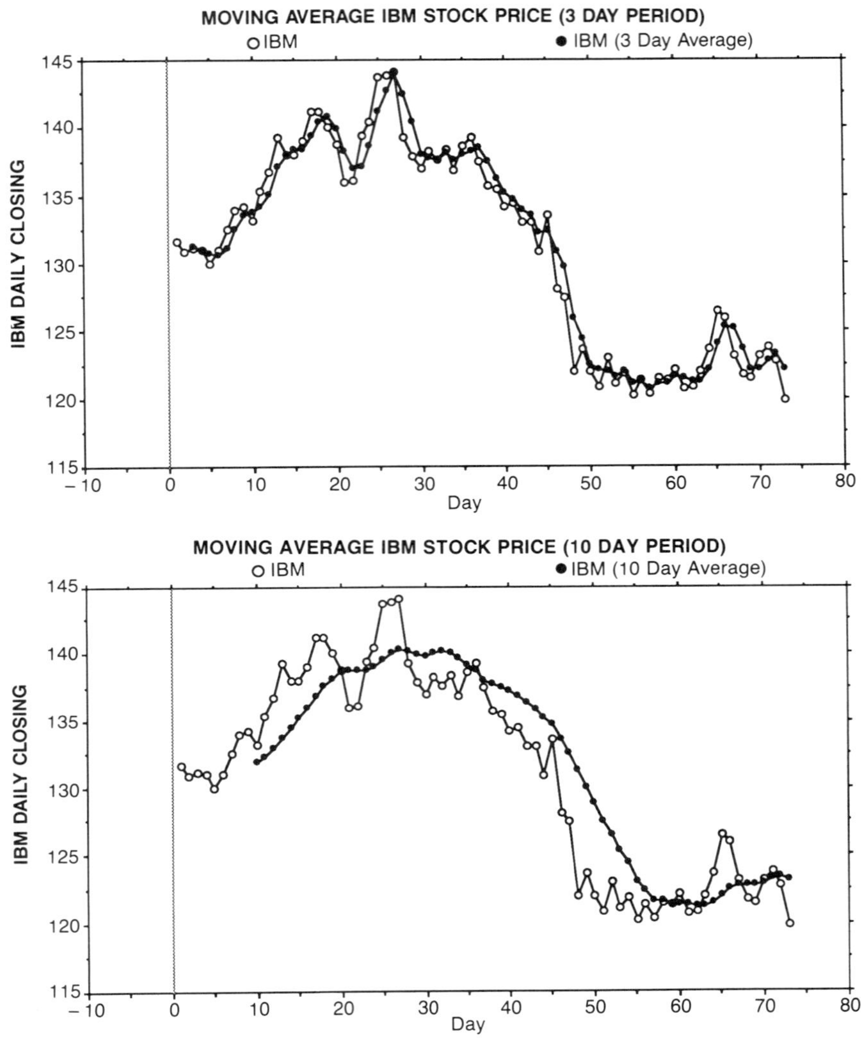

EXHIBIT 9–15 Using Moving Averages to Smooth Out Daily Stock Exchange Prices. *Courtesy of* Brain Power, Inc.

- ☐ Given a fixed amount of manpower, funds, equipment, and material (input), how much can be produced (output) by the organization?
- ☐ How much of each resource will be required to satisfy a specific workload.

Input/output methods are well-suited to workload and resource projection problems because the support resources needed to administer the resources themselves are included in the analysis. An effective analogy is the requirement to make one pound of grated cheese. If we take a pound of solid cheese (the input) and process it through the grater, we will end up with less than a pound of shredded cheese (the output) because some remains clogged in the machine. Organizations are essentially the same (Exhibit 9–16). Input/output analysis measures not only the amount of resources that go directly into the final product but also the amount required to acquire, service, and maintain the resources. For example, in preparing the estimated budget for an organization, the manager needs to compute both the direct labor, funds, and material for the product along with the resources needed to train, hire, purchase, stock, and administer the resources (what it takes to actually run the "machine").

WHAT TO USE AND WHEN

Choosing the correct quantitative technique can be one of the most crucial and difficult considerations to the effective application of a DSS. Often there are several quan-

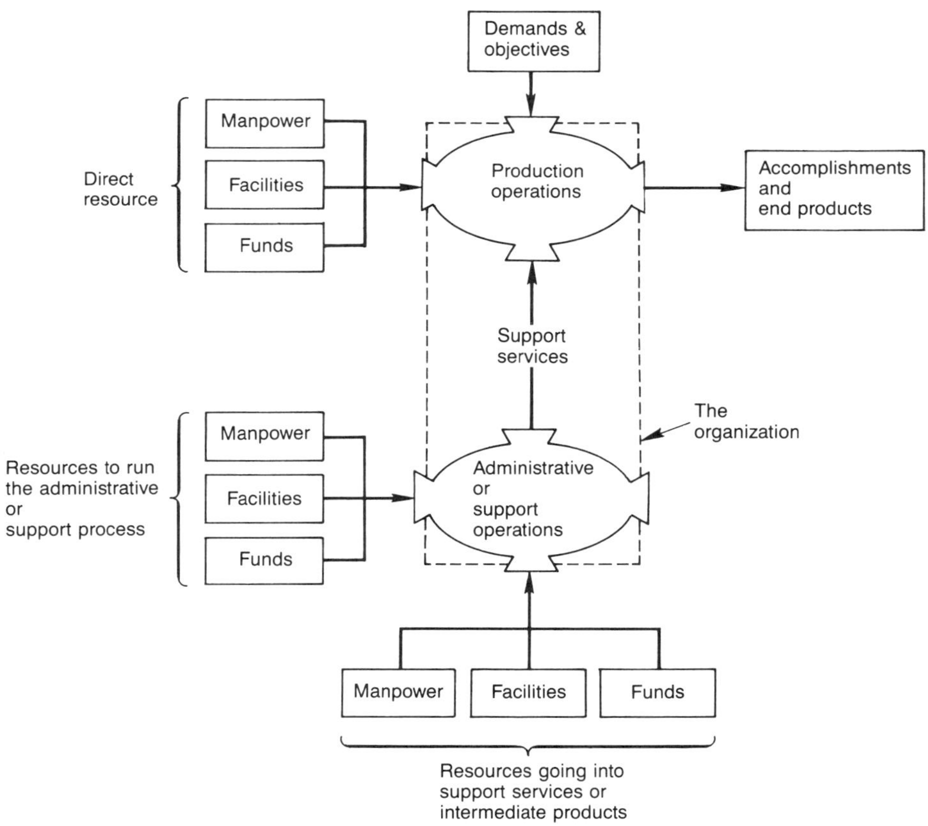

EXHIBIT 9–16 An Organization Viewed As An Input/Output Process.

titative procedures that can be used, but only one is best suited to solve a particular problem (like cutting a board with a jigsaw, hacksaw or broadsaw; all will do the job, however, the broadsaw results in the quickest cut and the straightest edge). In other situations there is but one correct choice (like trying to use a slothead screwdriver for a phillips headed screw). Unfortunately there is no steadfast rule that can be applied in choosing the best quantitative tool.

In practice there is no "absolute truth" that can be used in all cases to guide in the proper selection of a mathematical model or quantitative procedure. In many cases the analytical methodology that is used to build a DSS is based on the developers background and training, not so much on common ground rules that exist in the profession. To illustrate, four independent teams were tasked to design the mathematical model for a workload planning system. Each team worked independently without knowledge of the other groups. The first team of economists chose input/output analysis. The second team, consisting mainly of statisticians, decided to use time series techniques. The group from the computer department felt that discrete event simulation was the only way to go. Finally, the operations research team used a combination of Markovian analysis and linear programming. Experience has shown that the path selected is not necessarily based on insight as to which route provides the best approach, but depends more frequently on which roads are the most comfortable to the developer. Although the choice is not always clear cut, various criteria can be used to select a quantitative technique. This section will discuss several of the factors that influence the choice of one procedure over another.

Problem Structure

The underlying structure of the problem, as well as the type of decisions being made, help to determine the general class of quantitative procedures that can be used. Consider the manager who must decide how to apportion limited resources across various programs. Each program will result in a different profit or gain to the organization. Each program requires various amounts of resources (staff time, funds, material, etc.). As noted earlier, this type of decision is ideally suited to mathematical programming techniques such as linear or integer programming. The manager would be attempting to force "the square peg into a round hole" should he choose another approach. In a different situation, the manager may wish to establish recruiting policies that provide a specific workforce level within each job series (engineers, programmers, technicians, etc.) five years from now. Markovian analysis is well-suited to this type of workforce planning decision. The point is that certain decisions lend themselves to a solution using techniques designed specifically for that class of problem. Exhibit 9-17 provides a general match up between some of the more common areas of application and the quantitative procedures frequently used to support that type of decision.

Complexity

The complexity of the real world often necessitates that a course of action other than the simplest approach be taken. For example, in cases where mathematical programming

AREA OF APPLICATION	Mathematical programming	Network optimization	Decision trees	Flowgraphs	VERT	Simulation	Inventory	Queing	Markovian	Regression	Time series	Input/output analysis
Resource allocation	X											
Material distribution	X	X										
Workshift scheduling	X	X										
Process analysis			X	X	X	X	X	X				
Workload projection									X	X	X	X
Resource assignment	X	X										
Market forecasting						X			X	X	X	
Workforce planning	X	X							X			
Organizational analysis					X	X			X			X
Budgetary planning	X											X
Production scheduling	X	X										
Financial analysis	X		X		X	X				X	X	
Vehicle dispatching	X	X										
Routing problems	X	X										
Combat evaluation					X	X	X	X	X			
Incident/accident forecasting					X	X			X	X	X	
Portfolio analysis	X	X	X	X	X							
Maintenance planning					X	X			X	X		
Equipment replenishment					X	X	X	X				
Productivity analysis					X	X						X
Patient bed allocation	X	X										
Facility location	X	X										
Emergency operations	X	X			X	X	X		X			
Venture evaluation	X	X	X	X	X							

EXHIBIT 9–17 General Uses of Quantitative Techniques

fits the mode, the ideal tactic is to use linear programming procedures since they provide the easiest and quickest solution, plus there is an abundance of commercially available software packages. If, however, the results must have integer values (that is, 6.5 warehouses is illogical) or the mathematical relationships used to define the problem are not "neat" linear expressions (that is, shipping costs are typically a disjointed function of load size), then more complicated methods (such as integer/non-linear programming) must be employed.

Problem Size

Although computers are typically thought to operate in the "wink of an eye," the computational procedures to mathematically manipulate large bundles of data can be quite involved. Some of the problems are so complex that traditional techniques can require hours to reach a solution. The DSS is expected to function as an interactive and direct link with the decision process. Response times measured in seconds or minutes are realistic in a decision support environment. As a result, the sheer size of a problem can play an important part in the selection of an effective quantitative procedure. For example, although standard integer programming techniques can be used to solve virtually any type of production scheduling problem, the solution time becomes prohibitively long (hours) even for moderately sized applications. Most production operations are so large that standard integer programming methods are impractical. Instead, specially designed network optimization procedures can generate a production schedule in a matter of minutes.

Precision

The prime concern of many decisions is not so much the resolution of the answer, but merely to obtain general guidance as to a preferred direction. There are many quantitative techniques that can obtain a quick approximation (say 95 to 98 percent of the best possible solution). Using precise mathematical procedures to gain the few extra percentage points can require hours (assuming that the best solution is ever reached). For example, heuristic scheduling techniques are often used in place of more exact methods because a "good" solution can be obtained rather quickly and the result provides significant improvement over trying to create a schedule manually.

Software Availability

The choice as to which technique is used may be predicated on what commercial or in-house software is readily available and not which procedure best fits the particular problem. For example, the designer may convert a problem that is naturally nonlinear into a linear approximation because of the abundance of linear programming software. As new analytical procedures are created and more versatile software becomes "widely" marketed, the availability of specific types of quantitative packages will become less of an issue.

Designer Preference

It was inferred earlier that the dominant force in the selection of a quantitative procedure may be the background and experience of the developer, not necessarily the characteristics of the problem itself. It is natural for the designer to "latch onto" one or two techniques that have been used extensively. The classic example is the overuse of simulation techniques when in many cases a closed form solution exist. Overcoming this tendency requires that a development team be well-rounded and experienced in a broad range of applications.

EXERCISES

1. List the factors that can contribute to the reason why one particular quantitative technique is selected over others.
2. For the systems you classified as DSS in Exercise 1 of Chapter 2, identify which quantitative model (resource allocation, activity scheduling, etc.) applies to that particular application.
3. Based on the material and examples discussed in this chapter, identify which quantitative technique (simulation, statistical analysis, etc.) appears appropriate for the following problems (note that in some cases more than one procedure may be appropriate):
   a. Projecting next year's sales using historical data of customer demands over the last three years.
   b. Determining what the average time is for an individual to progress from an intern position to a management role, and what percentage of starters succeed in the program (for example, make it to a management position).
   c. Evaluating the risk of terrorist infiltration at a sensitive site (military center, nuclear facility, etc.) based on the random nature of the situation (chance of sensor malfunction, sensing the intrusion at each security level, neutralizing security personnel, etc.).
   d. Determining the best way to send petroleum through an existing nationwide pipeline system to minimize waste and pumping costs.
   e. Determining the best allocation of available funds across various investments over the next five years based on the given rate of return, maturity period, interest rate, and so on.
4. At the end of Chapter 2 (AREAS OF APPLICATION), we discussed various groupings of DSS applications (Operations Planning and Management, Resource Allocation and Acquisition, etc.). Examine Exhibit 9–2 and estimate where each grouping (for example, management functions) fits into the management process. (*Hint:* review the narrative that describes each area.)

REFERENCES AND SUGGESTED READING

Introduction and Survey of Quantitative Methods

1. Ackoff, R., E. Arnoff, and C. Churchman, *Introduction to Operation Research,* Wiley & Sons, 1957.
2. Hillier, F. and G. Lieberman, New York, N.Y.: *Introduction to Operations Research,* Oakland, CA: Holden-Day Inc., 1967.
3. Moder, J. and S. Elmaghraby, *Handbook of Operations Research,* New York, N.Y.: Van Nostrand-Reinhold Publishing, 1978.
4. Rivett, P., *Principles of Model Building,* New York, N.Y.: Wiley & Sons, 1973.

5. Thesen, A., *Computer Methods in Operations Research,* Orlando, FL: Academic Press, 1978.

6. Wagner, H., *Principles of Operations Research,* Englewood Cliffs, N.J.: Prentice-Hall, 1975.

Mathematical Programming and Multicriteria Methods

7. Bracken, J. and G. McCormick, *Selected Applications of Nonlinear Programming,* New York, N.Y.: Wiley & Sons, 1968.

8. Dantzig, G., *Linear Programming Extensions,* Princeton, N.J.: Princeton University Press, 1963.

9. Dyer, J., "Interactive Goal Programming," *Management Science,* Vol. 19, 1972.

10. Dennardo, E., *Dynamic Programming: Theory and Application,* Englewood Cliffs, N.J.: Prentice-Hall, 1975.

11. Dreyfus, S. and A. Law, *The Art and Theory of Dynamic Programming,* Orlando, FL: Academic Press, Inc., 1977.

12. Duffin, R., E. Peterson and C. Zener, *Geometric Programming: Theory and Application,* New York, N.Y.: Wiley & Sons, 1967.

13. Garfinkel, R. and G. Nemhauser, *Integer Programming,* New York, N.Y.: Wiley & Sons, 1972.

14. Garvin, W., *Introduction to Linear Programming,* New York, N.Y.: McGraw-Hill, 1960.

15. Geoffrion, A., *Perspectives On Optimization,* Reading, MA: Addison-Wesley, 1972.

16. Geoffrion, A., and R. Marsten, "Integer Programming: State-of-the-Art Survey," *Management Science,* May, 1972.

17. Goicoechea, A., A. Hansen and B. Duckstein, *Multiobjective Decision Analysis With Engineering and Business Applications,* New York, N.Y.: Wiley & Sons, 1982.

18. Hu, T., *Integer Programming & Network Flows,* Reading, MA: Addison-Wesley, 1969.

19. Hwang, C. and K. Yoon, *Multiple Attribute Decision Making Methods and Applications—State-of-the-Art Survey,* New York: Springer-Verlag, 1979.

20. Keeney, R. and H. Raiffa, *Decisions With Multiple Objectives: Preferences And Value Tradeoffs,* New York, N.Y.: Wiley & Sons, 1976.

21. Mangasarian, O., *Applied Nonlinear Programming,* New York, N.Y.: McGraw-Hil, 1969.

22. Saaty, T., *The Analytic Hierarchy Process,* New York, N.Y.: McGraw-Hill, 1980.

23. Simmonard, M., *Linear Programming,* Englewood Cliffs, N.J.: Prentice-Hall, 1966.

24. Steuer, R., "An Interactive Multiple Objective Linear Programming Procedure," *TIMS Studies in the Management Sciences,* Vol. 6, 1977.

25. Wendell, R., "Multiple Objective Mathematical Programming With Respect To Multiple Decision Makers," *Operations Research,* Vol. 28, no. 5, 1980.

26. Wilhelm, J., *Objectives and Multi-Objective Decision Making Under Uncertainty,* New York: Springer-Verlag, 1975.

27. Yu, P., "Linear Multiparametric Programming by Multi-Criteria Simplex Method," *Management Science,* Vol. 23, no. 2, 1976.

28. Zeleny, M., *Multiple Criteria Decision Making,* New York, N.Y.: McGraw-Hill, 1982.

29. Zionts, S., *Linear and Integer Programming,* Englewood Cliffs, N.J.: Prentice-Hall, 1974.

Network Optimization

30. Baker, K., *Introduction To Sequencing and Scheduling,* New York, N.Y.: Wiley & Sons, 1974.

31. Ford & Fulkerson, *Flows in Networks,* San Francisco, CA: University Press, 1962.

32. Glover, F. and D. Klingman, "Network Applications In Industry and Government," *AIIE Transactions,* December, 1977.

33. Jersen, P. and J. Barnes, *Network Flow Programming,* New York, N.Y.: Wiley & Sons, 1975.

34. Potts, R. and R. Oliver, *Flows In Transportation Networks,* Orlando, FL: Academic Press, 1972.

Network Analysis

35. Hespos, R. and P. Strassman, "Stochastic Decision Trees for the Analysis of Investment Decisions," *Management Science,* no. 11, 1965.

36. Lee, S., G. Moeller and L. Digman, *Network Analysis For Management Decisions,* Derenter, Netherlands: Kluwer-Nijhoff Publishing, 1982.

37. Lee, S. and L. Moore, *Introduction To Decision Science,* Princeton, N.J.: Petrocelli, 1975.

38. Moore, L. and E. Clayton, *GERT Modeling and Simulation: Fundamentals and Applications,* Princeton, N.J.: Petrocelli, 1976.

39. Pritsker, A., *Modeling and Analysis Using Q-GERT,* New York, N.Y.: Halsted Press, 1977.

40. Raiffa, H., *Decision Analysis,* Reading, MA: Addison-Wesley, 1968.

41. Raiffa, H., and J. Pratt, *Introduction To Statistical Decision Theory,* New York, N.Y.: McGraw-Hill, 1965.

42. Whitehouse, G., *Systems Analysis and Design Using Network Techniques,* Englewood Cliffs, N.J.: Prentice-Hall, 1973.

Program Management

43. Moder, J. and C. Phillips, *Project Management With CPM and PERT,* New York, N.Y.: Reinhold Publishing, 1964.

44. Wiest, J. and F. Levy, *A Management Guide To PERT/CPM,* Englewood Cliffs, N.J.: Prentice-Hall, 1977.

Stochastic Methods

45. Cruon, R., *Queuing Theory-Recent Developments and Applications,* New York, N.Y.: Elsevier Publishing, 1967.

46. Emshoff, J. and R. Sisson, *Design and Use of Computer Simulation Models,* New York, N.Y.: MacMillan, 1970.

47. Fishman, G., *Concept and Methods in Discrete Event Simulation,* New York, N.Y.: Wiley & Sons, 1976.

48. Gaver, D. and G. Thompson, *Programming and Probability Models in Operations Research,* Monterey, CA: Brooks-Cole, 1973.

49. Grinold, R. and D. Marshall, *Manpower Planning,* New York: North-Holland, 1977.

50. Hadley, G. and R. Whitin, *Analysis of Inventory Systems,* Englewood Cliffs, N.J.: Prentice-Hall, 1963.

51. Kemeny, J. and J. Snell, *Finite Markov Chains,* Van Nostrand, 1960.

52. Lee, A., *Applied Queuing Theory,* New York, N.Y.: St. Martin's Press, 1966.

53. Maier, R., Newell, T. and A. Puzer, *Simulation in Business and Economics,* Englewood Cliffs, N.J.: Prentice-Hall, 1969.

54. Mize, J. and G. Cox, *Essentials of Simulation,* Englewood Cliffs, N.J.: Prentice-Hall, 1968.

55. Nadder, E., *Inventory Systems,* New York, N.Y.: Wiley & Sons, 1966.

56. Newell, G., *Applications of Queuing Theory,* London, England: Chapman & Hall Ltd., 1971.

57. Shannon, R., *Systems Simulation: The Art and Science,* Englewood Cliffs, N.J.: Prentice-Hall, 1975.

58. Watson, H. and D. Christy, "The Application of Simulation: A Survey of Industry Practice," *INTERFACES,* October, 1983.

Statistical Forecasting Techniques

59. Anderson, O., *Time Series Analysis and Forecasting,* London, England: Butterworths, 1979.

60. Anderson, T., *Statistical Analysis of Time Series,* New York, N.Y.: Wiley & Sons, 1971.

61. Box, G. and G. Jenkins, *Time Series Analysis Forecasting and Control,* San Francisco, CA: Holden-Day, 1970.

62. Brillinger, D., *Time Series Data Analysis And Theory,* New York, N.Y.: Holt, Rinehart, and Winston Inc., 1975.

63. Daniel, G. and F. Woods, *Fitting Equations to Data,* New York, N.Y.: Wiley & Sons, 1971.

64. Draper, N. and H. Smith, *Applied Regression Analysis,* New York, N.Y.: Wiley & Sons, 1966.

65. Ostle, B. and R. Mensing, *Statistics in Research,* Ames, Iowa: Iowa State University Press, 1975.

66. Winters, P., "Forecasting Sales by Exponentially Weighted Moving Averages," *Management Science,* no. 6, 1960.

10

Software Considerations

This chapter examines the software aspects of a DSS. We will discuss the hierarchy (shells) of software, summarize some of the software development tools that can be used to create the application, and finally present several approaches to software development. We will start by exploring the various layers of software that can be encountered in a computer application and how they pertain to a DSS.

LAYERS OF SOFTWARE

Without a set of instructions to tell the computer how a specific task is to be conducted, automation would be of little value. "Software" ties together the various parts of a computer system to meet the needs of each application. Software consists of a set of instructions that define how computations are to be performed, data is to be entered, or results are to be listed. Typically, software is made up of one or more "programs." Programs identify the step-by-step procedures that are to be followed by the computer for each task. Software comprises the major effort in creating a DSS. In each application there are several layers of software that play a part in making up the total system (Exhibit 10–1).

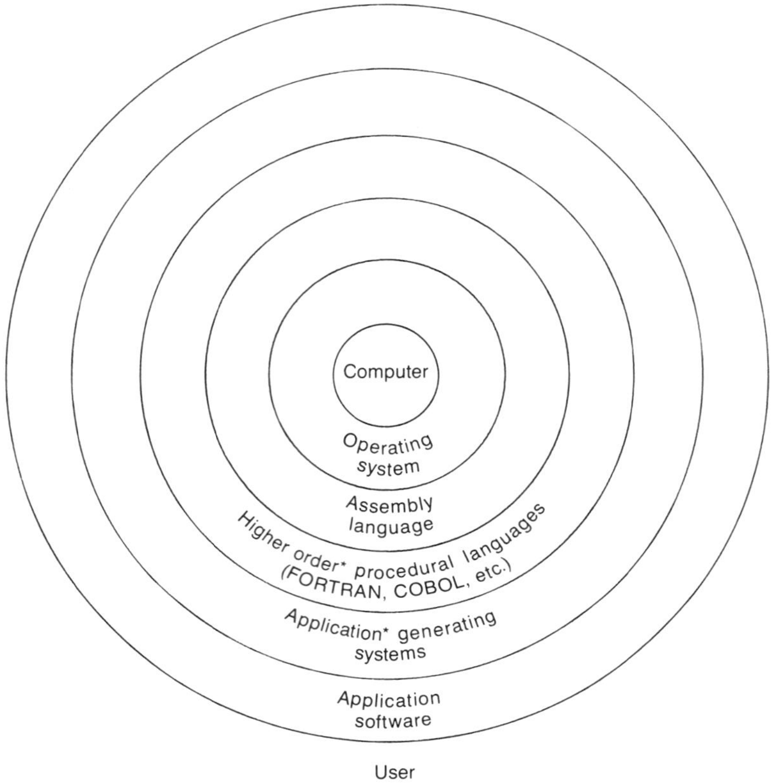

* An application can be created using either a procedural language (FORTRAN, COBOL, etc.) or an application generating system

EXHIBIT 10–1 Layers of Software.

Operating System

The operating system provides a mechanism by which the user can perform "low level" operations such as: logging into the system; copying, erasing, or naming files; creating applications programs; and so forth. Operating systems are "usually" associated with one particular computer manufacturer for mini/mainframe systems. For example: TSO (IBM), MPE (HP3000), TOPS (DEC20), and MCR (VAX), to mention a few. (UNIX is an example of a common operating system that can be used on many computers.) Operating systems for microcomputers are not generally specific to only one system. Some of the more prevalent operating systems for microcomputers include: CP/M, DOS and P-systems.

Programming Facilities

To create an applications package, software designers rely heavily on a variety of programming facilities. These programming "tools" help the software engineer to describe an operation, activity, or task as a set of instructions that can be executed by the computer. Programming facilities are typically referred to as "programming languages" because they have a dialogue and interpretation of their own. At the lowest level we have what is commonly called the "assembly language." The format and syntax of an assembly language is particular to each machine and extremely difficult for normal humans to comprehend (system's programmers are the most frequent users of assembly). Because assembly languages are so difficult to use, "higher order" programming languages (frequently referred to as "procedural" languages for reasons we will discuss later), have been developed over the years. A few examples of higher order languages include: FORTRAN, COBOL, PASCAL, ADA, and BASIC. These languages appear closer to normal spoken English than does an assembly language. In addition to being easier to use, higher order languages offer more machine compatibility. For example, a program properly developed in FORTRAN on a VAX minicomputer can usually be converted to a microcomputer with only minimal changes.

Because software design constitutes such a large portion of a system's cost, one of the areas of current development and technological endeavor deals with programming facilities that "short-cut" the coding effort (translating an operation or task into programming steps). Applications Generating Systems (AGS) [1,21,25] provide programming facilities that either generate their own code to perform specific tasks in a larger program or can be used to create a specific application. For example, a software developer might use an AGS to design analysis capabilities, prompts for user entry, routine and repetitive reports, etc. The AGS would then create the package necessary to perform this function. At a somewhat higher level, an AGS could be used on an ad hoc basis to accomplish specific operations requested by an implementer (Chapter 1) or a sophisicated user. Application Generators are sometimes referred to as nonprocedural languages and differ from traditional languages (like FORTRAN, PASCAL, COBOL, etc.) in their *nonprocedural* approach to creating an application. Procedural languages require the developer to describe the logic and flow of a program (the procedure) to accomplish a specific set of tasks or operations. For this reason they are often referred to as *procedural languages.* Conversely, nonprocedural languages concentrate the developer's efforts on what the program is to accomplish, not on the steps and procedures necessary to achieve the result. In other words, nonprocedural languages allow the application developer to focus on what the system is to do, not how it is to do it.

Applications Packages

At the outer rim of software is the package applied by the user to perform the specific job or task. Examples include word processing packages, telecommunication software, financial planning systems, resource allocation package, Expert Systems, and so forth.

In general, the software element of a decision-support application centers around the last three layers. Accordingly, our discussion will focus on this aspect of DSS software.

PROCEDURAL (Third Generation) LANGUAGES

Procedural programming languages provide the mechanism through which the operations and procedures being automated can be translated from a form that humans can understand and work with to a form the machine can interpret. The current roster of procedural (often referred to as Third Generation or 3GL) languages is extensive with new and "improved" 3GLs added each year. Decision-support applications can be developed in virtually all of the current languages, however, some are more appropriately suited to designing a DSS than others.

Selecting the right 3GL is somewhat like buying a new pair of shoes. The pair chosen can depend on personal preference, how often they will be used, their purpose (for leisure, dress, or work), and many similar factors. To understand which language best satisfies the needs of a particular application requires an overview of their various attributes and capabilities.

Types of Applications

Procedural languages can be classified into three categories based on their purpose and the general functions for which they are used:

- ☐ *General Purpose/Business Languages* are designed for programming the tasks associated with most business functions or personal activities such as accounting, bookkeeping, record tracking, cash management, and so forth. Examples include COBOL, BASIC and PASCAL.
- ☐ *Scientific Languages* are intended for automating procedures that are analytical in nature. The need for performing complex mathematical computations occurs in the fields of engineering, operations research, physics, and similar disciplines where it is necessary to manipulate large quantities of numbers. FORTRAN is an example of a programming language designed primarily for scientific applications.
- ☐ *Special Application Languages* are used in areas where specialized features can expedite programming efforts by exploiting the characteristics and structure of a particular class of problems. Examples include SIMSCRIPT [22] and GPSS [30,36] which are tailored to simulation problems, APL which is tuned specifically to manipulating large data arrays, and LISP which is designed for creating expert systems and artificial intelligence applications.

Mode of Operation

Programming languages operate in two basic modes: interpretive and compiled. Interpretive languages (like APL and BASIC) are targeted at applications where the major concern is the time required to write and debug the program. They operate in an interactive programming environment where the developer can quickly enter, test, and debug the program. Although interpretive languages can be used to design a DSS, they are more suitable for relatively small and expendable programs where computational speed is not an issue. The bulk of DSS applications are developed using "compiled" languages.

The difference between interpretive and compiled languages stems from how the program is translated from the lines of instructions entered by the programmer to what the machine uses. In an interpretive language program, statements are translated into the machine's language each time they are executed. If part of the program is used repeatedly, those statements must again be translated into machine instruction each time they are "reused." This "line-by-line" process is ideal for interactive programming but not for speed. The translation process takes a significant amount of time. If the program has to cycle through many interations (as in most DSS applications), then an interpretive program can take an exorbitant amount of time to run. Compiled languages are more efficient for "number crunching" exercises. The total program is translated all at once using a "code translater" package (called a "compiler"). This makes compiled languages more suitable for complex mathematical procedures that will be used repeatedly (as with a DSS).

Attributes and Features

Each language has its own profile of operational and functional characteristics. These attributes can be clustered into two groups: those dealing with the external features of the final product (what the user sees); and those dealing with the internal properties of the language. This section will explain some of the more prevalent characteristics that have traditionally influenced the choice of a programming language for a particular application.

- ☐ *Machine Portability.* Virtually at the instant a new language is introduced into the marketplace, vendors begin developing their own versions. Each version will typically have its own innovative features. Until the language is old enough for common standards to be established, the functional characteristics vary so widely that a program developed on one computer will be incompatible with most other computers. This causes no problem if the software package will only be used on the original computer series during its entire lifetime. However, in the event that the package will be used on many different brands of computers, the lack of compatibility can be a serious consideration. Generally, the older and more frequently used languages are more portable in going from one hardware configuration (like an IBM 3033) to another (like a VAX).
- ☐ *Availability.* The languages that are more readily available are those that have been used more extensively and make up the greater market base. Special purpose languages are less commonly available. For example, FORTRAN and COBOL compilers can be found on virtually every main, mini or microcomputer system. Conversely APL and SIMSCRIPT are usually available only on a case-by-case basis.
- ☐ *Functional Versatility.* For the more sophisticated applications, the functional capabilities and features of the programming language can play a vital role in design-

ing a DSS. Languages intended for "quick and dirty" applications (like BASIC) are usually more difficult for programming complicated large scale operations that require special mathematical and structural features (as is necessary with most DSS applications).

- *Text Manipulation.* The ability of a programming language to readily perform text and file manipulation can be very important in the development of user-oriented systems. Newer languages provide a broad spectrum of easy to use text and file manipulation features. Although the more scientific languages can perform comprehensive file and text manipulation, it usually requires that special programs be written to provide these functions. With the advent of microcomputers many of the scientific languages provide special support programs that can perform text manipulation functions.
- *Readability and Ease of Upgrade.* Each language uses its own special syntax. How close the syntax is to the spoken language will affect how easy it is to understand and eventually upgrade the program. Some of today's programming languages provide a reasonable facsimile to English (like PASCAL) while others appear as clusters of random characters (as with APL).
- *Conciseness.* There is an inverse relationship between the readability of a language and the amount of required programming effort. For example, COBOL is extremely readable but requires a large number of statements to accomplish even the simplest tasks. Conversely, APL is probably one of the most difficult languages to follow but can perform very complex operations using only three or four characters. One line of an APL program can equate to hundreds of lines of another language.

Summary of Several Popular 3GLs

As previously noted, a multitude of procedural languages are available to the developer (LISP, ADA, COBOL, ALGOL, DYNAMO, MODULA, C, SNOBOL, APL, FORTRAN, GPSS, SIMSCRIPT, represents just a fraction of the currently available languages). This section attempts to establish a basic understanding of some of the more commonly used procedural languages. The references [4,17,19,31,38,41,42] provide a historical perspective of 3GLs, a consolidated source of sample programs for many of the modern languages, and a general comparison of their advantages and disadvantages.

- *FORTRAN* was one of the first "high level" tools designed to replace the machine oriented assembly languages [10,14,34]. FORTRAN (FORmula TRANslation) was released in 1957 and intended for automating scientific and engineering problems. FORTRAN is a well-rounded language, however its syntax is oriented toward "number crunching" operations typical to DSS applications. The language offers one of the most portable programing tools where a package developed on one hardware system can be transferred to a different one with very few (if any) revisions.
- *COBOL* is one of the more commonly used languages for business applications [5,16]. COBOL is a very "wordy" language designed specifically for file manipulations and business activities (records tracking, accounting, billing, etc.). Because of its age, COBOL is also a very standardized language.

- ☐ *PL/I* was developed in 1964 in an attempt to combine the best features of FORTRAN and COBOL [20,27]. Although the language is quite flexible, it never gained the favor of the programming community as originally expected. PL/I has not been standardized and is not as widely used as many of the other common languages. As a result it is not one of the more machine to machine compatible languages.
- ☐ *BASIC* was developed specifically for the novice [3,40]. It is widely used on micro and personal computers. BASIC (Beginner's All purpose Symbolic Instruction Code) is well-suited for small programs but difficult to use for developing large scale applications that require a high degree of mathematical power. Although BASIC is widely used, it is one of the least standardized languages.
- ☐ *RPG* is a specialized language designed specifically for report generation. Although RPG can be a valuable asset for providing the report generating capabilities necessary in a DSS, it is not widely available and lacks the functional features required for the quantitative aspects of a DSS.
- ☐ *PASCAL* is a powerful language that combines many of the positive features of other languages [18,32,35]. It is well-suited to both business and scientific applications. PASCAL features a self-documenting style and uses structured programming techniques. Although PASCAL is a viable candidate for DSS development, it has not reached the popularity of the more common languages (like COBOL and FORTRAN).
- ☐ *ADA* is "somewhat" similar to PASCAL in syntax but with even greater programming power and flexibility [2,37,43]. The primary proponent of ADA is the Department of Defense (DOD). Several policy initiatives are currently in the process of trying to establish ADA as the standard language for DOD systems. Although ADA programming systems are appearing in the market for many computers, common use across the industry is not likely in the near future.
- ☐ *APL* is another specialized language [12,13,44]. It is very powerful and concise for manipulating large arrays of data. As a result, APL is well-suited to complex statistical, engineering, and scientific applications. APL (A Programming Language) was developed by Kenneth Iverson in the early 1960s while at Harvard. Because of its propensity for performing complex operations in remarkably few steps, APL quickly spread in the analytical community. However, the very features that make it ideal for mathematical operations result in the language being difficult to follow and revise. The syntax of the language consists primarily of mathematical symbols. It is also not readily available in any but the more specialized areas.
- ☐ *SIMSCRIPT* was developed specifically for solving simulation problems [22]. The language is very English-oriented and easy to read. SIMSCRIPT provides a powerful and expeditious tool for developing DSS applications that require a simulation model. It is not, however, one of the more commonly available languages.
- ☐ *LISP* was developed at MIT by John McCarthy in the late 1950s specifically for the purpose of creating Artificial Intelligence (AI) and Expert Systems applications. LISP (short for "LISt Processing") is structured for coding the logical relationships and decision rules that are necessary to create the *knowledge base* used by Expert Systems and AI applications. As a result, LISP has a technically-oriented syntax that is difficult for the novice to understand. There are also many versions of LISP and it is not one of the more common languages. LISP is a powerful tool for AI oriented systems but less flexible than other languages for developing general decision-support applications.

Making the Right Choice

Deciding which 3GL is best for a particular situation requires that several questions be answered:

- ☐ Will the DSS ever be used on more than one computer system?
- ☐ Is it likely that modifications will be required by different work groups?
- ☐ Which is more important—development time and cost, or operation speed and subsequent modification?

The predominant factor that usually determines which programming language is used is the designers background and experience. Assume, however, that the development staff is proficient in each language. A comparison of language capabilities with the characteristics of the application will help in selecting the most appropriate programming facilities. Exhibit 10–2 provides a qualitative assessment of the various languages. The following "rough" guidelines are offered in situations where the DSS is being developed from scratch:

- ☐ If the DSS will be used on only one type of hardware, then use the language available on that system with the best properties (Exhibit 10–2) for ease of modification, functional power, and text/file manipulation.
- ☐ If the DSS will only be used in a specific community (military, academic, etc.), then exploit the features of the appropriate specialty languages (ADA, SIMSCRIPT, etc.).

	Availability	Standardization	Portability	Facilities for large scale applications	Text/file manipulation capabilities	Readability	Conciseness	Mathematical and scientific features
FORTRAN	Excellent	Excellent	Excellent	Excellent	Moderate	Moderate	Good	Excellent
COBOL	Excellent	Excellent	Excellent	Good	Good	Good	Low	Fair
BASIC	Good	Low	Low	Low	Good	Fair	Fair	Moderate
PASCAL	Moderate	Moderate	Fair	Excellent	Excellent	Excellent	Moderate	Good
ADA	Fair	Fair	Moderate	Excellent	Excellent	Good	Moderate	Good
SIMSCRIPT	Low	Good	Good	Good	Moderate	Excellent	Good	Good
PL/I	Fair	Good	Good	Good	Good	Good	Fair	Moderate
APL	Low	Moderate	Moderate	Fair	Good	Low	Excellent	Excellent

EXHIBIT 10–2 Comparison of Procedural Programming Languages and Their Properties. Properties are ranked in the following order: Low, Fair, Moderate, Good, Excellent.

- ☐ If the DSS will be used on many different computer systems across various sectors (government, commercial, academic, military), then use the more portable/common languages (like FORTRAN or COBOL).
- ☐ If the DSS is expected to have a long lifetime and go through many revisions, then readability and ease of modification should be given top priority.

The following comments provide general observations about specific procedural programming languages:

- ☐ FORTRAN provides a well-rounded candidate designed specifically for the type of analytical procedures that are required in many of the large scale DSS applications. Although the older versions were weak in file/text manipulation, new versions (FORTRAN 77 and above) alleviate most of the earlier shortcomings. It is also well-suited to the modular programming required for large applications, and is one of the more common/portable languages.
- ☐ PASCAL is a very powerful and well-structured language. Internal utilities provided with the language can reduce development time significantly. Where portability is not an issue, PASCAL provides a versatile programming language.
- ☐ APL and BASIC are not, in general, well-suited to DSS applications unless the system is to be a quick and simple tool.

NON-PROCEDURAL (Fourth Generation) LANGUAGES

We mentioned earlier that creating software from scratch is both time consuming and labor intensive. The process of translating the requirements of a user (query information, sort data, perform computations, etc.), into program statements that will accomplish the desired effect, is an involved procedure. Over the past ten years, Fourth Generation Languages (4GL) have shown promise in helping to facilitate the process through which certain types of decision-support applications are created. Although 4GLs are rooted in the late 1960s, they have become more prominent in the last decade [8]. The nonprocedural products of today can roughly be partitioned into two spheres of application: those oriented toward facilitating system development by computer professionals (INGRESS, ORACLE and IDEAL are examples), and 4GL systems aimed at supporting users (EMPIRE, FOCUS, and IFPS represent the latter category). Although the objective of improved productivity is the same, the central difference stems from the targeted audience and the user interface environment that is employed. Our discussion will concentrate on the more user-oriented domain of 4GL applications.

General Capabilities

In essence, 4GLs provide a wide range of "already developed" procedures and programming facilities that can be enacted by interactively issuing succinct commands. To illustrate, consider the requirement to view sales by product type, by month, within each geographic region, and summarized for each customer (see Case Study 4 in Chapter 12). To generate the report with a 4GL, only a few command lines would be needed such as:

```
TABLE FILE SUM UNITS
BY MONTH BY REGION BY CUSTOMER BY PRODUCT
ON CUSTOMER SUBTOTAL
END
```

A procedural language (like COBOL) would require 500 to 1,000 lines of programming instruction to accomplish these tasks [7].

As with any new concept, 4GLs suffer the same "bandwagon" syndrome of most marketable automation products (similar to that incurred by DSS itself (Chapter 2) and Artificial Intelligence [Chapter 13]). The result has been a marketplace saturated by a variety of products, with broadly different features and capabilities, all promoted as 4GLs. There are, however, certain attributes that are typical to most 4GLs [7,8,26,28]. In general, it can be stated that 4GLs:

- ☐ Permit interactive ad hoc inquiry (for example, the user defines what information will be exhibited, how it will be displayed, and how it can alter the process at will while sitting at a terminal).
- ☐ Provide information entry, editing, and deletion in a user-oriented fashion.
- ☐ Facilitate the development of specific applications (sales reports, market projects, inventory tracking, production status updates, etc.).
- ☐ Result in substantial productivity improvements over procedural languages (estimates range between a 5 to 1 and a 30 to 1 saving depending on the application).
- ☐ Incur a return on investment of roughly nine to 15 months.
- ☐ Provide a broad range of general decision-support capabilities (spreadsheet analysis, business graphics, statistical analysis, financial forecasting, etc.).

A Sampling of Commercial 4GL Products

Because of the competitive and dynamic nature of the software industry, specific features, capabilities, and hardware environments change rapidly. The following discussion provides a static view of four nonprocedural products as seen in the 1986 time frame. Each of the products discussed in this section have been in service for several years across a broad user base, have established customer support facilities, and provide free introductory seminars or demonstrations of their products. A more complete and detailed discussion of available 4GL products can be found in reference [26].

RAMIS II is a 4GL available through Martin Marietta Data Systems. In 1985, RAMIS II was in operation in over 1,000 installations and in use by more than half of the Fortune 100 companies. The system's capabilities focus primarily on supporting user needs for ad hoc data query. RAMIS II allows the user to choose from any three of the methods of user interaction discussed in Chapter 8 (succinct command lines, menu driven, or a natural language interface). RAMIS II will also allow the user to establish an interface between programs created outside the 4GL environment with a procedural language such as FORTRAN, COBOL or PL/I.

Exhibit 10–3 illustrates how RAMIS II can be used to query a database to generate

```
TABLE
FILE SALES
.
SUM REVENUE AND UNITS
BY PRODNUM ACROSS MONTH
IF MONTH IS FROM 8301 TO 8303
.
END
```

PRODTYPE	TOT REVENUE WITHIN PRODTYPE	PRODUCT	REVENUE	PER REVENUE WITHIN REPORT
ELECTRONICS	$237,000.00	CALCULATOR/PRINTER	$4,500.00	63
		TYPEWRITER	$66,500.00	9 29
		WORD PROCESSOR-1	$129,000.00	18 02
		WORD PROCESSOR-4	$37,000.00	5 17
FILES	$76,078.60	4-DR. FILE	$12,676.60	1 76
		4-DR. FIREPROOF FILE	$62,503.00	8 73
FURNITURE	$186,963.60	CONFERENCE TABLE	$13,906.36	1 94
		EXECUTIVE CHAIR	$66,692.80	9 31
		EXECUTIVE DESK	$26,926.55	3 82
		SIDE CHAIR	$16,392.10	2 16
		TYPIST CHAIR	$7,870.40	1 10
		TYPIST DESK	$24,276.40	3 39
		WOOD BOOKCASE	$31,890.00	4 46
TERMINALS	$217,976.00	PRINTING TERMINAL	$110,975.00	15 50
		VIDEO TERMINAL	$107,000.00	14 94

QUARTERLY SUMMARY BY PRODUCT TYPES

```
TABLE
FILE SALES
.
SUM REVENUE AND PERCENT REVENUE WITHIN REPORT
BY PRODTYPE DISPLAYED WITH TOTAL REVENUE
BY PRODUCT
IF MONTH IS FROM 8301 TO 8303
.
END
```

PAGE 1

PRODNUM	MONTH 8301 REVENUE	UNITS	8302 REVENUE	UNITS	8303 REVENUE	UNITS
DK0114	$10,600.00	37	$10,800.00	37	$10,490.00	35
CA1430	$1,200.00	16	$1,650.00	22	$1,650.00	22
CH1307	$2,473.80	19	$3,443.60	27	$1,963.00	16
CH1310	$3,913.80	44	$6,496.30	64	$6,963.00	70
CH2470	$21,366.00	67	$22,404.80	70	$22,033.00	75
D51065	$9,888.20	16	$6,364.80	17	$8,022.40	22
D52130	$7,082.06	16	$9,936.15	21	$8,906.38	19
FI1204	$4,293.80	15	$4,427.60	26	$3,854.20	22
FI2734	$16,696.00	18	$22,672.00	26	$24,135.00	20
TA7396	$3,943.36	10	$6,267.80	12	$4,706.20	11
TE0700	$41,886.00	21	$33,560.00	26	$36,730.00	18
TE3214	$33,760.00	28	$36,000.00	29	$37,250.00	30
TY7402	$21,000.00	14	$27,600.00	19	$18,000.00	12
WP1961	$39,000.00	3	$30,000.00	3	$61,000.00	4
WP4400	$0.00	0	$0.00	0	$37,000.00	1

MATRIX REPORT

```
TABLE
FILE SALES
.
SUM REVENUE AND PERCENT REVENUE WITHIN REPORT
BY PRODTYPE DISPLAYED WITH TOTAL REVENUE
BY PRODUCT
IF PERCENT REVENUE WITHIN REPORT EXCEEDS 6
IF MONTH IS FROM 8301 TO 8303
.
END
```

PAGE 1

PRODTYPE	TOT REVENUE WITHIN PRODTYPE	PRODUCT	REVENUE	PER REVENUE WITNIN REPORT
ELECTRONICS	$237,000.00	TYPEWRITER	$66,600.00	9 29
FILES	$75,078.60	WORD PROCESSOR-1	$129,000.00	18 02
FURNITURE	$186,963.60	WORD PROCESSOR-4	$37,000.00	6 17
TERMINALS	$217,975.00	4-DR. FIREPROOF FILE	$62,503.00	8 73
		EXECUTIVE CHAIR	$66,692.80	9 31
		PRINTING TERMINAL	$110,976.00	16 60
		VIDEO TERMINAL	$107,000.00	14 94

SUMMARY SELECTION

```
TABLE
NOTE AT TOP OF PAGE
CENTER SALES IN FIRST QUARTER SKIP LINE
FILE SALES
.
SUM REVENUE AS DOLLAR AMOUNT AND UNITS
BY PRODNUM DISPLAYED WITH TOTAL REVENUE WITHIN PRODNUM
ACROSS MONTH
IF MONTH IS FROM 8301 TO 8303
ON REPORT COLUMN TOTAL
.
END
```

PAGE 1

SALES IN FIRST QUARTER

PRODNUM	TOT REVENUE WITHIN PRODNUM	MONTH 8301 DOLLAR AMOUNT	UNITS	8302 DOLLAR AMOUNT	UNITS	8303 DOLLAR AMOUNT	UNITS
DK0114	$31,890.00	$10,600.00	37	$10,800.00	37	$10,490.00	35
CA1430	$4,500.00	$1,200.00	22	$1,650.00	16	$1,650.00	22
CH1307	$7,870.40	$2,473.80	27	$3,443.60	19	$1,963.00	16
CH1310	$16,392.10	$3,913.80	64	$5,496.80	44	$5,983.00	70
CH2470	$66,662.80	$21,366.00	16	$22,404.80	67	$22,933.00	75
D61065	$24,276.40	$9,888.20	17	$6,364.80	16	$8,022.40	22
D62130	$25,926.55	$7,082.05	21	$9,938.15	16	$8,906.36	19
FI1204	$12,575.60	$4,293.90	26	$4,427.60	28	$3,854.20	22
FI2734	$62,603.00	$15,696.00	16	$22,672.00	18	$24,135.00	28
TA7396	$13,906.35	$3,943.36	12	$6,257.80	10	$4,706.20	11
TE0700	$110,975.00	$41,886.00	26	$33,560.00	21	$36,730.00	18
TE3214	$107,000.00	$33,760.00	29	$30,000.00	28	$37,250.00	30
TY7402	$66,600.00	$21,000.00	19	$27,500.00	14	$10,000.00	12
WP1961	$120,000.00	$39,000.00	3	$30,000.00	3	$61,000.00	4
WP4400	$37,000.00	$0.00	0	$0.00	0	$37,000.00	1
TOTAL	$716,007.20	$216,881.10	343	$228,611.96	404	$271,614.16	384

QUARTERLY REPORT

EXHIBIT 10–3a Using a 4 GL to Query a Database. RAMIS II, *Courtesy of* Martin Marietta Data Systems.

```
TABLE
FILE FINANCE
SUM LTDEBT AND CURLIABILITY BY YEAR
IF CO IS 'ABC LTD.'
END
```

```
PLOT BAR
ON 7221
HEADING 'ABC LTD.'
  'LONG TERM DEBT AND CURRENT LIABILITY'
LABEL Y AS 'DOLLARS'
BAR TYPE LTDEBT 82 IN BLUE AND LIABILITY
84 IN PURPLE  MOVE LEGEND (4.57)
FOOTNOTE LEFT 'FISCAL YEARS 1979–1982'
END
```

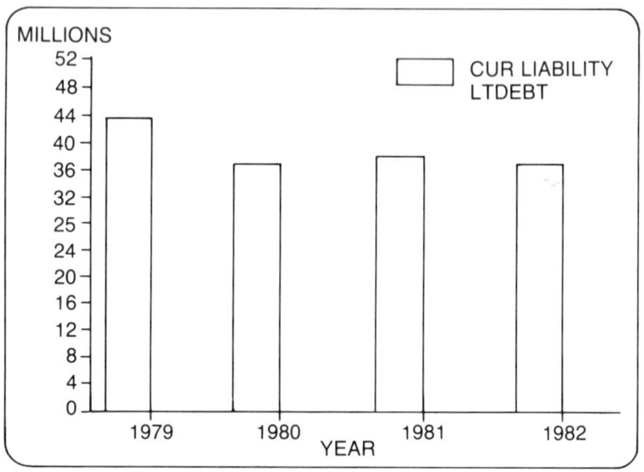

DEFAULT GRAPH

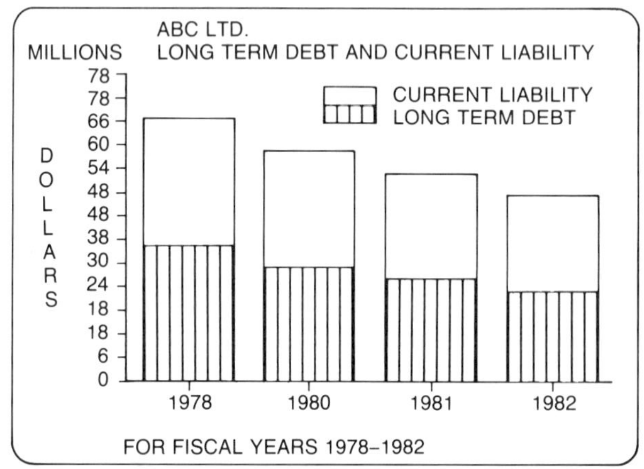

GRAPH WITH EDITING

EXHIBIT 10–3b Using a 4GL to Generate Graphics. RAMIS II, *Courtesy of* Martin Marietta Data Systems.

various reports. The top figures depict the commands entered by the user while the figures at the bottom provide the resulting report. In Exhibit 10–3a the user generates a report summarized by product type (top left), in a matrix format by product number (top right), for a selected set of months and products where revenue exceeds 6 percent (bottom left), and in a quarterly report context for revenue totals (bottom right). Exhibit 10–3b shows how the user would summarize information from a financial database and display it in either a simple (left figure) or a more elaborate (right figure) bar graph.

FOCUS is a nonprocedural product marketed by Information Builders Inc. By 1985 FOCUS was in use in over 1,100 installations worldwide. Although primarily oriented toward supporting ad hoc data query, FOCUS does provide statistical analysis and spreadsheet capability. As with many of the 4GL products of today (see Chapter 13), FOCUS allows the user to select which interactive environment is preferred (command line, menu drive, natural language). FOCUS offers its natural language option by use of INTELLECT, a natural language processor available through Artificial Intelligence Inc. (Chapter 13). The product is available in a variety of main/mini/micro configurations including IBM, VAX, IBM PC/XT and Wang. The user also has the option of

```
TABLE FILE SALES
PRINT NAME AND AMOUNT AND DATE
BY REGION BY SITE
IF AMOUNT GT 1000
ON REGION SKIP-LINE
END
```

PAGE 1

REGION	SITE	NAME	AMOUNT	DATE
MA	NEWK	ELIZABETH GAS	$2,877.30	82 AUG
	NEWY	KOCH RECONSTRUCTION	$6,086.23	82 APR
	PHIL	ROSS INC	$3,890.22	82 JUL
		LASSITER CONSTRUCTION	$1,120.22	82 SEP
MW	CHIC	BAKESHORE INC	$5,678.23	82 OCT
		ROPERS BROTHERS	$2,789.20	82 AUG
	CLEV	BOVEY PARTS	$6,769.22	82 MAY
		ERIE INC	$1,556.76	82 JAN
NE	ALBN	ROCK CITY BUILDER	$1,722.30	82 JUL
	BOST	HANCOCK RESTORERS	$8,246.20	82 FEB
		WANKEL CONSTRUCTION	$2,345.25	82 JUN
		WARNER INDUSTRIES	$3,155.25	82 OCT
	STAM	ACORN INC	$2,006.20	82 MAR
		KANGERS CONSTRUCTION	$2,790.50	82 JUN
		DART INDUSTRIES	$7,780.22	82 MAY
		ARISTA MANUFACTURING	$4,295.90	82 FEB
SE	ATL	RICHS STORES	$1,345.17	82 AUG
	WASH	CAPITOL WHOLESALE	$3,789.00	82 JUN
		FEDERAL DEPOT	$2,195.25	82 MAR

EXHIBIT 10–4 Using FOCUS to Query a Database for Client Sales By Region and Site. *Courtesy of* Information Builders, Inc.

```
TABLE FILE SALES
PRINT NAME BY REGION
RANKED BY HIGHEST 3 AMOUNT
ON REGION SKIP-LINE
IN DATE GE 8201
END
```

PAGE 1

REGION	RANK	AMOUNT	NAME
MA	1	$75,120.22	LASSITER BUILDERS
	2	$56,086.23	KOCH RECONSTRUCTION
	3	$52,877.30	ELIZABETH METAL WORK
MW	1	$66,789.20	ROPER BROTHERS
	2	$56,769.22	BOVEY PARTS
	3	$54,978.34	COACH AND BODY WORKS
NE	1	$86,295.90	ARISTA MANUFACTURING
	2	$68,345.25	WANKEL BROTHERS
			WARNER CONSTRUCTION
	3	$68,246.20	HANCOCK RESTORERS
SE	1	$82.195.25	FEDERAL DEPOT
	2	$56,345.17	RICHS STORES
	3	$53,789.00	CAPITOL WHOLESALE

EXHIBIT 10–4b Using FOCUS to Sort Top Three Clients within Each Region. *Courtesy of* Information Builders, Inc.

creating support programs outside the 4GL environment in FORTRAN, COBOL or PL/I.

Exhibit 10–4 demonstrates some of the features and capabilities provided with FOCUS. In Exhibit 10–4a the user enters nonprocedural commands (top) to query a sales database and displays client's sales by region and site. Next the user repeats the query (top of Exhibit 10–4b) to sort the highest three in each region. Exhibit 10–4c depicts how sales data would be displayed by product across each region. Exhibit 10–4d illustrates how the information would be displayed graphically in both a bar (top) and pie (bottom) chart. Finally, Exhibit 10–4e demonstrates how a statistical analysis would be performed.

IFPS was released in 1975 by Execucom Inc. and represented one of the early attempts at providing a nonprocedural tool to analyze complex financial models. By late 1985 IFPS was in its tenth release and in use worldwide. Although IFPS can provide ad hoc data query capability, its major application centers around modeling complicated financial problems. The product can be used for inventory management, market simulation, venture/portfolio analysis, budget forecasting, cash management, trend analysis, resource allocation decisions, etc. IFPS is available on main/mini-systems such as IBM, DEC, HP, Prime, Sperry and also can be operated from the IBM-PC/XT microcomputer. IFPS provides the additional flexibility of providing the user access to other 4GL products (such as FOCUS, SAS and INFO) or to procedural programs created in FORTRAN, COBOL, or PL/I.

```
DEFINE FILE SALES
REGION/A12= DECODE REGION(NE 'NORTH EAST'
            SE 'SOUTH EAST' MW 'MID WEST'
            MA 'MID-ATLANTIC'):
 END
 TABLE FILE SALES
 HEADING CENTER
"PRODUCT UNIT SALES ANALYSIS </1"
 SUM UNITS AND ROW-TOTAL AND COLUMN-TOTAL
 ACROSS REGION
 BY PRODNUM AS 'PRODUCT,NUMBER'
 END
```

PAGE 1

PRODUCT UNIT SALES ANALYSIS

PRODUCT NUMBER	REGION MID WEST	MID-ATLANTIC	NORTH EAST	SOUTH EAST	TOTAL
10524	164	181	184	115	644
10526	40	126	150	45	361
11275	189	219	133	168	709
11302	179	130	288	172	769
11303	99	121	220	30	470
11537	90	260	110	124	584
11563	297	245	520	371	1433
11567	86	80	*	20	186
12275	*	*	*	30	30
12345	*	10	*	*	10
13737	*	*	29	*	29
13797	110	160	65	389	724
13938	324	186	441	164	1115
13979	*	12	*	*	12
14156	200	538	120	169	1027
15016	94	257	156	245	752
16394	252	210	187	40	689
16436	*	132	52	20	204
16934	*	50	*	*	50
17434	166	378	84	174	802
17905	164	70	108	199	541
34562	25	*	*	*	25
34567	100	*	*	*	100
56267	146	190	910	255	1501
TOTAL	2725	3555	3757	2730	12767

EXHIBIT 10–4c Using FOCUS to Display Sales By Product Across Regions. *Courtesy of* Information Builders, Inc.

```
JOIN PRODUCT IN SUPPLY TO ALL PRODUCT IN SALES

DEFINE FILE SUPPLY
PNUM/A2=EDIT (PRODNUM, '99');
END

GRAPH FILE SUPPLY
SUM UNITS AS 'ORDERED UNITS' AND
     QOH AS 'ON HAND'
ACROSS PNUM AS 'PRODUCT SERIES'
IF PRODNUM FROM 10000 TO 19999
END
```

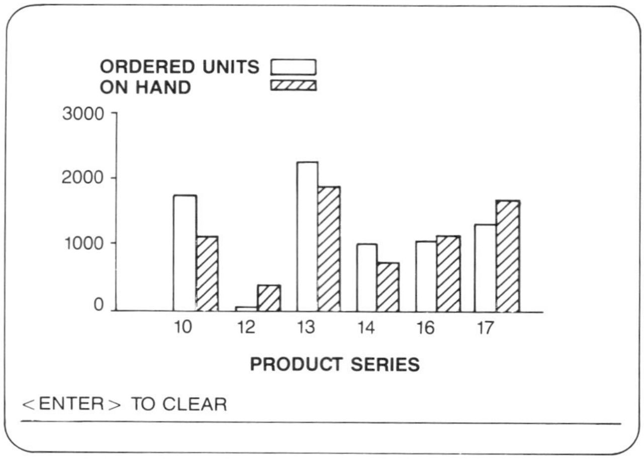


```
SET PIE=ON,BARNUM=ON
GRAPH FILE SALES
SUM RPCT.AMOUNT
AS 'MID ATLANTIC REGION SALES ANALYSIS'
ACROSS STORE
IF REGION EQ 'MA'
END
SET PIE=OFF
```

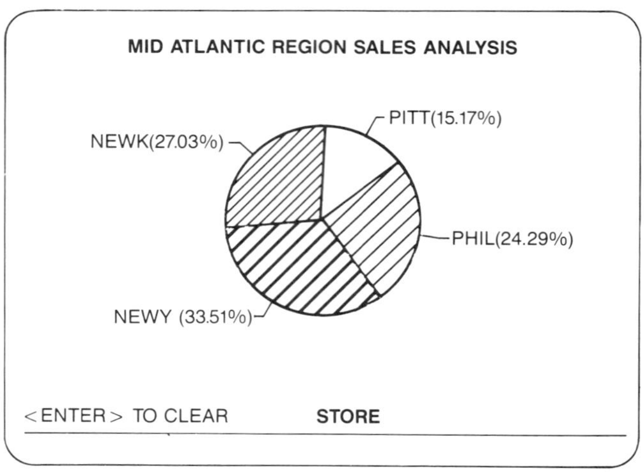

EXHIBIT 10–4d *Courtesy of* Information Builders, Inc.

O.T. INDEX	DATE	QUANTITY	LF. QUANTITY	EF. QUANTITY
10	82 OCT	855.0000	1077.902	1046.330
11	82 NOV	1336.000	1176.874	1199.613
12	82 DEC	1511.000	1275.846	1375.352
13	83 JAN		1374.818	1576.835
14	83 FEB		1473.790	1807.837
15	83 MAR		1572.762	2072.678
16	83 APR		1671.734	2376.319
17	83 MAY		1770.706	2724.439
18	83 JUN		1869.678	3123.561
19	83 JUL		1968.650	3581.150
20	83 AUG		2067.622	4105.777
21	83 SEP		2166.594	4707.254
22	83 OCT		2265.566	5396.852
23	83 NOV		2364.539	6187.469
24	83 DEC		2463.510	7093.914

ANALYSE command issued which produces a menu of available functions. (All ANALYSE prompts shown in bold face).

```
ANALYSE FILE HOLD
  STATISTICAL OPERATIONS...
    ANOVA    CORRE   EXPLAIN   EXSMO   FACTO     MDISC   MULTR
    POLRG    STATS   STATSET   STEPR   TIMESER   XTABS   FILESIZE
  ENTER STATISTICAL OPERATION DESIRED—
STATSET HOLD = STATHOLD
  ENTER STATISTICAL OPERATION DESIRED—
```

Timeser function selected.

```
TIMESER
NUMBER OF OBSERVATIONS = 12
  ENTER NAME OF TIME VARIABLE—
```

TIMESER function prompts for necessary date.

```
DATE
  ENTER TIME FOR 1 INTERVAL (E.G. "1", "2 DAYS", "1 MONTH")—
1 MO
  ENTER COMMAND (OR ? FOR HELP)—
FIT
  ENTER NAME OF VARIABLE—
QUANTITY
  DO YOU WISH TO KEEP PREDICTED VALUES (TYPE "KEEP" OR "NOKEEP")—
KEEP
  HOW MANY PERIODS DO YOU WISH TO EXTRAPOLATE—
12
  DO YOU WISH TO KEEP RESIDUALS (TYPE "RESID" OR "NORESID")—
RESID
  ENTER THE TYPE(S) OF EQUATION YOU WISH TO FIT—
```

A linear and exponential fit is requested.

```
LIN EXP
```

The fit equations and goodness of fit statistics are displayed.

```
NOTE: TIME VARIABLE HAS DATE FORMAT: THUS FITTING IS AGAINST T.INDEX
LINEAR:                Y=88.18188+98.97203 ★ T
PREDICTED IN LF. QUANTITY   RESIDUALS IN R.LF.QUANTIT
MEAN ABS ERR   = 105.1666   MEAN SQ ERR   = 17961.14   MEAN PCT ERR   = 16.44229
CORRELATION    = .9309397   R-SQUARED     = .8666487   T-STATISTIC    = 8.061625
F-STATIC       = 64.98979   VARIANCE      = 21553.40   ST ERR OF EST  = 146.8108
DURBIN-WATSON  = 1.116933
EXPONENTIAL:           Y= 266.6501 ★ EXP(.1367106 ★ T)
PREDICTED IN EF. QUANTITY   RESIDUALS IN R.EF.QUANTIT
MEAN ABS ERR   = 77.38672   MEAN SQ ERR   = 9077.281   MEAN PCT ERR   = 10.77330
CORRELATION    = .9658486   R-SQUARED     = .9328635   T-STATISTIC    = 11.78770
F-STATISTIC    = 138.9501   VARIANCE      = .0192346   ST ERR OF EST  = .1386887
DURBIN-WATSON  = 1.785422
  ENTER COMMAND (OR ? FOR HELP)—
```

Requests display of forecasted results.

```
DISP
  ENTER UP TO 4 VARIABLES TO DISPLAY—
QUANTITY LF.QUANTITY EF.QUANTITY
  ENTER FIRST TIME PERIOD TO DISPLAY OR "BOT"—
8210
  ENTER LAST TIME PERIOD TO DISPLAY OR "TOP"—
TOP
  ENTER COMMAND (OR ? FOR HELP)—
```

Results are saved in a HOLD file for further analysis and graphing.

```
HOLD

HOLDING...
  ENTER COMMAND (OR ? FOR HELP)—
END
ENTER STATISTICAL OPERATION DESIRED—
END
```

EXHIBIT 10–4e Using FOCUS to Perform Statistical Analysis on the Sales Data. *Courtesy of* Information Builders, Inc.

Exhibit 10–5 depicts how IFPS could be used to create and analyze a comprehensive financial model. In Exhibit 10–5a the user defines the variables (PAYROLL, TRAVEL AND ENTERTAINMENT, COMMISSIONS, etc.) and their relationships (PAYROLL = 19000*NUMBER OF SALES PERSONS, TRAVEL = 15000* NUMBER OF SALES PERSONS, COMMISSIONS = 15 PERCENT*SALES REVENUE, etc.). Exhibit 10–5b displays the results for four periods. At the top of Exhibit 10–5c the user performs a sensitivity analysis to assess what will happen if certain conditions prevail (commissions change from 15 percent to 16 percent or sales price

```
10   COLUMNS 1980HALF1,1980HALF2,1981HALF1,HALF2
20   *    THIS MODEL IS FOR SIX MONTH PERIODS
30   *    EXPENSE SECTION
40   PAYROLL = 19000*NUMBER OF SALESPERSONS, PREVIOUS*1.05
50   NUMBER OF SALESPERSONS = 4
60   TRAVEL AND ENTERTAINMENT = 15000 * NUMBER OF SALESPERSONS
70   PROMO SUPPORT = 11000 * NUMBER OF SALESPERSONS
80   ADMINISTRATIVE SUPPORT = 53000,PREVIOUS*1.05
90   COMMISSIONS = 15% SALES REVENUE
100  TOTAL EXPENSES = SUM(PAYROLL THRU COMMISSIONS)
110  *    REVENUE SECTION
120  SALES REVENUE = NUMBER OF SALES*SALES PRICE
130  NUMBER OF SALES = 5*6*NUMBER OF SALESPERSONS
140  SALES PRICE = 4350 FOR 2,4695
150  *    SUMMARY SECTION
160  GROSS CONTRIBUTION MARGIN = SALES REVENUE-TOTAL EXPENSES
170  EXPENSE RATIO = TOTAL EXPENSES/SALES REVENUE
```

EXHIBIT 10–5a Defining the Variables with IFPS. *Courtesy of* Execucom, Inc.

?SOLVE
ENTER SOLVE OPTIONS
?ALL

	1980HALF1	1980HALF2	1981HALF1	1981HALF2
EXPENSE SECTION				
PAYROLL	76000	79800	83790	87980
NUMBER OF SALESPERSONS	4	4	4	4
TRAVEL AND ENTERTAINMENT	60000	60000	60000	60000
PROMO SUPPORT	44000	44000	44000	44000
ADMINISTRATIVE SUPPORT	53000	55650	58433	61354
COMMISSIONS	78300	78300	84510	84510
TOTAL EXPENSES	311304	317754	330737	337848
REVENUE SECTION				
SALES REVENUE	522000	522000	563400	563400
NUMBER OF SALES	120	120	120	120
SALES PRICE	4350	4350	4695	4695
SUMMARY SECTION				
GROSS CONTRIBUTION MARGIN	210696	204246	232664	225552
EXPENSE RATIO	.5964	.6087	.5870	.5997

EXHIBIT 10–5b Displaying Four Periods with IFPS. *Courtesy of* Execucom, Inc.

varies). The user can also determine what conditions would be necessary to achieve a specific objective or goal. For example, establishing an expense ratio of .57 (Exhibit 10-5d).

```
?WHAT IF
WHAT IF CASE 1
ENTER STATEMENTS
?COMMISSIONS=16% *SALES REVENUE
?SALES PRICE=4450 FOR 2,4750
?SOLVE
ENTER SOLVE OPTIONS
?SALES REVENUE THRU EXPENSE RATIO
                          WHAT IF CASE 1
2 WHAT IF STATEMENTS PROCESSED
                        1980HALF1  1980HALF2  1981HALF1  1981HALF2
SALES REVENUE              534000     534000     570000     570000
NUMBER OF SALES               120        120        120        120
SALES PRICE                  4450       4450       4750       4750
 SUMMARY SECTION
GROSS CONTRIBUTION
MARGIN                     215556     209106     232574     225462
EXPENSE RATIO               .5963      .6084      .5920      .6045
```

EXHIBIT 10-5c Performing Sensitivity Analysis with IFPS. *Courtesy of* Execucom, Inc.

```
ENTER SOLVE OPTIONS
?GOAL SEEKING
GOAL SEEKING CASE 1
ENTER NAME OF VARIABLE TO BE ADJUSTED TO ACHIEVE PERFORMANCE
?SALES PRICE
ENTER COMPUTATIONAL STATEMENT FOR PERFORMANCE
?EXPENSE RATIO = .57
                          GOAL SEEKING CASE 1
                        1980HALF1  1980HALF2  1981HALF1  1981HALF2
SALES PRICE                  4623       4751       4885       5026
EXPENSE RATIO                 .57        .57        .57        .57
```

EXHIBIT 10-5d Searching for a Specific Expense Ratio with IFPS. *Courtesy of* Execucom, Inc.

Factors to Consider in Choosing a 4GL

Although vendors promote 4GL products as the ultimate "catchall" solution to virtually every decision-support requirement, 4GLs are still evolving and there are limitations. When considering 4GLs as an alternative for establishing decision-support capabilities, there are various factors, and shortcomings that must be taken into account [9,15,23,24, 28,29,39]:

☐ *Vendor Experience and Support Facilities.* One benefit to considering 4GL products is that many of the currently marketed systems have gained feedback through operation by a broad base of users and several years of experience to work out system problems and enhancements. Most of the reputable vendors provide the additional advantage of established customer support facilities (training, problem assistance, etc.) as well as offering free seminars or demonstrations that allow potential users to sample the product's capabilities and optional features.

- ☐ *Standards.* Procedural languages (like FORTRAN, COBOL, PASCAL) are driven by standards established by industrial and professional societies. 4GLs march to the tune and specifications of each vendor. The result is that each 4GL has its own command syntax, rules and features.
- ☐ *User Friendliness.* What a vendor declares as user friendly is frequently quite different from what a manager considers friendly. Many 4GLs rely on rigid command syntax, require significant training, and necessitate continuous use to maintain user familiarity. Some of the current products attempt to overcome this problem by providing optional approaches to user interaction (command structure, menu driven, natural language interface). Chapter 13 provides a further discussion of this trend.
- ☐ *Computer Resources.* Industry experience has demonstrated that although the productivity of application development improves radically with 4GLs, computer operations can degrade significantly in comparison with an application that has been developed with a procedural language.
- ☐ *Programming Flexibility.* Decision makers encounter many problems that require sophisticated quantitative methods and analytical techniques to analyze a complex set of issues and influential factors (Chapter 3). Such applications (type B and type C problems described in Chapter 4) rely on intense mathematical procedures to analyze the problem. By their very nature, 4GLs are limited in their procedural flexibility. The more sophisticated applications depend on the procedural capabilities inherent in traditional programming languages to provide the array operations, mathematical functions, looping logic, and so forth, that is necessary to create the algorithmic procedures used in modeling complex decisions. Many of the current 4GLs try to circumvent this shortcoming by allowing the user to link with programs written outside the 4GL environment in procedural languages (like FORTRAN, COBOL, PL/I). Although this increases algorithmic flexibility (Chapter 9) to a certain degree, there are still the inherent difficulties associated with such composite applications (as will be discussed in the next section).

The fact that 4GLs exhibit shortcomings does not infer they should be discarded from consideration in establishing certain types of decision-support capabilities. Quite the contrary. It does mean that the user requirements be thoroughly examined and compared with the features and capabilities of the particular 4GL in question. For applications oriented toward selective review and inquiry of large databases or for decisions requiring relatively straightforward computations (statistical analysis, graphic projects, financial forecasts, etc.), 4GLs can be valuable assets.

APPROACHES TO SOFTWARE DEVELOPMENT

Three methods of software development will be discussed: using off-the-shelf packages; patching together existing software modules (DBMS, analytical packages, etc.); and designing a totally integral system from scratch.

Off-The-Shelf Packages

Whenever possible, the most economical and expeditious approach is to obtain a "ready-to-go" package that is appropriate to the problem at hand. Such packages come in two forms: a DSS designed specifically for a special type of problem (workforce planning, inventory management, market forecasting, etc.); and packages developed to solve a wide range of generic applications that pertain to a special class of problems (Thought Structuring Systems, flow distribution, resource allocations, etc.).

Prepackaged software rarely comes with the source code. This means that in order for an off-the-shelf package to meet the need, two prerequisites must be satisfied. First, the problem must be fully defined at the outset. Second, the features and capabilities of the system must be reviewed in action to insure that the package totally meets the perceived requirements. Both prerequisites are easier to satisfy with generic systems than with packages designed for a specific application (Chapter 5).

Generic systems are generally designed with greater flexibility since they are intended to handle a broad class of problems. This increase in flexibility is most often achieved at a cost of fewer specific capabilities. Packages designed for a particular application have less latitude for future alterations. In most situations the first attempt to scope the requirements usually defines only about 80 percent to 90 percent of the problem. The remaining portion is identified after the system has been in use for a while. Purchasing an off-the-shelf package without the option for subsequent modification can be a risky proposition unless the manager spends a significant effort up front to define the problem (Chapter 11). This also means that demonstration of the package is essential.

Off-the-shelf systems offer the most cost effective alternative for supporting the decision process. Implementation cost is but a fraction of developing a new system from scratch. The option to "try before you buy" provides another significant advantage to consider with prepackaged software. Even if the system has to be modified to fit the needs of a new application (assuming that the vendor offers such services), the cost is minimal compared to the lengthy process of designing a completely new sysem. Appendix A provides a brief survey of a few commercially available packages.

Composite Systems—The Patchwork Approach

When the search for an off-the-shelf package fails, the "next best" alternative is to assemble the various components of the DSS from commercially available functional packages (DBMS, analytical systems, etc.). The "patchwork" approach can be very successful but it usually requires that the developer create interface modules to tie the various units together. Although this typically costs more than a prepackaged system, the cost is still far below that necessary to create a DSS from scratch.

There are a variety of commercially available packages that perform well in a narrow role (data management, report generators, graphic units, quantitative packages, etc.). Linking these units together is another matter. Packages that are developed independently offer special problems in trying to combine them into an integral system. Because each system is designed for a special purpose, programming languages and file structures are used that are most effective for each particular function (data management, user interface, etc.). This can make it extremely difficult to interface the separate packages and can even limit the total system from providing all of the capabilities required in a particular application. Although mating together specialized packages allows the developer to combine the best features of many programming tools, it does require special care and attention. Personnel with expertise in each functional area can best link together independent systems. Post development test and evaluation is very important to composite systems. Frequently, the features and functions that work well when the packages are used independently provide "weird" results when the output from one package is used as input to another.

This is not to say that composite systems should not be considered. If each separate package has been designed with sufficient foresight and features to allow mating with other functional packages, integrating individual systems can be a viable approach. There are a few functional packages that mate easily with other systems. Products designed to permit interaction with other systems are becoming increasingly available each year. As the merit of the composite approach becomes more apparent, the marketplace will move further in this direction.

From Scratch—An Integral Approach

When all else fails, management must resort to building the DSS up from ground zero. This approach should only be considered as the last alternative. The cost of total development and implementation can far exceed that of an "off-the-shelf" system.

There are basically three reasons why an organization may have to create the DSS from scratch:

- ☐ The application is unique and no other system exists that satisfies the requirements.
- ☐ There are systems that would provide a portion of the necessary features and capabilities but the cost to revise or patch up the package is prohibitive.
- ☐ The search, if any, was not extensive enough to identify an existing DSS that does, in fact, provide a reasonable facsimile.

Conditions 2 and 3 are usually the most prevalent cause for starting from scratch. Whatever the reason, the decision to develop the DSS from the ground up carries certain benefits (and disadvantages) over the other two approaches:

THE PROS

- ☐ Virtually all the requirements and management preferences can be satisfied.
- ☐ The best match between operational efficiency, user interface and hardware configuration becomes feasible.
- ☐ Control over equipment compatibility and upward expansion falls within the preview of the organization.

THE CONS

- ☐ Economically the "scratch" approach costs roughly five to 100 times that of a "ready-to-go" package (depending upon whether the system is implemented on a main/miniframe or microcomputer).
- ☐ Depending on the scope and complexity of the application, design and implementation can range between several months to a few years.
- ☐ The system remains "sight unseen" until completion of a test configuration (demonstration of prepackaged systems is usually possible).

Unless an off-the-shelf package is available, programming facilities become an important consideration. Choosing the most appropriate programming language can depend on many factors: what is available on the subject hardware, what features are required, the need for compatibility with other machines, and so on.

EXERCISES

The selection of which programming language will be used in building a DSS is not always within the preview of the manager responsible for development of the system. Assume for the moment that you can specify which programming facilities will be used. Given the circumstances described in the following four situations, state which programming language you would select as the most appropriate in each case:

1. The system will be used on a routine basis (daily) and depends on complex mathematical procedures being performed repeatedly to analyze each scenario. The system must provide answers in real time (for example, no more than a few minutes required for each solution). We would also like to market the final product to as wide a customer base as possible.

2. The system will be used infrequently (four or five times a year). The application requires that large arrays of data be analyzed, but computation time is not an issue. It is crucial, however, that the system be up and running in just a few days with minimal staff time.

3. Management wishes to establish an integrated reservoir of information that can be accessed across the total organization. The primary focus of the application will be to allow managers to cull out and review selected subsets of a large database in an ad hoc fashion, view the information graphically, and on occasion perform straightforward statistical analysis of the subject data. The system must be operational in just a few months and must pay for itself in less than a year.

4. You must develop a system that will support a large scale production and distribution process. The application will require a significant amount of file and text manipulation, but also depends on sophisticated analytical procedures. Compatibility is not a concern since all hardware in the organization is from the same vendor and uses the same operating system. However, since revisions and upgrades will be required frequently, the program must be well structured and easy to interpret.

5. For a DSS to be effective, the internal mechanics of the system must remain phantom to the user. However, the manager responsible for implementing the system must be

familiar with the general properties of programming facilities discussed in this chapter. Explain why this is true.

REFERENCES AND SUGGESTED READING

1. Babb, D., "Increasing Productivity with the Application Generator Interface," *Journal of Information Management,* Spring, 1985.
2. Barnes, J., *Programming In ADA,* New York, N.Y.: Addison and Sons, 1983.
3. Boillot, M. and L. Horn, *BASIC,* St. Paul, MN: West Publishing, 1983.
4. Broadwell, B., and P. Edward, *Data Processing,* Belmont, CA: Wadsworth Publishing Co. Inc., 1979.
5. Brown, G., *Advanced ANS COBOL,* New York, N.Y.: Wiley & Sons, 1977.
6. Christoff, K., "Building a Fourth Generation Environment," *Datamation,* September 15, 1985.
7. Cobb, R., "In Praise of 4GLs," *Datamation, July 15, 1985.*
8. Cobb, R., "Fourth Generation Languages: From Backwater to Mainstream," *Computerworld,* October 14, 1985.
9. Desmond, J., "Language Barrier: The Fourth Generation at Work," Computerworld, November 11, 1985.
10. Didday, R. and R. Page, *FORTRAN For Humans,* St. Paul, MN: West Publishing, 1981.
11. Dunning, K., *Getting Started In GPSS,* San Jose, CA: Engineering Press, 1981.
12. Geller, D. and D. Freedman, *Structured Programming In APL,* Cambridge, MA: Winthrop Publication, 1976.
13. Gilman, L. and A. Rose, *APL: An Interactive Approach,* New York, N.Y.: John Wiley & Sons, Inc., 1979.
14. Gottfried, B., *Programming With FORTRAN IV,* New York, N.Y.: Quantum Publishing, 1972.
15. Grant, F., "The Downside of 4GLs," *Datamation,* July 15, 1985.
16. Grauer, R., *COBOL—A Vehicle For Information Systems,* Englewood Cliffs, N.J.: Prentice-Hall, 1981.
17. Hofeditz, C., *Computer Programming Languages Made Simple,* New York, N.Y.: Doubleday and Co., 1984.
18. Holt, R. and J. Hume, *Programming Standard PASCAL,* Englewood Cliffs, N.J.: Prentice-Hall, 1980.
19. Horowitz, E., *Programming Languages: A Grand Tour,* Rockville, MD: Computer Science Press, 1983.
20. Hughes, J., *PL/I Structured Programming,* New York, N.Y.: Wiley & Sons, 1979.
21. Jenkins, M., "Surveying the Software Generator Market," *Datamation,* September 1, 1985.

22. Kiviat, P., R. Villanueva, and H. Markowitz, *SIMSCRIPT II.5 Programming Language,* Santa Monica, CA: CACI, 1978.

23. Kull, D., "Anatomy of a 4GL Failure, *Computer Decisions,* February 11, 1986.

24. Lukac, E., "The Impact of 4GL on Hardware Resources," *Datamation,* October 1, 1984.

25. Martin, J., *Application Development Without Programming,* Englewood Cliffs, N.J.: Prentice-Hall, 1982.

26. Martin, J., *Fourth Generation Languages,* Englewood Cliffs, N.J.: Prentice-Hall. Volume 1 (August 1985) and Volume 2 (February 1986).

27. Marcolly, M., *Structured Programming With PL/I,* Englewood Cliffs, N.J.: Prentice-Hall, 1977.

28. Mimno, P., "The 4GL Debate," *Computerworld,* August 26, 1985.

29. Myers, E., "A Natural Fit?" *Datamation,* January 15, 1986.

30. O'Donovan, T., *GPSS Simulation Made Simple,* New York, N.Y.: Wiley & Sons, 1979.

31. Pratt, T., *Programming Languages: Design and Implementation,* Englewood Cliffs, N.J.: Prentice-Hall, 1975.

32. Price. D., *PASCAL—A Considerate Approach,* Englewood Cliffs, N.J.: Prentice-Hall, 1982.

33. Rose, A. and B. Schick, *APL In Practice,* New York, N.Y.: Wiley & Sons, 1980.

34. Sass, C., *FORTRAN IV Programming and Applications,* Oakland, CA: Holden-Day, 1974.

35. Schneider, M. and S. Weingart, *An Introduction To Programming And Problem Solving With Pascal,* New York, N.Y.: Wiley & Sons, 1978.

36. Schriber, T., *Simulation Using GPSS,* New York, N.Y.: Wiley & Sons, 1974.

37. Shumate, K., *Understanding ADA,* New York, N.Y.: Harper and Row Publishing, 1984.

38. Tennent, R., *Principles Of Programming Languages,* Englewood Cliffs, N.J.: Prentice-Hall, 1981.

39. Tinnirello, P., "Users Find Problems with Fourth Generation Tools," *Computerworld,* August 26, 1985.

40. Walsh, B., *Proper BASIC,* New York, N.Y.: Wiley & Sons, 1983.

41. Wegner, P., "Programming Languages—The First 25 Years," *IEEE Transactions on Computers,* December, 1976.

42. Wexelblat, R., *History Of Programming Languages,* Orlando, FL: Academic Press, 1981.

43. Young, S., *An Introduction To ADA,* New York, N.Y.: Wiley & Sons, 1983.

44. Wiedmann, C., *Handbook Of APL Programming,* Princeton, N.J.: Petrocelli, 1974.

11

Creating DSS Capabilities

In comparison to the other classes of information processing systems, the development of decision-support capabilities is by far the most demanding. In addition to understanding the intricacies of the operation being automated, the developer must comprehend the decision-making environment itself. Functional knowledge must go beyond the systems analysis and programming expertise necessary with other systems. The designer(s) must rely on a multitude of diverse skills and draw from a broad spectrum of disciplines in mathematics, computer technology, operations research, decision science, economics, engineering, statistics and management science, to mention a few. Pure analytical expertise is not enough. Team members must possess real-world experience to differentiate between what is practical and what is done for the sheer pleasure of personal edification. The veteran understands that delivery of a new and innovative capability to support decision makers does not necessarily equate to the system becoming functionally useful. Successful application requires that the behavioral and motivational aspects of human nature be taken into account during every step of the process.

This chapter focuses on the logical steps to establishing decision-support capabilities. A systematic approach to creating a DSS consists of four major phases (Exhibit 11–1): conducting a preliminary survey; performing a needs assessment; developing the computerized system; and implementing the system within the decision process. The scope and level of effort at each phase will depend on the complexity of the decision environment (Chapter 3) and whether the computerized portion will result from

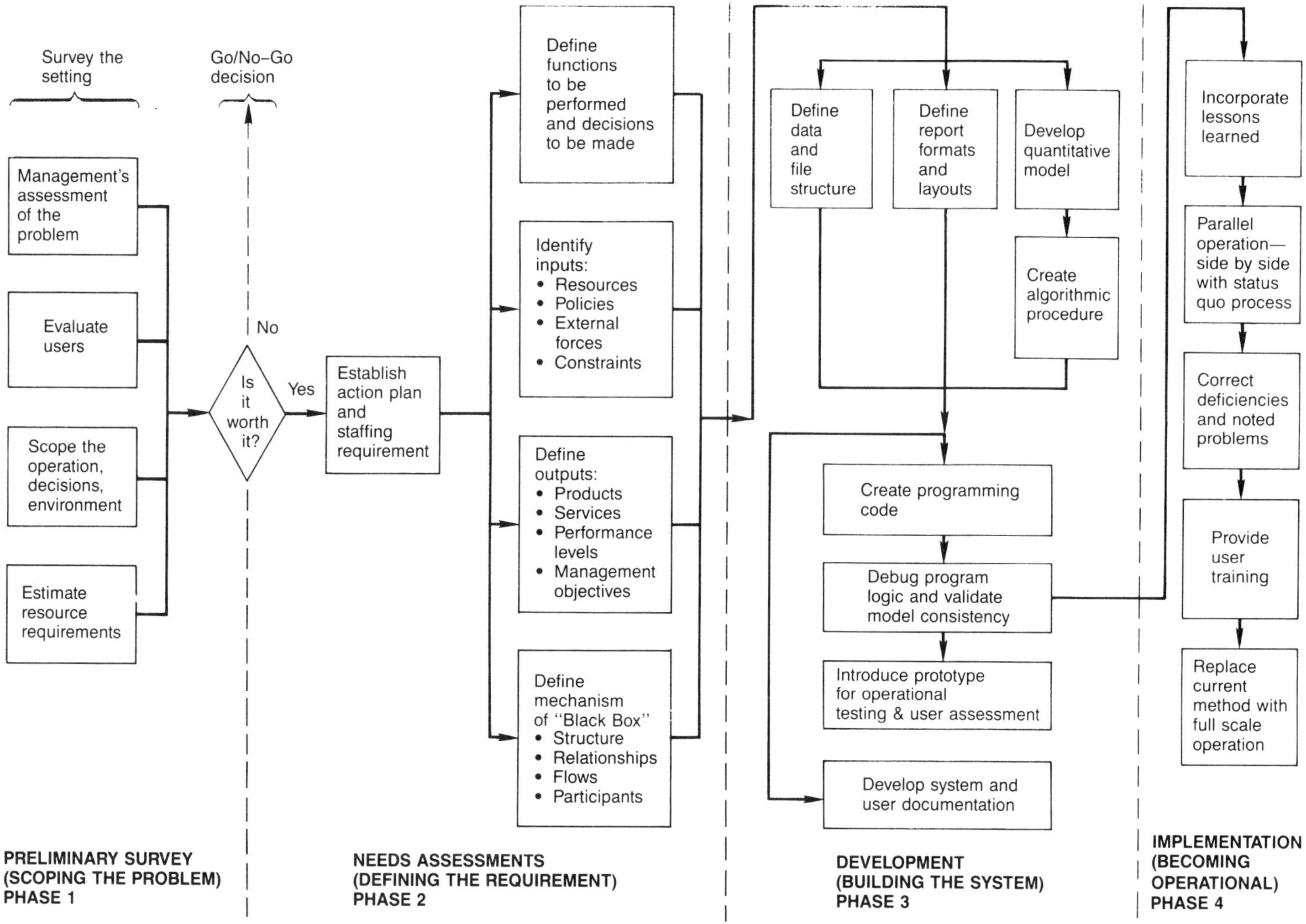

EXHIBIT 11–1 Creating the DSS—The Total Process.

an "off-the-shelf" package, composite system, or be developed from scratch (Chapter 10). This chapter does not attempt to cover every aspect of the process but instead highlights the concept and major considerations behind the design, development and implementation of a DSS. Additional material on system development and implementation methodologies can be found in the noted literature [11,15,18,40,41].

SURVEY THE SETTING

Before any decision to commit resources, the first step must be to gain a "feel" for the breadth and difficulty of the situation. A preliminary survey can help to: reduce the chance of unrealistic action plans; circumvent early misconceptions and unlikely expectations within the management hierarchy; and evaluate the feasibility of eventual success. At the very least, the preliminary survey should consider the following key areas.

- ☐ *Examine the decision process* to answer questions about the environment and characteristics of decision making such as:
  - What is the reason and purpose for the application (financial planning, material distribution, resource allocation, etc.)?
  - Who participates in reviewing the results and reaching the final decisions?
  - How will it be used (quick and dirty, everyday, budget cycle, voluntary, required by policy, etc.)?
- ☐ *Evaluate the user populace* to assess their level of experience (novice, technically informed, technically oriented) and their impressions about establishing automated support (apprehensive, fearful, hostile, supportive, etc.).
- ☐ *Investigate the motives* behind obtaining DSS capabilities. This usually requires a subjective assessment to determine the proponent's true intentions such as:
  - To come of age in a "new" technology.
  - Impress higher authority.
  - Part of a merit pay contract for executive management (a strong motivator).
  - Improve productivity, performance or control.
  - Eliminate recurring shortfalls, bottlenecks, disruptions, and so forth.
- ☐ *Explore the "powerbase"* behind the decision to establish DSS capabilities. With few exceptions, changing the style of decision making from a traditional "seat of the pants" approach to a more quantitative method is rarely a smooth transition. Territorial conflicts, lack of organizational interaction, or an inability to visualize personal gain can often be diverted by the impression that the right channels are directly interested in the endeavor. This is especially true when the application is expected to cut across the organization. Managers whose positive contribution is crucial to success must be aware of their role in the overall process. All parties who participate in the operation or maintenance of the system must understand (either through policy statements or joint financial reward) that their personal support and involvement is essential.
- ☐ *Determine the scope and complexity* of the application. Obtain estimates of the size

of the problem in terms of data elements, geographic considerations, organizational impact, operational complexity, etc.

- ☐ *Consider alternative* hardware and software approaches for satisfying the requirement. This would include determining what level of hardware is appropriate (microcomputers, existing internal mini/mainframe, time sharing facilities, etc.) and whether or not a commercially available package is likely to meet the basic requirement.
- ☐ *Estimate the resources* that will be necessary for each phase of the process. Obviously precision estimates are not likely until a detailed needs assessment (phase 2) can be completed. "Ball park" figures are possible using the information obtained during the preliminary survey. Rough estimates of staff, funds, and duration can help to prevent misconceptions that might lead to controversy later in the process.

In addition to providing insight about the size and boundaries of the problem, the preliminary survey can answer many questions about issues that might eventually lead to the demise of the application, for example:

- ☐ What level of user friendliness will be tolerated by the user populace?
- ☐ Can organizational and behavioral barriers be overcome?
- ☐ Is management willing to commit the funds and staff time necessary for system development, implementation, and training, in addition to understanding the temporary disruption that will occur in transitioning to a new mode of decision making?
- ☐ Can the user populace be convinced of the need and benefit that will result from the system?

The next logical step is to make a qualitative and quantitative assessment as to the practicality of the application[7,21,24,31,38,43]. Assuming there is a choice as to whether or not the effort should be undertaken then the "go/no go" decision should be based on the following criteria:

1. *Is is practical?* If the decision is so simple that automated support would be more of an encumberance than an aid (as with type 0 problems discussed in Chapter 4), or the problem is so difficult that modeling the situation is a "pipe dream," then a DSS is impractical.
2. *Is it worth it?* To determine whether the return outweighs the cost, the developer must compare both direct (funds, operational improvements, etc.) and indirect (quality control, reduced risk, less disruption, etc.) savings with the total expenditures necessary to implement and operate the DSS.
3. *Is it likely to succeed?* In most situations, estimating the likelihood of success is a total judgment call. It requires that the potential developer review various qualitative conditions about the organization and make a subjective assessment. For example:
   - Is the management style flexible enough to accept change?
   - Is the user populace openly hostile or reluctant to the new approach?

- Are personnel within the organization functioning at a sufficient level to adapt to a new technology?

DEFINING THE REQUIREMENTS

After management has decided to commit the anticipated resources, the next step is to identify the total requirement. A "rough and ready" examination is sometimes used to try and define the requirement. For the most elementary problem, such a haphazard approach may suffice, but it is generally the exception and not the norm. DSS applications typically apply in areas of extreme complexity. Identifying the intricate relationships and complicated process behind the more difficult decisions warrants a thorough and systematic methodology.

Over the years, a variety of methods have evolved for defining the requirements for information systems. Examples include: structural analysis [5,9,19], information analysis [8], Business Systems Planning [1], and action oriented flow analysis [15], to mention a few. Many of the approaches are similar in nature, differing primarily in terminology. In general, however, there are both benefits and disadvantages to each methodology (references [30,31] provide a comparison of some of the various approaches to defining requirements).

Regardless of what method is used the eventual outcome should be a detailed description of the total problem to include:

- ☐ Definition of all relevant factors that influence the process (Chapter 3).
- ☐ Determination of the relationships and structure between the influential factors and how they affect the behavior of the process.
- ☐ Explanation of the operational mechanism that governs how the process reacts to various conditions, resource levels, policies, and performance characteristics.

The developer's background (systems analyst, operations research analyst, engineer, economist, etc.) will strongly influence the underlying philosophy used to define the requirements. For example:

- ☐ Engineers typically rely on a bottom-up approach (start at the elementary component level and work up).
- ☐ Economists prefer an input/output methodology based on their supply/demand experience.
- ☐ Operations research analysts view complex problems with a flow model perspective (recall many of the quantitative techniques described in Chapter 9 are formulated around a flow model).

Methodology

The methodology presented in this section is referred to as the "Stratified Input/Output" approach (SIO) and provides a useful tool in helping to "divide and conquer" a complex problem into workable parts. The intent of this discussion is not to linger on the specifics of any single tactic but instead to provide an appreciation for the logic and need to a structured approach. The SIO approach views all problems (organizations, operations, physical systems, etc.) as systems that obtain input from their environment, convert this input into some product (material shipped, personnel recruited, enemy destroyed, profit obtained), and undergo a dynamic interaction and exchange with their surroundings. Prior to this chapter, we purposely reserved the word "system" to refer to automated devices. Here we will use the word system in a more general context to represent an input/output oriented process.

The SIO approach expresses each layer of the decision-making arena (Chapter 3) in terms of what goes in, what comes out, and what goes on in between. The various levels of the operation (resources, information, organizational factors, etc.) must be defined to explain the conversion process between what enters the system and how items are manipulated by the internal mechanism in order to evolve into the final output. In essence, the problem is represented as a flow model that describes how entities (funds, material, policies, communications) move through the process. Viewing complex problems as a system with resources flowing in and products flowing out is a useful device. Most real-world phenomenon deal with the transfer or movement of entities from one source to another. For example:

- ☐ Parts are moved through a production line and assembled into the final product.
- ☐ Personnel are recruited, advance through the organization, and eventually leave.
- ☐ Material is shipped from production through warehousing and finally to the customer.
- ☐ Funds are deposited in a bank, transmitted electronically, and withdrawn by other institutions.
- ☐ Combat forces are deployed, moved into tactical positions, encounter enemy forces, and expire through attrition.
- ☐ Data is gathered, entered into a storage media (like a computer), manipulated, and output in a form that can be used by management.
- ☐ Legislative actions or federal regulations start as bills or proposals, are processed through the review channels, modified, recycled, and are eventually enacted as laws, or are discarded.

In areas where a DSS is applicable, the underlying structure is often so complicated and involved that the analyst can quickly drown in detail and lose sight of how the total process fits together. To ensure participants are not overwhelmed, the analysis must be conducted in stages so that the requirements can be defined (or stratified) into several tiers, each with an increasing focus on the amount of detail. An example will help visualize the logic behind why a requirements analysis should be stratified.

To fix an inoperative vehicle, the mechanic could start by testing each piece of each component until the problem had been isolated. This would result in thousands of components being examined unnecessarily and possibly several weeks to complete. The more practical approach would be to first take a macro view and identify which major automotive systems are causing the problem. Based on the symptoms, the mechanic determines whether the problem results from the ignition system, starter circuit, fuel system, and so forth. If the failure is isolated to the fuel system, the next step would be to identify which component (carborator, fuel pump, etc.) was the culprit. Once the faulty component had been found, the mechanic would finally search at the most elementary (micro) level to locate the bad part (like a leaky gasket).

In larger applications, the SIO approach provides a structured methodology that helps to guide the analysis and reduce the chance of crucial elements being missed or buried in specific detail. Later we will examine how this methodology can be used in a setting more appropriate to a decision-support application. For now, consider that practically any requirements analysis can be organized and conducted at three or more generic levels:

- ☐ *Macro Perspective (Functions).* The first step is to look at the overall application with a macro (high level) perspective that views the total scope and breadth of the situation. The problem is partitioned into major *functional* areas (such as, fuel system, electrical system, research, engineering, marketing or production).
- ☐ *Medium Level (Activities).* Next each function is divided into its basic *activities.* For the fuel system we have storage (the tank), fuel delivery (the pump), and carboration and distribution (the manifold).
- ☐ *Micro View (Components).* Finally each activity must be broken into its most elementary level of detail, generally referred to as *components* (for example, carboration is disassembled into the float chamber, gaskets, injection device, mixture channel, etc.).

The amount of effort necessary to completely describe the problem will depend on the operational complexity, the sheer size of the application, and the volume of information required to support decisions. Regardless of the situation, the most effective procedure for defining the problem is to interview managers, observe the operation in action, and question personnel at each level of the organization. At each step, insight and understanding will expand geometrically.

The specific tasks associated with performing a needs assessment will vary. There are, however, certain activities common to virtually all applications, namely: analyzing the decision process, identifying inputs and outputs, and defining the internal operating mechanism of the system.

Analysis of the Decision Process

The preliminary survey provides general insight about the decision-making environment, but not in sufficient detail to establish the specific needs of management. Both the proponent of the effort and the actual user must be consulted to identify the perception of what the DSS is expected to do, how it will be done, and under what governing rules.

- ☐ *Management Objectives.* The designer(s) must query each affected level of management for its "must have" and "would like" objectives, for example:

- Preordained solutions (answers that "must" conform to preconceived notions).
- Targeted priorities (which problems should be addressed first).
- Untouchables (things that cannot or "will not" be touched).
- Organizational involvement (who will participate).

☐ *Types of Decisions.* The preliminary survey identifies the general areas of applications (financial planning, workforce management, material distribution, etc.) but not the specific concerns or types of support that the system must address, such as:

- What factors are the most unstable (attrition, shipping cost, vendor support, etc.)?
- Which conditions are of prime concern to management (maintaining a stable workforce, controlling cost, customer satisfaction, etc.)?
- What kinds of "what if" questions are most prominent such as:
  - .. How will recruiting policies affect end-of-year staff levels?
  - .. What happens to delivery time if 30 percent of the workforce goes on strike?
  - .. How will production be affected by a change in supply lines?
  - .. Where should additional resources be used and what kind should they be?

☐ *Required Characteristics.* Chapter 4 discussed how the characteristics and properties of a DSS will depend on the particular application. Management must decide up front what is expected of the information generated by the system in terms of its:

- Precision (within plus or minus two percent of targeted objectives).
- Reliability (the result reflects reality 95 percent of the time).
- Frequency of use.
- Required response time.
- Level of detail.

Inputs—The Limiting Factor

Whether the system represents an organization, physical system, operation or similar process, the fundamental principle is the conversion of some form of input into a desired outcome. In all practical situations the inputs into the process are not infinite but are limited by nature. To establish a quantitative representation of the process, the types of input must be defined, as well as the role they play in constraining the final output. Inputs to the process come in various forms.

☐ *Resources.* Although long term actions (such as recruitment, stock issue, new facilities) can expand the pool of available resources, in the short term, practically all resources are restricted. Resources fall into several categories:

- Staffing
- Funds
- Material
- Equipment
- Facilities

☐ *Internal Policies.* Virtually all systems are affected by policies that are set internally to provide common rules that strive for consistency across the organization. These governing principles act as regulating forces that meter how inputs will be used, acquired, or administered. Examples include:

- Skill mix (one secretary for five professionals).
- Promotion practices.
- Minimum stocking levels.
- Retained earnings ratio.
- Contingency plans (for example, what to do in case of catastrophic failure).
- Acceptable rejection or failure rates.
- Permissible production delays or order backlog.

☐ *External Factors.* Whether the application is in the commercial, public service or military sector, there are always restrictive factors that must be dealt with as givens (beyond management's ability to change). Some of the most common external factors that influence the realm of possible options during the decision process include:

- Affirmative action
- Minority quotas
- Government regulations
- Laws
- Union contracts and practices
- Available labor pool for specialized skills
- Geographic conditions (existing transportaion, inclement weather, etc.)
- Public pressure

Often managers envision constraints or restrictions as rigid when, in fact, they are actually dealing with desirable goals and targets. For example, management might confine the solution to only those possibilities that use current resource levels (personnel, funds, material, equipment, etc.). The more cost effective approach, however, is to consider a broader area of possibilities (temporary staff, venture capital, leased warehousing, equipment replacement, etc.). The best decisions typically result where the greatest latitude of alternatives is allowed. This is not to say that decision makers never encounter rigid restrictions and barriers. Many requirements can, however, be formulated as objectives that allow more flexibility. For example, instead of confining inputs to fixed levels (staff size less than 600, external loans no greater than 10 percent of capital worth, no new facilities, etc.) the possibility of "floating" the restrictions should be considered where it is effective (for example, reduce the number of additional staff, minimize any dependence on outside finances, new facilities must provide a minimum return on investment period, and so forth).

Output—The Desired Results

Whether the system in question is an organization, a physical system (air traffic control, material distribution) or a procedural process (like a regulatory agency), the purpose is to produce or accomplish certain end results. The characteristics of the output must be known so that they can be linked to the input side of the process. Output typically falls into three categories:

- ☐ *Physical Products.* Output that possesses physical properties and attributes, as in:
  - Mining operations—coal excavated, sites explored, acreage restored.
  - Assembly operations—automobiles assembled, buildings constructed, chemicals manufactured.
  - Warehouse operations—inventory storage, stock control, products delivered.
  - Military operations—bombs delivered, enemy destroyed.
- ☐ *Services.* Items of an operational or activity oriented nature that provide support such as:
  - Vehicle maintenance—units repaired, preventive maintenance, depot refurbishment.
  - Computer support organizations—time sharing, computer programs.
  - Consulting firms—studies, model development, needs assessments.
  - Medical institutions—examinations performed, surgery, emergency services.
  - Public service—student grants, farm loans, commodity and crop reports.
- ☐ *Procedural Output.* Examples include:
  - Judicial/legislative activities—laws passed, cases resolved, incarcerations.
  - Regulations—discrimination investigations, environmental laws, import taxes.
  - Inspections—custom inspections, immigration monitoring, audits.

Defining the Internal Mechanism

Understanding the input and output side of the process is of little value without knowledge as to how the internal mechanism links everything together. This is generally the most difficult phase of the analysis. It requires that the developer(s) be able to explain (often in a mathematical model) how the complex mechanism converts inputs into their final form so that the behavior of the process can be emulated by the DSS. To describe the process completely the analyst must obtain knowledge about:

- ☐ How entities flow through various parts of the system?
- ☐ What is the relationship and structure between the various parts?
- ☐ How does this overlay within the framework of the organization?
- ☐ What are the various performance criteria that govern the conversion process such as:
  - Control—product rejection rate, mid air incidences, employee accident rate.
  - Productivity—units per time period.
  - Response—military operational readiness, product delivery time.
  - Consumption—attrition rate, resources per product.
  - Efficiency—extent of waste, cost per item.

Flow models can be used at each level in a stratified analysis to explain (Exhibit 11-2): what is being used, how it is used, by whom, for what purpose, and who does

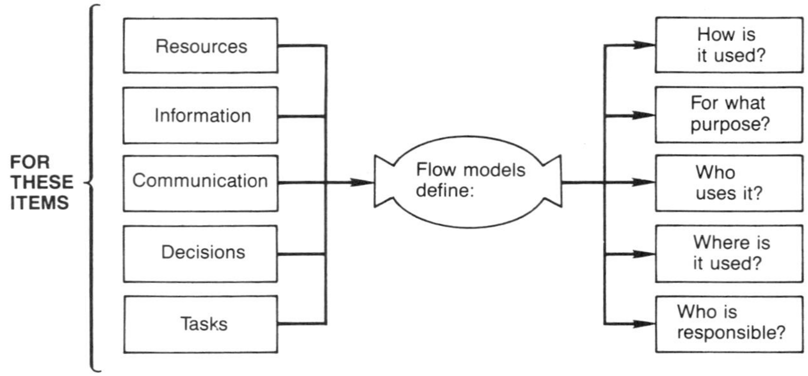

EXHIBIT 11–2 Flow Models and Their Functions.

it? To illustrate how flow models can be used, consider a simplified corporate example of a large manufacturing firm. First the process is partitioned (at a macro level) into its major functions, namely: sales, marketing, engineering, manufacturing, and administration. The relationship and exchanges between these functions are expressed in a flow model (Exhibit 11–3). Each function is then divided into its basic activities. For example, the manufacturing function consists of replenishment (supply), production, storage (inventory), and distribution (Exhibit 11–4). Finally, each activity is dissected into its fundamental components or tasks (for example, production is made up of scheduling, product machining, assembly, packaging, quality control, etc.). After all functions and associated activities have been subdivided to their lowest level, the relationship and interactions between each component or task must be defined in terms of information needs, performance characteristics, organizational responsibilities, and so forth (Exhibit 11–5).

Depicting the relationship and flow between each part of the process, across all dimensions of the problem, can become unwieldy and impractical for large scale applications. "Interaction matrices" can be used to supplement the flow diagrams and help visualize the relationships between the various parts of the process. Exhibit 11–6 provides a hypothetical sample of the interactions that might exist between the information and the decision/tasks of our corporate example. Some of the typical interactions that provide insight during the development phase include:

- ☐ Information elements compared to their organizational users (who uses the data).
- ☐ Information elements matched to required decisions or operational tasks (how it is used).
- ☐ Tasks or decisions overlayed with the organization (who is responsible and where does it come from).

Once the total process has been completely defined, the analyst is in a position to visualize potential areas for decision support. Obviously, every situation is not as comprehensive and elaborate as in the previous case. For example, management may

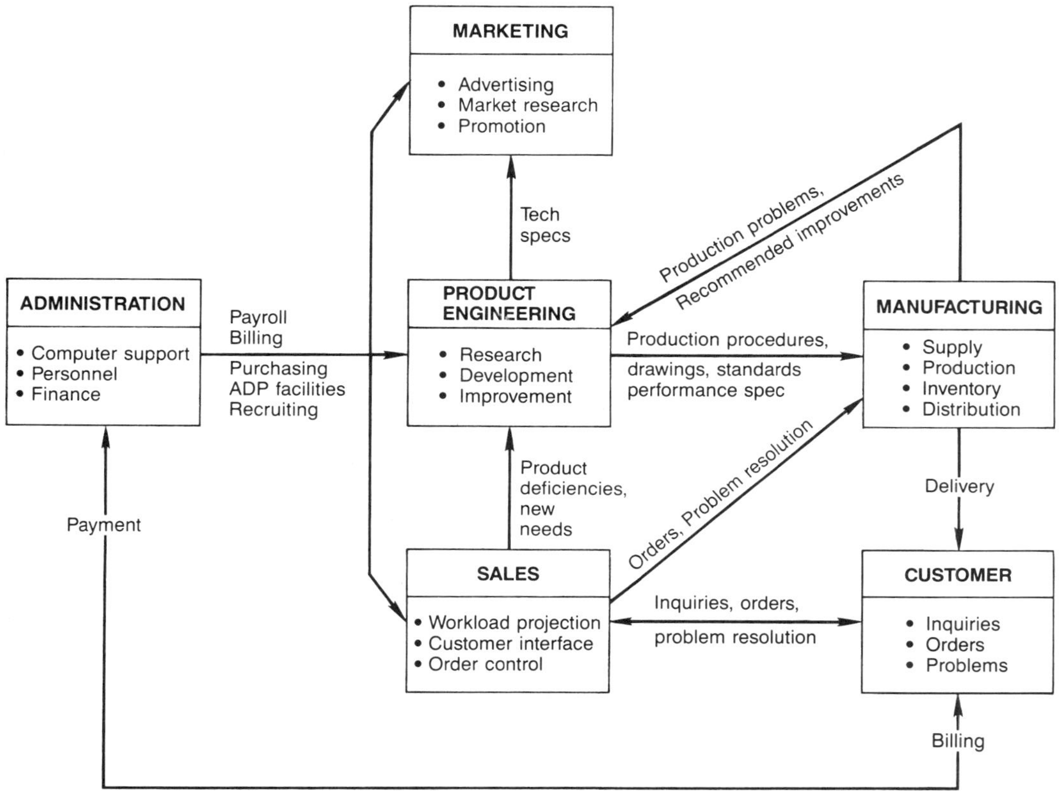

EXHIBIT 11–3 Macro View of the Total Process.

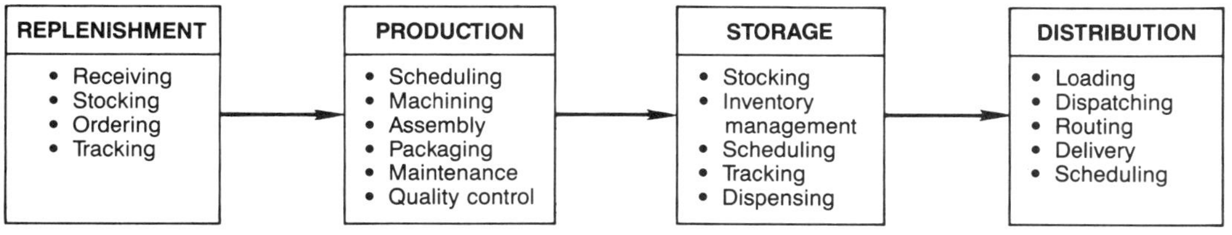

EXHIBIT 11–4 Activities of the Manufacturing Function.

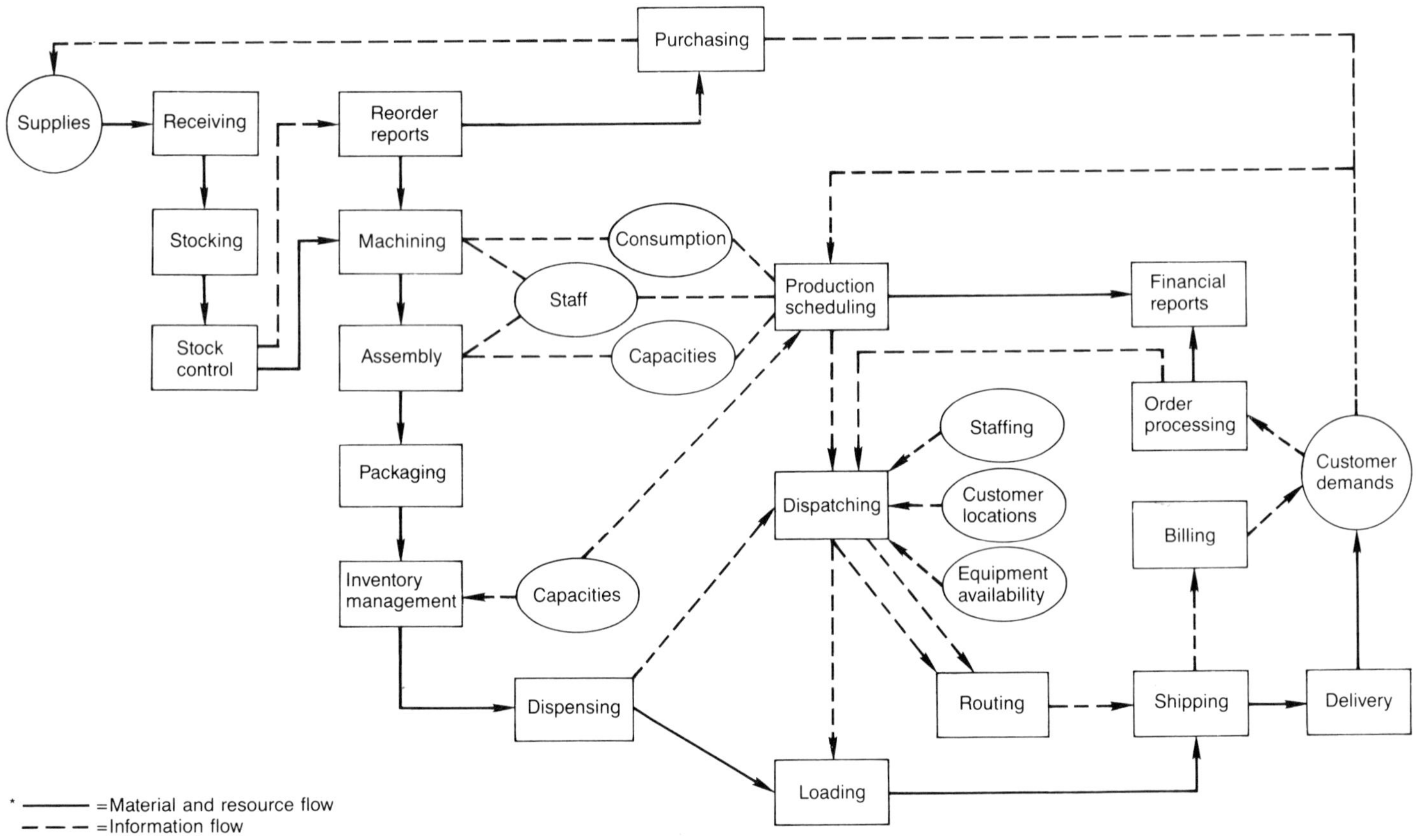

EXHIBIT 11–5 Relationships and Flow of Manufacturing Activities.

DECISIONS AND TASKS

Information components	Production scheduling	Workforce planning	Personnel services	Purchasing	Billing	Dispatching	Financial analysis	Inventory management	Quality control	Equipment maintenance
Production volume	G	U		U	U		U	U		U
Inventory levels	U			U			U	G		
Stock capacities				U				U		
Maintenance records				U			U			G/U
Staff skills	U	U	U							
Personnel availability	U		U							
Equipment capacity						U	U			
Staff costs		G					U			
Consumption rates	U						U	U	U	
Rejection rate							U		U	
Equipment status	U								U	U
Customer demands	U	U		U	U	U	U	U		
Customer locations						U	U			
Vehicle capacities						U				
Revenue/expense reports				G	G	G	U			

U=Used by
G=Generated by

EXHIBIT 11–6 Interaction Matrix for This Manufacturing Function.

specify during the preliminary survey that only selected activities and decisions are to be supported (inventory management, production scheduling, etc.). However, even in the simplest application, the principles and techniques behind systematically defining the requirements still apply.

SYSTEM DEVELOPMENT

Once the overall requirement has been defined, the developer must model the problem then select which software strategy is appropriate to this application [29,35,42]. The required capabilities are used to estimate the necessary system characteristics in terms of the data management facilities (Chapter 7), user interface features (Chapter 8), quantitative procedures (Chapter 9), and report generator requirements. This information is used to decide whether an off-the-shelf package will suffice, a composite system is possible, or whether the only practical approach is to start from scratch (Chapter 10).

The actual development of a DSS is rather technical. It depends on a heavy concentration of programming skills, a quantitative background and experience in recognizing what is and is *not* user friendly. Although specific design procedures are beyond the scope of this text [8,34,35,42], the following general principles apply to virtually every application.

Segmented Development

Depending on the size of the problem and the software support facilities, the time to totally design, code, and debut a DSS can range from a few months to a year or more. Experience has shown that the longer the gap between initial interest and the point when users can gain their first "hands on" view of the system, the greater the risk of failure due to disenchantment, changes in command, and so forth. For large scale applications, the most effective approach is to segment the development so that parts of the system are made available to the user as soon as possible. This can be accomplished by partitioning the system into "functional modules" that can be designed and implemented incrementally.

A large portion of the effort will go toward defining the common baseline (file structure, data elements, etc.) and the links between the modules. The system is then made operational in increments by making each module available to the user as it is completed. Obviously the functional models must be implemented in the particular sequence that will allow the partial stages of the system to be of value and meet the preferences of the users. Several of the case studies in Chapter 12 illustrate how segmented development can contribute to a successful implementation.

Operational Flexibility

Essentially every dimension of the business world changes continually: technology advances, markets change, enemy threats shift, organizations restructure themselves, and so forth. The rate of change may vary, but the affect is the same. To prevent the system from becoming immediately obsolete, a DSS must be designed with sufficient operational flexibility so the user can adjust to a dynamic environment. Chapter 8 discussed many of the features that can lead to a more flexible design.

User Experience

It is impossible to perform a task on a day-to-day basis and not gain insight as to the "dos and don'ts" of an application. The proficient developer turns an open ear to the experienced user to stay in tune with changing conditions and to exploit his knowledge as to what should and should not be done. The seasoned veteran can provide insight as to:

- ☐ What actions are feasible?
- ☐ What are some of the hidden pitfalls that can only be learned through trial and error?
- ☐ Which capabilities will and will not be used (and why)?
- ☐ Are the results produced by the system logical in terms of real-world experience?
- ☐ Where is the environment (policies, organization structure, required capabilities, etc.) likely to change?

It may be difficult to believe, but there is actually debate as to the value and effectiveness of user involvement. There are both advocates and opponents to the philosophy of user participation [6,14,22,23,33,37]. In the author's opinion, there are very few exceptions where user involvement is not a sound approach to establishing decision-support capability.

User Background

Conforming to the background of the user populace is an important consideration to the eventual success of a DSS. Even when the system is turned over to the user incrementally, the quickest way to lose support is for users to become disillusioned by frequent failures and a "less than" user-friendly interface. Although the more extensive self-teaching features (tutoring modules, help options, etc.) can be delayed until later, the user should always feel comfortable in dealing with the system.

Practicality

Essentially any task can be automated. There is, however, a limit to what is practical. For many applications there is a diminishing return or trade off in trying to support every facet of the decision process. The effort required to computerize selected operations or various management activities may not be offset by the potential gain. There are also many tasks that are best left to the human element. Before significant time and resources are expended to create each capability, users should be queried to assess whether or not a perceived need does exist. Obviously a certain degree of judgment is necessary on the part of the developer(s). It may be difficult for users to totally visualize the eventual worth of a particular feature until the capability is seen in action. Reluctance and hostility can also deter user inputs. Nonetheless, users should be given the opportunity to evaluate the usefulness of each capability.

IMPLEMENTATION

Throughout this chapter the central theme has been user involvement. The story remains the same during the implementation phase. Who else has the corporate memory and expertise to determine whether the proposed system matches the demands of the real world. If the DSS is an off-the-shelf package, then the organization typically has few options for correcting or improving the design.

Even with the best implementation plans, errors and shortfalls can still arise during the initial period of operation. A consistent and thorough implementation effort can, however, minimize the number and severity of long-term system discrepancies and user dissatisfaction. The following actions can help to achieve a smoother transition from system development to full scale operation. The reader should note that many of these steps overlap into the development phase because of the strategy of early and continued user involvement.

Prototype

Before the total user populace is exposed to the DSS, it is important that a small sample be given the chance to evaluate the system. Prototyping is a developmental and implementation process through which a preliminary version of the system is placed in the user's hands as soon as possible. The "prototype" version provides the first opportunity to gain hands on user experience and to "test the water" early to sound out major problems. The prototype is not used in the actual operation. The chance of error and failure is high at this stage and disruption of normal operation would be extremely detrimental to eventual success. If the development team implements the DSS in segments (as previously suggested), each section should undergo a prototype evaluation.

There are a variety of issues that can be circumvented with prototyping. The user can assess:

- ☐ Whether the general approach and concept is valid.
- ☐ Whether there are specific requirements and capabilities that are missing.
- ☐ Does the language and terminology conform to the background of the user populace?
- ☐ Are the results provided by the system logical and consistent with the real world and user experience?

Why go through a "preimplementation" phase? Why not just allow all users to test the DSS during performance of their normal duties? The reason is to minimize the damage to future user acceptance when problems occur (as they inevitably do). History has shown that disenchantment often occurs when a system goes directly from development to full testing by the total populace. Nothing illustrates this better than an actual horror story.

The executive leadership at a large federal institution decided it was time to bring their organization into the modern ages. A management consulting firm was contracted to analyze their requirements and implement the necessary system. The firm determined that a large multi-station system was necessary for tracking, scheduling, reporting, and analyzing the total operation. After the package was designed and tested at the firm's internal site, the decision was made that a full scale operational test was in order and would help to gain the favor of all the users. The firm was confident that their experience in computerized systems was sufficient to have circumvented any major difficulties. When the "test" configuration was installed, all of the 200 stations were brought on-line and 500 users eagerly gained access to the system. After four weeks, only about 10 percent of the organization was still trying to use the system. When users were questioned to find out why they were no longer accessing the system, it was determined that the current configuration, in the user's eyes, fell far short of their expectations. Terminology was unclear, too much time was required to learn and use the system, the capabilities provided did not address the major problems and decisions they faced, and many other assorted difficulties. The developers tried to explain that this was just the test version and the full scale system would correct all these problems. Unfortunately, the users had turned a deaf ear and no longer supported the concept. Management decided that the application was now doomed to failure. They informed the company that the contract for the full scale version would not be issued.

Not all concur with the usefulness and practicality of prototyping. As with other topics we have discussed, there are both those in favor and those against the prototyping approach [3,12,13,20,32]. In most situations, prototyping an application can be a viable alternative to the lengthy (and risky) proposition of waiting until the final version of the DSS is available. When coupled with the segmented approach (for example, prototype each functional module), prototyping can help to preclude shortfalls in the design before they can mature to major issues once the DSS is turned over to the user populace.

Pilot Operation

Once the DSS has undergone prototype testing, the next step is to expose the system to the real world. Assuming all major difficulties have been weeded out with the prototype, the package must still undergo an operational shakedown. A "pilot operation" is the final stage before the DSS is ready for full scale implementation.

The pilot operation is conducted under normal conditions, in an operational environment, solving actual problems by the total user populace. As a result, it must be carried out side by side with the existing status quo procedures. It must also incorporate full scale user interface features (help options, tutoring facilities, etc.). Although significant testing has been performed prior to this phase, the pilot operation is the first time all parts of the organization will be tied to and dependent on the system. Failures at this point can be a catastrophe if a fall back position does not exist.

The primary purpose of the pilot version is to provide "fine tuning" of the design. This includes reporting formats, added options, improved wording, missed "error proofing," and a variety of other minor flaws that usually surface with a broader user base. A valuable mechanism to uncover and identify noted problems and obtain recommendations is to provide users with a "user report." This approach not only records beneficial information and circumstances that would otherwise be missed, but also provides users with the opportunity and impression that their concerns have been taken into account.

Full Scale Operation

The final step is to move into full scale operation. Once the lessons learned during the pilot operation have been incorporated, the DSS is ready to become functionally independent. It is at this point where implementation is considered complete and the system is suitable to replace the previous method or procedures that were used.

Documentation

System documentation provides continuity throughout the life of any information system. Preparation of the documentation should begin during the development period and continue through the implementation phase. Although documentation is essential, it can also be an albatross if the proper blend between detail and brevity is not reached. Too much detail and the busy user becomes overwhelmed. Too little information and the newcomer will never grasp the range of possible applications. We will first examine some common principles that apply to all user-oriented systems and conclude with special considerations pertaining to DSS documentation. The most effective approach is to partition the documentation into three parts:

- *The User Manual* provides instruction to the newcomer and a refresher for the veteran. It is written in clear concise everyday English. The manual should be structured to indoctrinate the novice as to the concept behind the application, provide sufficient detail to bring the user on line, contain an actual sample session, and consolidate advanced features in a separate section, that can be explored once the user is comfortable with the basic operating principles and capabilities. A road map of available options (Exhibit 8–1) provides an excellent quick reference for menu driven systems. An easy to understand and complete user manual is especially important for microcomputer based applications where the user is often left on his own. Although it requires significant effort on the part of the developer, suitable instructions and detail for even the most sophisticated DSS can be provided without requiring multiple sets of manuals. The ideal test is to have a virgin user read the manual and operate the system without any further direction from the developer. Although user documentation is a key element, it should not be viewed as a substitute for providing a conversational interface to the user. If the system is truly user friendly and the user manual is well prepared, the newcomer should be qualified to use the major components and capabilities of the system in a very short period.
- *The System's Specification Manual* describes all of the technical aspects of the system. This includes code structure, model development, file and data layout, and an explanation of how the components of the system function and fit together. The primary purpose of the technical manual is to provide an audit trail that can be used to upgrade or modify the system once the initial development team has departed. Without such documentation, future alterations are not only difficult but extremely costly.
- *An Installation Guide* should be prepared if there is any chance that the DSS will be installed at a different site other than the one on which it was developed (this is especially true for microcomputer applications). The installation manual provides peculiar characteristics and requirements that must be accounted for in transferring the soft-

ware to either an equal or different hardware configuration. A test problem should also be included to insure that the package can be verified as totally operational.

When dealing with a decision-support application, there are several additional considerations that must be taken into account in the user documentation. For example:

- *Operational Flexibility.* User manuals for virtually any type of information system must explain the functional flexibility available to the user (for example, the latitude and extent of activities that the system can be used to support). For the DSS, however, it is especially important that the user understand how the system can adapt to a changing environment. Remember that one of the distinctions between DSS and other information systems is its ability to function in a dynamic and ever changing environment. The documentation must demonstrate how the system can conform to changing conditions, and explain how each capability is used to evaluate alternatives (resource cutbacks, new pricing strategies, productivity improvements, etc.).
- *Scenarios.* Nothing demonstrates the potential value of a DSS more than to illustrate how the system is used to solve actual problems. The user manual should depict several real-world scenarios, highlight what factors and conditions the user is investigating/evaluating, and explain (interpret) what the results mean in each case.
- *Sensitivity Insights.* Remember that the system will be used by a decision maker to formulate alternative policies and strategies. The user manual should explain how the DSS can be used to explore the sensitivity of each alternative to changes in the influential factors (resource constraints, consumption rates, personnel attrition, interest rates, etc.), and identify which factors "typically" cause the greatest change (for sensitivity) in the solution. Such information can be useful in helping the decision maker to formulate a course of action that is "robust" (relatively stable) to a changing environment.
- *Limitations.* In the more sophisticated applications, involved mathematical procedures are required to model and analyze the problem. Although such procedures are invaluable for transforming a complex situation into a mathematically equivalent form, it is usually only an approximation to the real world. The decision maker must understand any limitations in applying the system to actual problems. The user must be aware of situations where the analysis breaks down, changes in the precision of the system under different conditions, factors that are not accounted for in the model, and so forth.

Training

Chapter 8 stated that one of the properties of an effectively designed DSS is that it permits a manager to sit down and feel instantly at ease with the system. Using help options, tutoring facilities, and other instructional devices, the user should be able to "learn as you go." Why then is providing user training important to successful implementation of the system? If the user interface is indeed conversational, and documentation is well prepared, why waste the time with unnecessary training? The answer stems from the fact that the background, experience, and prior knowledge of the user populace usually varies significantly across the organization. All three conditions will affect how readily each user adapts and what the best approach is for indoctrinating a particular user. For example:

- ☐ Many will never have seen a terminal, touched a floppy disk or typed in a command to a computer.
- ☐ Some may be familiar with the fundamentals (what is a cursor, return key, etc.), but will learn the basic capabilities of the system much more effectively through verbal instruction. Others are best left to themselves with the user manual and the systems help/tutor features. This is especially true of a user with a heavy workload that must learn incrementally in conjunction with their busy schedule.

In the majority of cases a large number of users will fall within the first category. The typical sign of an attempted application where training was not effectively applied is a room full of people surrounded by terminals with empty chairs and dusty cases. Too much training is just as bad. Many commercial DSS vendors survive by providing training sessions lasting for days. Individuals who will benefit the most from using the system rarely have the luxury of committing several days to training. They are more responsive to the daily pressure of trying to survive in a highly competitive environment.

The needs of all users can best be handled through the combined facilities of training, documentation, and a well-designed user interface. Training sessions should never be measured in days or weeks, but instead hours. Sessions should be provided in two stages: An indoctrination session that teaches the basics and provides users with their first hands on exposure; and an advanced session that illustrates the more extensive capabilities and applications of the system.

Finally, training should never be provided before users have the facilities on hand to practice what they learn. If the gap between training and independent use is more than a week, the combined benefit of training and hands on experience will be lost.

RULES OF THUMB—BEWARE THE PITS AND POTHOLES

The theme behind "the best laid plans of mice and men" is well suited to the successful implementation of a DSS. Even under the best of circumstances, the risk still exists that once operational, the system will function as nothing more than a dust collector. Experience has shown that the chance of success can be significantly improved by observing certain principles. This section discusses some of the rules of thumb that need to be considered in addition to several pitfalls that can lure the developer(s) to their eventual demise [4,26,38].

The User as a Positive Contributor

Anyone believing they possess sufficient knowledge to attack the problem in isolation of user insight is functioning with a cranial vacuum. Not only is user involvement priceless, it also helps to generate interest on the part of the user and to reduce some of the inherent reluctance humans exhibit when confronted by change. The alternative is that users become aliens instead of allies. Even the best of systems can die from apathy and sabotage. The experienced designer solicits user participation throughout the total process.

Terrible Toos: Too Much, Too Little, Too Late

In most situations there are several conflicting motivations: bring the system on line immediately, provide as much capability as possible, keep costs low, do not overwhelm the user with too many alternative choices, etc. Obviously, all these objectives cannot be satisfied. The developer(s) must, however, achieve a proper balance so that: resources are not expended in obtaining too much capability; implementation does not take so long that management support waivers; and enough features are included so that users view the system as beneficial and not a cumbersome burden.

Blinded By The Light

Most analysts thrive on the feeling of accomplishment in automating everything to the lowest level of detail and providing the decision maker with a multitude of alternative choices. Too much immediate capability can be "blinding." A moderate level of insight is helpful, but provide too much and the decision maker can become overloaded. In the more sophisticated applications, a DSS should provide an easily viewed record of previous solutions and "what if" scenarios.

The "Not Created Here" Phenomenon

Frequently, an external source will be called upon to establish DSS capabilities even though internal resources exist. Whether it be lack of expertise in the required disciplines, current workload of internal staff, or other conditions that justify seeking outside help, the incoming team must be conscious of potential negative feelings. The in-house personnel will inevitably be called upon to support the system. Hostility on the part of internal units can lead to the eventual death of the application. (Study 2 in Chapter 12 illustrates the "Not Created Here" phenomenon in action.)

The "Fear of Replacement" Syndrome

It is human nature that any automated system will cause many potential users to perceive the new capability as a substitute for human involvement. Both the developer(s) and upper management must insure that the phobia of being replaced is truly eliminated. Users must understand their role and participation in creating and operating the system.

Ownership

There must be several layers of responsibility if the DSS is to succeed: who will operate the system?; where will the input data be gathered and entered?; and which group of management will be responsible for oversight of the total process? The question of ownership must be resolved prior to implementation otherwise the system will dangle in a world of uncertainty, fragmented use, and lack of continuity when the DSS is turned over to successors. If the DSS is not institutionalized, it is likely that the system will drift into eventual oblivion.

The "Grab Bag" Approach

The pressures of surviving in the modern business world cause many management actions to be corrective versus preventive. As a result, decisions to upgrade the organization are often left to the end of a funding cycle. When the decision to create a more quantitative decision process occurs in "a hurry up" atmosphere, the DSS frequently exhibits the features of a "grab bag" system. The functions provided often do not match the true requirement. Establishing effective decision-support capabilities requires a sufficient planning horizon. The philosophy to create something quick (buy here; buy there) usually results in the development and/or implementation process being performed on the run. The likely result is a piecemeal proposition that eventually shakes apart.

The Fox in the Henhouse

In many situations decision-support capabilties can only be created through a cooperative effort with a well institutionalized Automated Data Processing (ADP) Department. Unfortunately, most traditional ADP groups are attuned to batch-processing operations and lack the expertise necessary to establish a quantitative user-oriented system. This often causes a dilemma to the DSS developer. The ADP group is generally out of touch with the characteristics and requirements behind a user-oriented system because of their batch-processing orientation and a focus toward hardware technology. They also frequently control the very resources needed by the DSS team to create a better environment for decision making. If, after the preliminary survey, it becomes apparent that the local ADP group exhibits all the characteristics of the "fox in control of the henhouse," the developer would be well advised to consider establishing separate automation facilities (for example, using a microcomputer or minisystem where appropriate). In Chapter 12, Case Study 4 provides a real-world example of this particular roadblock in action.

EXERCISES

1. We discussed three approaches to establishing decision-support capability: procure an off-the-shelf package, develop a composite system of existing and new components, and design the system from scratch. List the comparative pros and cons to each approach.
2. The cost to develop or acquire a DSS is obviously a major fraction of the initial cost. Identify some of the other costs associated with implementation and operation of the system.

3. Select a problem that you are familiar with from your own experience, or from other literature, that appears a likely candidate for a DSS application. Examples would include: a system to support development of preparedness plans for large scale catastrophes (floods, earthquakes); a system to plan, manage, and control the emparcation and deparcation process for distribution operations (docking, offloading, warehousing); a system to schedule and coordinate operations in a medical facility; or any similar situation. Use the SIO approach to "divide and conquer" the process into as many levels as are necessary, and be sure to show (flow) the relationships between the various parts.

4. At the end of Chapter 11, we cited several roadblocks and pitfalls to the successful implementation of a DSS. Based on either your own experience, or from other literature, identify two or three other "craters" that can lead to the eventual demise of an attempted application.

5. To describe the overall requirement for an application, we noted that it often helps to view the problem in terms of an input/output process where resources (people, funds, information, etc.) go in one side and products (petroleum, consulting services, studies, etc.) come out the other. This "systems" view is used in many professional areas to describe a problem or process. Name three or four disciplines or areas where the input/output model is applicable and explain how it would be used (what goes in, what comes out, and how things are transformed in between).

6. To bring together the various topics discussed thus far, consider the following applications:

   - ☐ A system that helps an organization develop its weekly workforce schedule at a retail store given the availability of personnel, hourly wages, overtime costs and regulations, projected workload in each period, skill requirements by department, and so forth.
   - ☐ A DSS that allocates weekly blood supplies across hospitals in a large area based on storage capacities, predicted demand, large civic events, transfer costs (to redistribute unused supplies), etc.
   - ☐ A system that helps a commander determine the best combination of aircraft and weapon systems to employ against different targets (artillary, tanks, personnel transports, infantry, railroads, radar sites) under various conditions (day/night operations, inclement weather) based on historical experience (munition experts, test data, commander insights, etc.).
   - ☐ A system that evaluates the favorability of a potential drilling or mining site based on survey studies, likelihood of success, cost of distribution, expected daily yield, and so forth. The system must couple the judgment and experience of a group of geological engineers with an appropriate quantitative procedure that predicts the risks and expected return associated with each alternative.

   Select one of these applications and perform the following:

   - ☐ Describe what type of DSS application we are dealing with (distribution problem, risk analysis, resource allocation, Expert System, Group DSS, etc.).
   - ☐ List some of the possible "inputs" and "outputs" of the problem.
   - ☐ Scratch a figurative model that depicts the overall process (inputs, outputs, flows, decisions, etc.).

- ☐ State what quantitative technique you feel would appear appropriate for this problem and note why.
- ☐ In the same context as Exhibits 2–5, 2–6, 2–7, 2–8, 2–9, 5–5, 8–7, 8–8, etc., illustrate a typical dialogue between the user and the system (for example, show what the interaction would look like, what would the user be asked to do, what type of questions would the system address, etc.).

REFERENCES AND SUGGESTED READING

1. Business Systems Planning, Information Systems Planning Guide, IBM Corp., Technical Publication, 1981.
2. Canning, R., "The Analysis Of User Needs," *EDP Analyzer,* January, 1979.
3. Connell, J. and L. Brice, "Rapid Prototyping," *Datamation,* October 15, 1984.
4. Davis, M., "The Pits Of Management Sciences And Gamesmanship To Skirt The Rim," *INTERFACES,* April, 1981.
5. De Marco, T., *Structural Analysis and Systems Specification,* New York, N.Y.: Yourdon Press, 1978.
6. Eason, K., "Human Relationships and User Involvement," *Computer Management,* May, 1977.
7. Emery, C., "Costs And Benefits Of An Information System," *Information Processing,* A. Rosenfeld, New York, N.Y.: Holland Publishing Co., 1974.
8. Fox, J., *Software And Its Development,* Englewood Cliffs, N.J.: Prentice-Hall, 1982.
9. Gane, C. and T. Sarson, *Structured Systems Analysis: Tools and Techniques,* Englewood Cliffs, N.J.: Prentice-Hall, 1979.
10. Gass, S., "Documenting a Computer Based Model," *INTERFACES,* May/June, 1984.
11. Hannan, J. (Ed.), *A Practical Guide To Systems Development,* New York, N.Y.: Auerbach Inc., 1982.
12. Harrison, R., "Prototyping and the Systems Development Life Cycle," *Journal of Systems Management,* August, 1985.
13. Harrison, T., "Techniques and Issues in Rapid Prototyping," *Journal of Systems Management,* June, 1985.
14. Hirschheim, R., "User Experience with and Assessment of Participative Systems Design," *MIS Quarterly,* December, 1985.
15. Hodge, B., C. Honess and R. Fleck, *Management Information Systems,* Chapter 11–13, Englewood Cliffs, N.J.: Prentice-Hall, 1984.
16. Hogue, J. and H. Watson, Management's Role in the Approval and Administration of Decision Support Systems," *MIS Quarterly,* June, 1985.
17. Huber, G., "Cognitive Style as a Basis for MIS & DSS Design: Much Ado About Nothing," *Management Science,* August, 1984.

18. Hussain, K. and D. Hussain, *Information Processing Systems For Management,* Chapter 11, Homewood, IL: Richard Irwin Inc., 1981.

19. Keller, R., *Practice of Structural Analysis,* New York, N.Y.: Yourdon Press, 1977.

20. Janson, M. and L. Smith, "Prototyping for System Development: A Critical Appraisal," *MIS Quarterly,* December, 1985.

21. Keen, P., "Value Analysis: Justifying Decision Support Systems," *MIS Quarterly,* March, 1981.

22. Keen, P. and E. Gerson, "The Politics of Software Design," *Datamation,* November, 1977.

23. King, W. and J. Rodriquez, "Participative Design of Strategic DSS," *Management Science,* June, 1981.

24. Lindgren, R., "Justifying A Decision Support System," *Data Management,* May, 1981.

25. Lucas, H., "User-Oriented Systems Analysis and Design," in Hannan, J. (ed.), *A Practical Guide to System Development Management,* New York, N.Y.: Auerbach, 1982.

26. Lynch, R., "Nine Pitfalls In Implementing Packaged Applications Software," *Journal of Information Systems Management,* Summer 1985, Vol. 2, no. 3.

27. Martin, M., "Determining Information Requirements For Decision Support Systems," *Journal of Systems Management,* December, 1982.

28. McKay, L., *A Common-Sense Guide To Creative Documentation,* Torrance, CA: Ashton-Tate Publishing, 1984.

29. Meader, L. and R. Mezger, "Selecting an End User Programming Language," *MIS Quarterly,* December, 1984.

30. Munro, M. and G. Davis, "Determining Management Information Requirements: A Comparison of Methods," *MIS Quarterly,* June, 1977.

31. Musket, M., "Applications Systems Planning," *Journal of Information Systems Management,* Winter, 1985.

32. Nauman, J. and A. Jenkins, "The New Paradigm for Systems Development," *MIS Quarterly,* September, 1982.

33. Nicholas, J., "User Involvement: What Kind, How Much, and When?" *Journal of Systems Management,* March, 1985.

34. Oliver, P., "Approaches to Software Engineering," *Journal of Information Systems Management,* Summer, 1985.

35. Peters, L. and L. Tipp, "Compare Software Design Methodologies," *Datamation,* November, 1977.

36. Robey, D. and D. Farrow, "User Involvement in Information Systems Development," *Management Science,* January, 1982.

37. Sanders, L. and J. Courtney, "A Field Study of Organizational Factors Influencing DSS Success," *MIS Quarterly,* December, 1984.

38. Smithin, T. and S. Jones, "Using MS For The Practice of MS," *INTERFACES,* May-June, 1984.

39. Sprague, R., "A Framework for the Development of Decision Support Systems," *MIS Quarterly,* December, 1980.

40. Sprague, R., and E. Carlson, *Building Effective Decision Support Systems,* Englewood Cliffs, N.J.: Prentice-Hall, 1982.

41. Sussman, P., "Evaluating Decision Support Software," *Datamation,* October, 15, 1984.

42. "Top-Down Software," NTIS, 5285 Port Royal Road, Springfield, VA 22161.

43. Wallace, R., "Cost/Benefit Analysis," *Journal of Information Systems Management,* Fall, 1984, Vol. 1, no. 4.

12

The Real World: Case Studies

Up to this point we have centered our attention on the framework around which decision support is applied and how the DSS is designed to work in that environment. The concepts and principles discussed thus far provide insight but not constant and rigid rules. Variance and imperfections in the real world require that the rules be bent and molded to each situation. Ideally, we strive to holistically combine the best of both worlds: the insight and corporate knowledge of human experience with the speed and thoroughness of automation. Rarely do we achieve this goal, but instead must revel in accomplishing only partial improvement. On occasion the total effort may result in a useless appendage because of some organizational, behavioral or external factor that was not taken into account.

This chapter reviews several real-world applications with the intent of "bringing it all together." Both successful and unsuccessful cases will be presented. Regardless of its success or failure, each case points out various issues that are relevant in applying decision support. The objective here is not to dwell on technical aspects, but to explore the environment in which the DSS is applied and the factors that lead to its success or failure. In each case the reader should examine:

- ☐ How were decisions made prior to the application?
- ☐ How was management convinced that decision support offered a solution?
- ☐ What organizational, behavioral and external issues had to be overcome?

- ☐ How was the problem structured and modeled?
- ☐ How was the new capability first perceived by the users?
- ☐ What procedures were used to make the system an integral part of the decision process?
- ☐ How did the organization benefit (cost savings, less risk, fewer bottlenecks, etc.)?
- ☐ What lessons were learned and what should have been done differently?

The case studies presented in this chapter were solicited from sources in the commercial, public service and military sector. They span a variety of management activities (Chapter 2) including: workforce planning, personnel assignments, market forecasting, workload scheduling, and organizational planning. An overview is provided at the beginning of each study with an assessment of how the application fits within the framework and topics discussed throughout the text.

STUDY 1

WORKFORCE LEVEL PLANNING

Large organizations are continually burdened with the requirement to maintain a suitable workforce without exceeding budgetary constraints. The complexity of such decisions is typically underestimated causing an organization to suffer from a workforce that is overloaded or underutilized. This section presents the successful application of a DSS to help executive managers project, plan, and monitor the level and expenditures of a workforce.

Background

In most technical or professionally-oriented institutions, the workforce accounts for between 40 to 60 percent of the budget and forms the organization's primary resource. One of the typical challenges managers face is how to control and manage the level of the workforce so that a stable base of expertise is maintained without exceeding funding or ceiling limits. The problem is complicated by a multitude of conditions that influence how a workforce will respond to various decisions. Factors such as seasonal attrition, time lags in the hiring process, freeze policies, and so forth, affect the manager's ability to make effective decisions. Such conditions cause a natural inertia in the workforce. It can take three to six months for the workforce to react to a policy or action directed at controlling end-of-year expenditures. Without proper planning and foresight the level of the workforce can porpoise up and down or fluctuate like a roller coaster. Such erratic behavior is costly in terms of staffing shortages, lost business opportunities, hiring/layoff expenses, and general morale problems.

Management at a large federal agency had repeatedly experienced difficulty in planning and controlling the level of their workforce. The number of on board staff typically ran far below the budgeted allocations. Each time actions were taken to "boost" the personnel level by increasing recruiting policies, the workforce would overcompensate and exceed authorized ceilings. The decision makers responsible for controlling personnel expenditures recognized the problem but were unable to come up with the proper corrective action.

Application Development

In an effort to resolve the problem, management initiated a project to improve the decision-making process. The major objective was to come up with a solution that could be quickly implemented and thereafter provide self-regulating control on the workforce level with minimum intervention by management. After a preliminary examination of the problem, project personnel recognized that a simple "quick and dirty" solution was impossible. The factors influencing the workforce level were too numerous and changed over time. To satisfy the requirement for a "quick" solution it was decided that the effort would be carried out in three steps:

- ☐ First, management would be provided with a "rule of thumb" indicator for establishing recruitment and freeze policies.
- ☐ A prototype DSS would then be designed to gain management support and recognition for the use of a continuous planning and monitoring tool.
- ☐ Finally, the full scale system would be designed and implemented.

A simple representation of an organization's workforce is to view it as a large reservoir (Exhibit 12–1a) with flow pouring in at the top (from recruiting replacements) and flow leaking out at the bottom (from attrition). The trick is to determine the rate at which flow (recruitment) must be piped in to compensate for the loss (attrition) leaving the organization. In the first step of the effort, the actual "workforce system" was simplified by assuming that the flow in and the flow out are constant. This assumption allowed an "approximation" technique to be developed to help managers set initial recruiting targets and ceilings. The basic approach consisted of the following concepts:

- ☐ If the rate of personnel attrition was constant and there was no time lag between when a vacancy occurred and when it was replaced, then a constant authorized recruiting level could be established by setting it equal to the desired workforce level. At the instant someone leaves the organization his replacement would report on board the next day and the level of the workforce would appear unchanged. Unfortunately, a time lag does exist in the hiring process. The time between when a vacancy occurs and the time when the new person reports on board can range from several weeks (for clerical and support staff) up to 12 months (for highly specialized skills). This time lag is complicated by the fact that if the replacement is filled from inside the organization then a new vacancy is created (the empty slot is just shifted within the organization) and the time to bring the workforce back up to its level before the initial loss is lengthened.
- ☐ Applying an inflation factor to the authorized level of recruiting provided a pool of "ripening" recruit actions. This inflation pool (Exhibit 12–1a) helped to compensate for the time lag in the replacement process. As the pool was depleted by a completed recruit action (the person reported on board) a new recruit action was started.

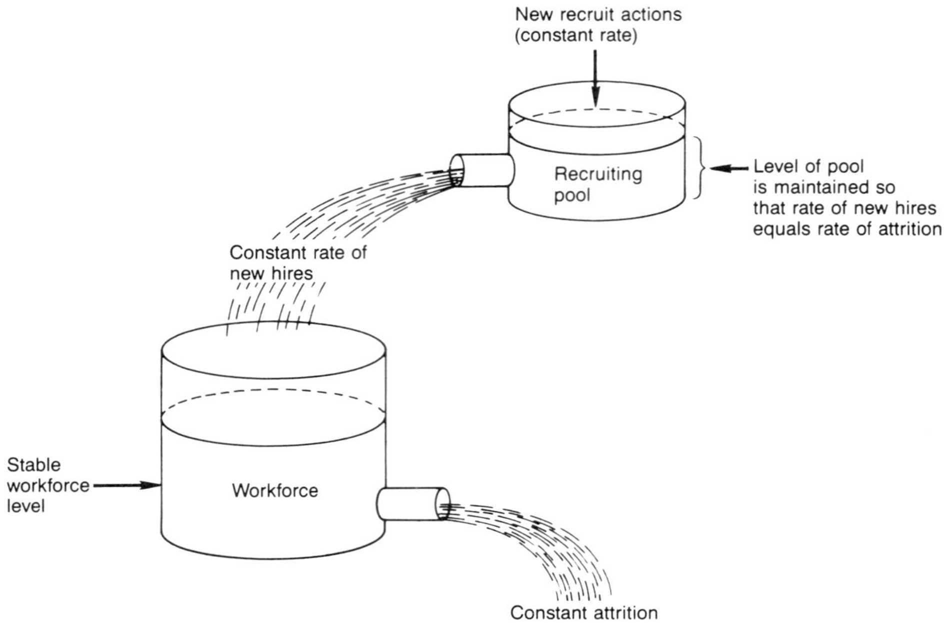

EXHIBIT 12–1a The Ideal Self-Regulating System.

- ☐ The level of inflated recruiting had to be set so that the rate of flow into the workforce equaled the rate of attrition leaving the workforce. This was accomplished by setting the amount of inflation to the product of the desired workforce, the annual attrition rate, and the average time lag in the hiring process.

To accomplish the basic "hands off" philosophy (once recruiting policies were established) divisions within the organization were allowed to "try" and recruit up to the inflated level. This meant that the total number on board plus the number of outstanding recruit actions had to remain constant. Divisions could not initiate new actions unless the number on board plus active recruitments was less than the authorized recruiting level (for example, the desired workforce level plus the inflation pool).

Implementation

The initial step was received positively by management for two reasons. It helped to establish the self-regulating policies that management wanted and it was logical, simple to understand, and easy to implement. The second step (creating a prototype DSS) was not as easy. A data base had to be established and procedures for continually gathering the information implemented within the organization. Because the forces influencing the workforce were so dynamic, an effective planning and control system had to be continually operated in order to monitor changes in the workforce.

A model was developed that considered the workforce as a continuous flowing process (Exhibit 12–1b) that took into account all of the major factors that influence the level of the workforce at each point in time (attrition, hiring freezes, etc.). A prototype software package was designed to project the workforce level over a two-year time horizon given conditions and policies entered by the user. The initial predictions indicated that current policies would result in a 30 staff year shortage at the end of the year. The workforce would grow to the desired level in the third quarter but again dip downward until the end of the year. Once these results were presented to management several gyrations of "what if" questions were proposed by the decision makers and projections were rerun. The best policy was chosen and implemented. The possibility of "short term" solutions resulting in the wrong "long term" effect convinced management that a permanent planning and control system was necessary. Managers were also convinced that a new version had to be developed that could be used directly by the decision maker. The final system allowed managers to evaluate their own decisions by providing the following capabilities:

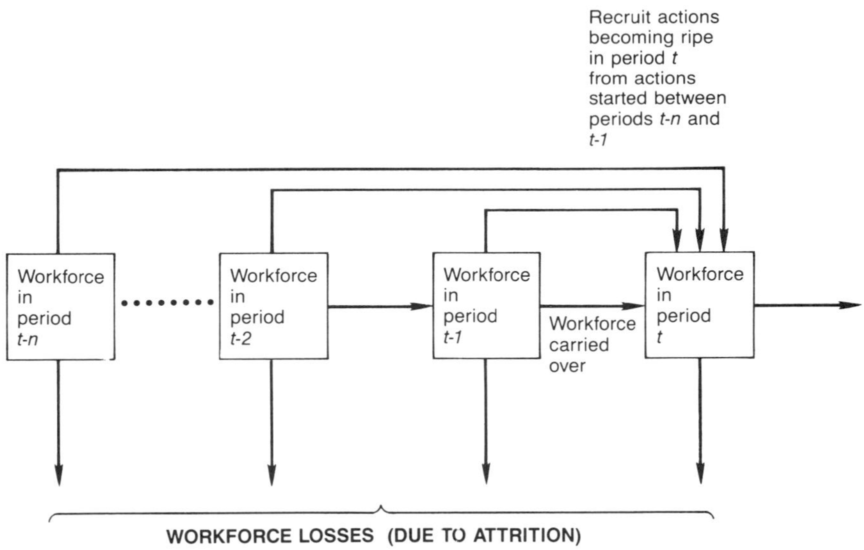

EXHIBIT 12–1b Continuous Flow Model of the Workforce.

- ☐ Tracking capabilities to record historical characteristics of the workforce.
- ☐ Monitoring capabilities to highlight and trigger undesired deviations from defined budgetary controls.
- ☐ Forecasting capabilities so that high level managers could evaluate alternative policies and their sensitivity to changes in attrition, freeze policies, hiring lags, and so forth.

The system was very effective in providing a totally integrated DSS (Exhibit 12-1c) and was strongly supported by management. The DSS provided operational insight as to whether or not the workforce was in control and also provided tactical directions that indicated what the affects of decisions and policies would be downstream in the next budget cycle. The total system became an integral part of the decision process.

Reflections

The success of this application can be attributed to three conditions: Management was up to its hips in alligators with no apparent way to turn; the total effort was implemented in parts, thus allowing the organization to "come of age" gradually; all of the concepts of the application were presented in terms that were logical to management; and the results were reasonable (not contrary to human senses). Prior to this application, the organization traditionally ran five to six percent under its allocations. Once the DSS

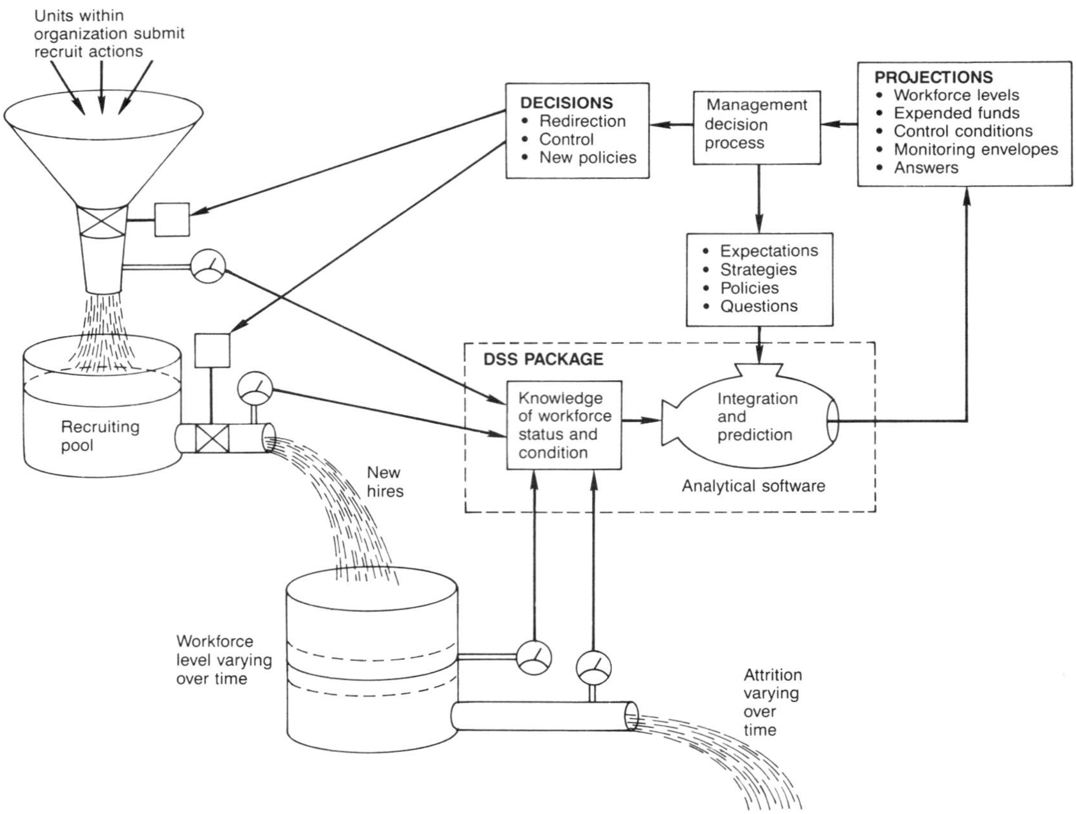

EXHIBIT 12–1c Operation of An Integrated Workforce Level Management System.

became an effective management tool the organization was capable of maintaining its workforce within one percent of the desired level. Use of the system also resulted in savings to the organization in other ways. During the first six months of operation, the full scale system projected an overrun of 16 staff years. Had workforce policies gone unchanged, a loss of over $400,000 in contracted funds would have been necessary (with associated penalties) to compensate for the overrun. The DSS was also useful in supporting budgetary requirements to upper management (outside the organization). At a budget hearing the system was used to demonstrate that an excessive reduction in output would occur if proposed cuts were enacted. Because the results could be quickly validated using the DSS, funds were shifted from a sister agency's budget in an attempt to balance the cuts. The sister agency was unable to quickly demonstrate the impact and loss such a cut would cause to their organization.

STUDY 2

MANAGING FLIGHT OPERATIONS IN A TRAINING ENVIRONMENT

In Chapter 11 several ''pits'' were discussed that can cause a potentially successful DSS to fall into one great abyss. The ''not created here'' syndrome often occurs when a party outside of the normal channels develops the system causing unintentional antagonism with in house resources. This case study illustrates such a situation where the proponent totally endorsed the application but could not obtain post development support from internal units.

Background

The complex nature of aircraft operations demands a dedicated effort to establish and maintain flight proficiency. Organizations involved in flight operations frequently employ comprehensive training and currency programs to maintain the continual safety and competency of their pilots. Managing such a program is a formidable task. Personnel responsible for planning and scheduling flight operations in a training environment must ensure compliance with a variety of flight restrictions, flight currency requirements, personnel and aircraft availability, and so on.

Administering a flight training program is a staff intensive and cumbersome process. When performed manually the sheer volume of possible alternatives is overwhelming. Deciding on a feasible set of flight assignments is more a manner of deadline than of efficiency.

The operations department at a military flight training facility was responsible for coordinating and scheduling flight assignments for up to 120 students with 20 instructors from a roster of approximately 90 aircraft. A staff of two individuals was responsible for generating two daily flight schedules. The director of the facility had long been aware that the flight operations department was a prime candidate for automation. The problem was one of resources. The computer services group that supported the facility estimated it would take one year for two programmers to develop a system that would only satisfy 40 percent of the requirement. To the director, this was totally unacceptable.

Application Development

The director decided to get a second opinion. An organization outside the umbrella of the training facility was requested to come in and size up the problem. Three days were spent observing the operations department. The operations personnel were surveyed to highlight any voids or misperceptions resulting from the preliminary review. Once a basic understanding of the requirement had been established, the director was queried for an assessment of his overall objectives and the major areas of the decision process that caused the most problems.

Aware that the director was expecting a "quick" solution to a very broad and extensive requirement, the development and delivery of an integrated DSS was initially out of the question. A segmented approach was proposed where the system would be designed and implemented in three separate stages:

1. *Flight Currency*—The director's major concern was that a small portion of both the student and instructor pilots were conducting flights when, in fact, they were not current (qualified) under military regulations. To alleviate this difficulty, the first phase would be completed in six weeks and provide operations personnel with the capability to interactively:
   - ☐ Track flight records for all personnel (previously each pilot maintained his own manual flight log).
   - ☐ Compute the qualifications of each person for 12 different types of required flight currency (ejection seat qualified, physiological standards, five flights in 30 days, etc.).
   - ☐ Project who would lose their qualifications in the near future and require immediate attention.
2. *Data Management*—Operations personnel had to maintain up-to-date records of student, instructor, and aircraft status (all of which changed daily). The second phase would provide record management capabilities that could be used to quickly assess:
   - ☐ Personnel and aircraft availability.
   - ☐ Student flight training programs (up to 50 events for each student with eight prerequisite requirements for each event).
   - ☐ Aircraft inventory, maintenance status, and special equipment configurations.
3. *Flight Scheduling*—The final segment would interface all of the previous requirements and develop flight assignments for available students, instructors, and aircraft according to personnel flight qualifications, student training requirements, and personnel/aircraft availability.

The overall concept was to provide an integrated system (Exhibit 12–2) that would:

- ☐ Automate roughly 90 percent of the tasks that operations personnel were performing manually.

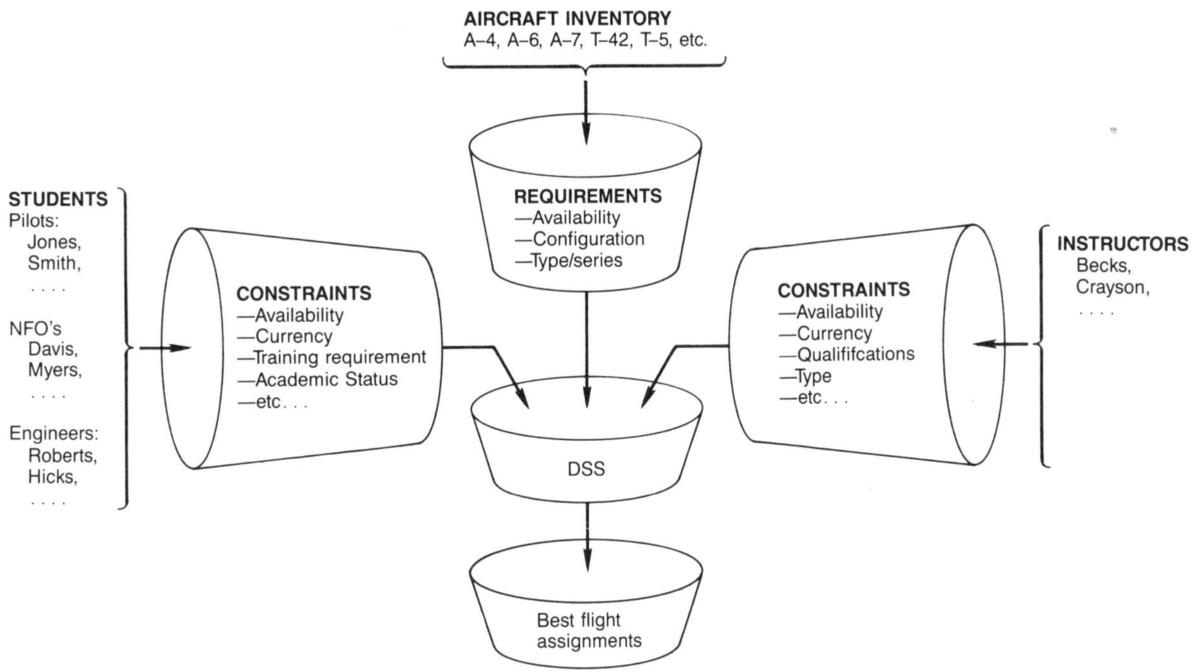

EXHIBIT 12–2 Components of a Flight Training DSS Application.

- ☐ Help executive personnel to evaluate the impact of external policies.
- ☐ Quantitatively search through all feasible flight assignments and generate a candidate list of assignments that maximized progress in the training programs.
- ☐ Allow operations personnel to review recommended assignments and make quick adjustments based on their experience and insight.

Implementation

Completion of phase 1 was anything but uneventful. The first projections made by the system indicated that roughly 40 percent of the pilots were unknowingly flying when they were unqualified. Obviously, neither the director nor the pilots were happy with this outcome but for diffent reasons. The pilots carried a "mental computation" of their currency and were alarmed that they might lose their flight privileges. The director was concerned that the total program had been running in violation of required regulations. In virtually every case, pilots would contest the results of the system only to find that they did, in fact, violate currency standards. To circumvent the problem, a new policy was instituted. No pilot that was identified by the system as nonqualified could fly without a written waiver from the director. This in turn caused another problem. Trying to keep the total roster of pilots "truly" current was causing significant impedence to normal training operations. After several months the director decided to request a special exception to the qualification requirements for the training facility. The phase 1 portion of the system was used to project long-term effects, design a tolerable qualification policy, and support the recommendation forwarded up to the executive command.

Phases 2 and 3 were completed without the controversy of phase 1. Nonetheless the results were remarkable. Although automating the recordkeeping efforts for maintaining status information (personnel availability, aircraft status, etc.) required roughly the same amount of time as the status quo operation, flight schedules could be generated in a matter of seconds with approximately 10 to 20 percent more flight assignments than when done manually. Operations personnel could also easily check out various "what if" scenarios (down weather conditions, additional aircraft becoming available, etc.) which allowed "backup" alternative schedules to be ready and waiting. The total integrated DSS was positively received by both the director and operations personnel. The system became a valuable asset to the organization resulting in both staff savings and long-term improvements in the progress of the training program.

Reflections

Although the software capabilities were readily accepted by the organization, hardware deficiencies led to the eventual demise of this application. The optimum configuration would have been to create an independent facility using microcomputers. Unfortunately, micro capacities had not yet achieved the level of today's systems. The only alternative was to use the mainframe currently available at the computer support facility (the same computer services group that was "unable" to participate in the development of the system). As luck would have it, the existing mainframe was not well suited to interactive operations. The computer was originally designed as a high speed "number cruncher" functioning primarily in a batch mode. Timesharing facilities were added as an afterthought. This caused a variety of hardware related problems. Two or three times a week the hardware would go down and literally lose track of where data was located on the storage units. The procedures required to "reload" the data were far beyond the skills of the user populace. Once the original developer was detailed to other duties, operations personnel could only rely on the assistance of the computer services group. For whatever reason, the computer services group took the position that their staff was not qualified to support the new DSS. Instead, they offered to create a batch operated program that would provide about 40 percent of the capabilities of the new system with a six hour turn around (on a good day). The training facility had no choice but to accept the offer. After several months of frustration the training department gave up and went back to the original manual operation. The total experience left a "bad taste" and a potential deterrent to similar efforts.

STUDY 3

PLANNING AND SCHEDULING OFFICE RELOCATIONS

The structure of modern organizations changes frequently. Associated with these changes is the need to consolidate and relocate offices and personnel. Managing such relocation exercises is an extremely demanding and complex effort. This case study discusses a DSS designed specifically to help managers plan and schedule office relocations. The application started as a success but ended as a failure because of behavioral issues and organization factors.

Background

Managing the relocation of office personnel, furnishings, and equipment is a difficult and resource intensive task. It requires a comprehensive effort to plan, schedule, and coordinate a variety of activities that are not only dependent on the successful completion of other moves, but also hampered by the availability of work crews. In a typical exercise, the manager must ensure that the occupants and furnishings of each office are moved out before the new residents are moved in. Renovations must also be scheduled to coincide with the vacancy of the office and the necessary sequence of refurbishing activities (first partition walls, then paint, then carpet, etc.). This complex maze of activities results in a complicated chain of events, where any change disrupts the total process much like a set of dominos.

Large organizations expend a significant portion of their effort shuffling offices around. Most institutions spend so much time in reorganization that special groups have to be permanently established just to manage associated relocation activities. In one such organization, a "rotary pool" philosophy was used to exchange mid-level managers between division supervisor slots. During the tenure of an enlightened manager, the new incumbent recognized the need for automated support. After discussing the problem with personnel specializing in DSS applications, the manager was convinced that quantitative support was feasible and authorized the project.

Application Development

The first step was to identify the "nature of the beast." The systems developer spent three days on site observing the operation. It was noted that approximately 70 to 80 percent of staff time was spent in trying to determine how moves should be sequenced and how to allocate the limited work crews across the various moving and renovation activities. Once a schedule had been created, changes would occur on a routine basis (new moves added, reduction in crews, etc.) necessitating that the total planning process be repeated. For example, to plan the relocation and refurbishment of 120 offices required eight weeks. After the initial plan was completed roughly 10 percent of the offices changed their destinations. This minor change required an additional two weeks to revise the master plan.

After a preliminary examination of the operation, the staff was surveyed for a potential wish list. There was basic agreement that the major areas of benefit would occur in helping division personnel to:

- ☐ Identify the required sequence of moves so that each office was vacated before the newcomer was scheduled to move in.
- ☐ Determine which moves could be separated into independent groups and managed separately.
- ☐ Schedule renovations to coincide with the required sequence of moves and the number of work crews available for each type of renovation.

The first prototype of the system was provided to selected staff members for an "early shakedown" just in time to support a major relocation exercise. The first version was intended to highlight problems in the general approach and the quantitative models used to solve each problem. Nonetheless, sufficient guidelines and user-friendly features were incorporated in the design, so that with only a half hour of instruction and a simple options "road map," users were able to apply the prototype directly.

Implementation

The first set of users received the new tool positively. Reductions in staff time were so significant that users had more time to work on other initiatives. For example, a small relocation effort (Exhibit 12–3a) required approximately 35 staff hours to develop a preliminary moving and renovation schedule. With the new DSS, a parallel planning effort was accomplished by one staff member in four hours. The system provided roughly 90 percent of the necessary planning requirements by separating moves into groups, computing the required sequence (Exhibit 12–3b), and then coming up with a feasible schedule of moves and renovation activities based on the available crews. When three

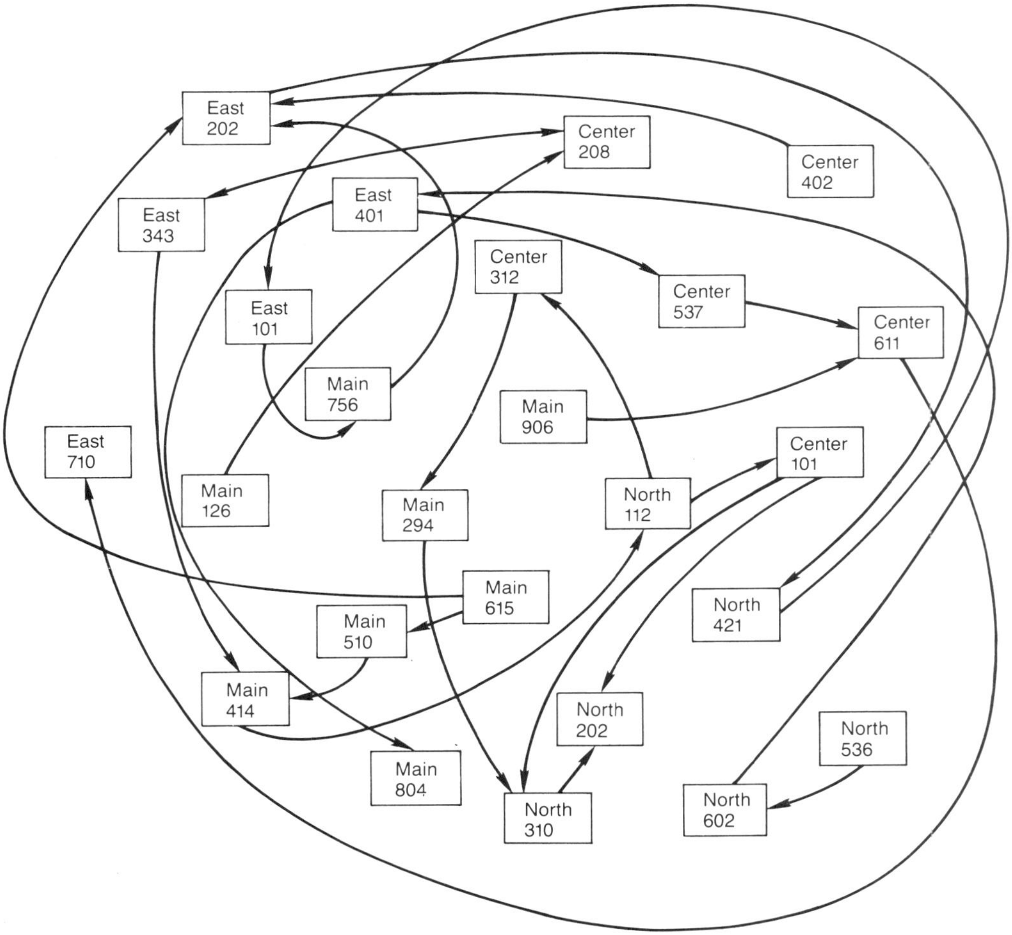

EXHIBIT 12–3a An Office Relocation Exercise (Maze of Complexity).

new offices were added to the exercise and one work crew was assigned to a different project, it took about four hours for the previous plan to be manually massaged. The staff member using the DSS required roughly ten minutes to incorporate the changes and the final solution was even better than that generated by the status quo method.

Based on these results a presentation was provided to the division manager and remaining staff. The manager was visually pleased with the outcome and requested that several features be added along with formal user documentation. The revised package and user manual was provided to staff members and both the manager and systems developer moved on to new horizons with the impression that the story had concluded with a happy ending.

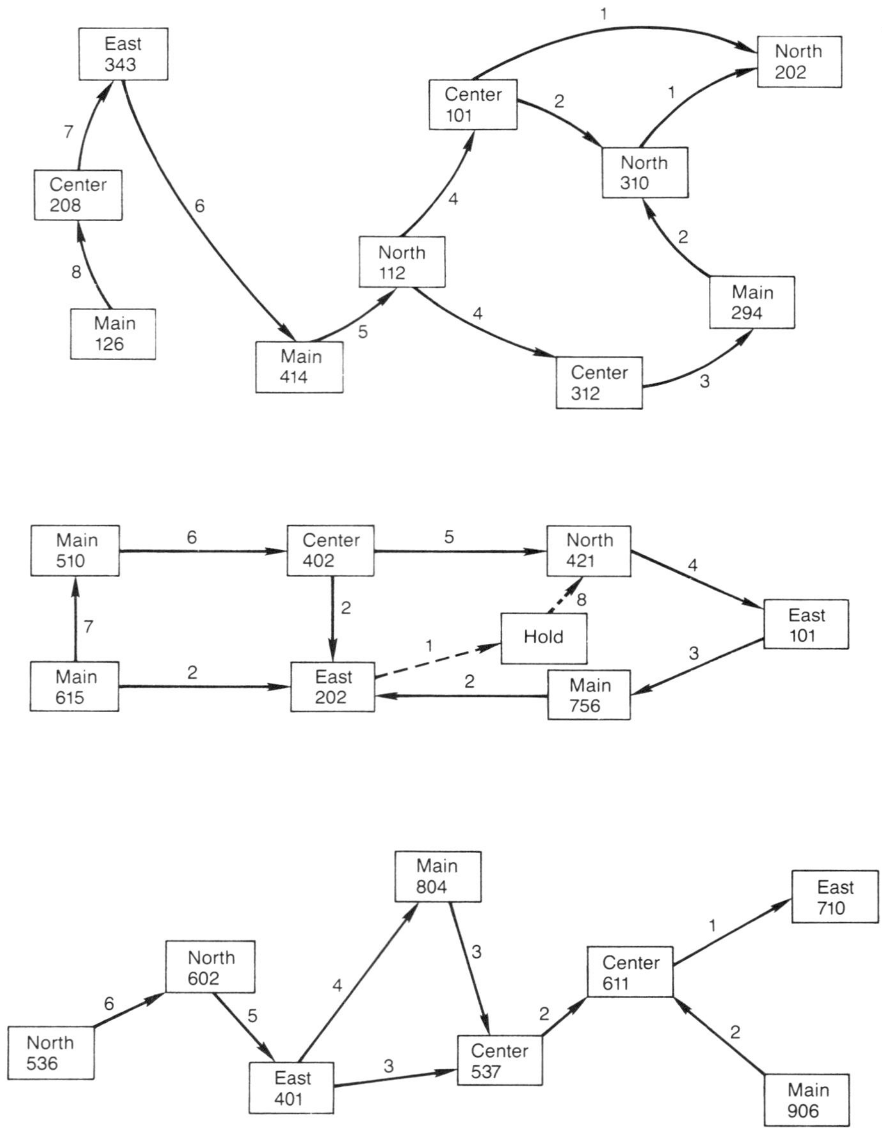

EXHIBIT 12–3b Transforming An Office Relocation into An Understandable Problem.

Reflections

Approximately six months expired and the new division manager was contacted in the hope of providing additional services. To the dismay of the developer, the system was not being used and the new manager had no intention of bringing it back to life. Further investigation disclosed that the new manager operated under a "seat of the pants" philosophy and was extremely apprehensive about computerized systems. Although staff members involved in the original effort continued using the system (until they had moved on to new jobs), others had not adapted to the new approach. They were perfectly satisfied to conduct their assignments in the same fashion that had been used for years.

In retrospect, several organizational and behavioral factors led to the failure of this application. The manager involved in the original effort had *assumed* that because the system provided real savings and improvements to the planning process, continual application would result naturally. However, because the tool had not been institutionalized (tied to the management process by executive policy), it was too easy to be ignored by traditionalists. Staff members content with the "old" approach were reluctant to any labor saving devices. The feeling was that the requirement to manually generate relocation plans provided job security. Self-motivation was not a viable stimulus in this case. Moral: 1. Ensure that upper management is involved in the decision to implement the DSS; and 2. Convince operational personnel that use of the DSS is not a substitute for the human element but instead a supplement to the process.

STUDY 4

A MARKET ANALYSIS AND FORECASTING APPLICATION

This case study illustrates the "fox in the hen house" pitfall in action (Chapter 11). The developer often finds himself in a "catch 22" position: He must depend on staff support from a centralized data processing department that is historically aligned with nonuser oriented systems. Most large institutionalized computer facilities have become accustomed to, and comfortable with, batch processing operations. If the success of an application depends solely on the commitment of an organizational unit with no experience (or appreciation) for user-oriented systems, the project may be doomed from the start.

Topic contributed by
Dr. Michael C. Stentz

Introduction

Organizations that are oriented toward consumer sales have a tremendous need to effectively "use" their sales data as a direct feedback on how their business is doing. Sales analysis is a branch of Marketing Research that uses sales data to make judgments about where the business may be going, where the problems and opportunities may lie, and which of the proposed improvements are likely to be the most effective and least risky for the organization in both the short term and the long run.

The mountain of internal sales data that exists in most consumer products organizations is the primary source of information for making decisions regarding marketing. Typical sales data includes: advertising, promotion, product modification, pricing, and miscellaneous operational issues. To make sense of the abundance of sales information, forecasting techniques are often used to project sales levels, their likely trends, and potential seasonal fluctuations in order to evaluate trial market entry. Sales data are usually voluminous. In most applications, sales information accumulates faster than it can be manually analyzed and evaluated.

Sales data can be viewed in most cases as a data "cube" with three important dimensions of recurring interest (Exhibit 12–4a): time, geography and product line. To analyze sales information, the manager typically uses different "slices" from the cube with varying levels of detail at various edges. For example, a slice might be taken at one point in time across several product lines for various geographic areas (Exhibit 12–4b) to examine differences between various regions. Another requirement might be to view two adjacent time periods that would depict the positive or negative "percent change" by geographic area (Exhibit 12–4c). The manager may also wish to take a slice across all time periods and across all geographic areas to analyze the trend of sales over time (Exhibit 12–4d). Such information would be helpful in forecasting sales fluctuations and trends to help predict the future.

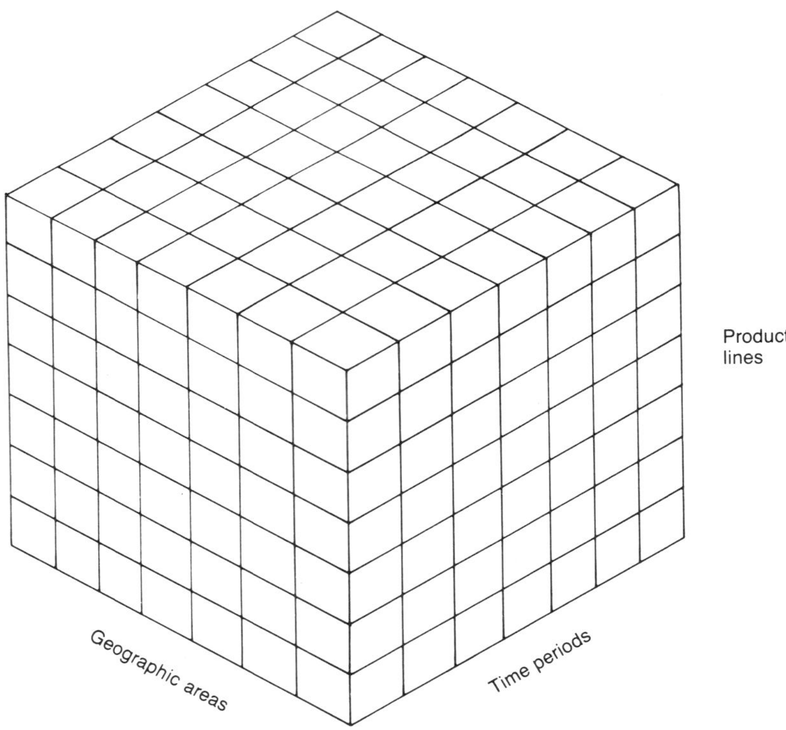

EXHIBIT 12–4a The Sales Data Cube.

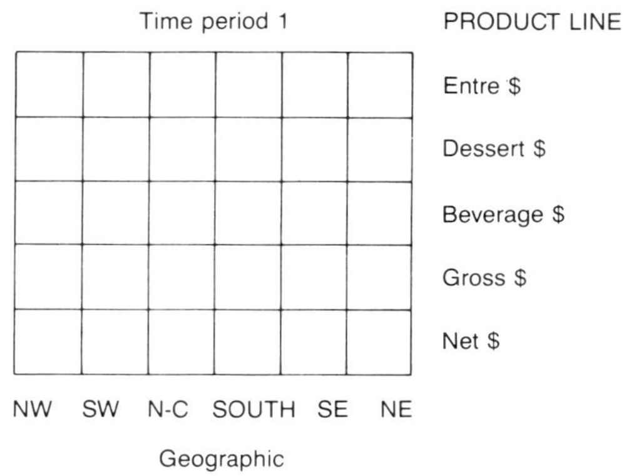

EXHIBIT 12–4b Examining Sales Differences By Product Line Across Geographic Areas.

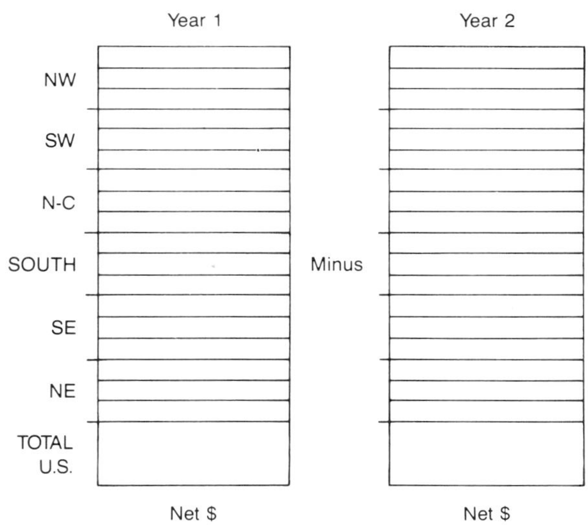

EXHIBIT 12–4c Measuring Gains (or Losses) Per Product Line for Geographic Areas.

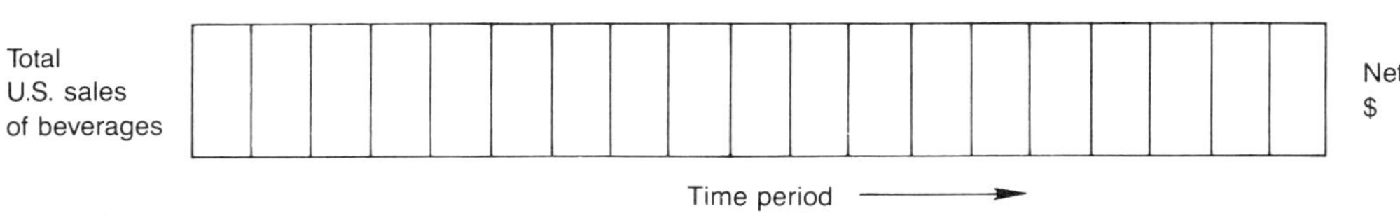

EXHIBIT 12–4d Total Sales for One Product Over Time.

At a moderately sized enterprise, the in-house Data Processing Department (DP) had initially been delegated the responsibility for managing the sales reporting function. Usually only a fraction of the data was entered, such as the monthly billing summaries by account. The report generated by the DP group had been relatively simple and rigid. The marketing personnel had been suitably "conditioned" by the DP group as to what could and could not be done, how long it would take to get changes and improvements programmed, and what other DP work had to "slide" in order to accommodate the demands of the marketing department for responsive reports.

Application Development

The company was a $500 million fast food chain, with half franchise and half company stores. They had excellent information on retail sales by geography and time, and fair information by item. Although sufficient information on advertising and promotion was available, it was unorganized and not in a computer-readable form. The Marketing Research department (MR) brought in a new sales research manager to try and manage this critical informational area. The manager hired an outside consultant to support efforts to improve the responsiveness and usability of sales information.

The task of the sales analysis group was to transition from a batch processing mode to a more flexible and readily usable form that could be extracted and analyzed on an as-needed basis. The DP department had no experience with software that exhibits a user-oriented interface. The development team consisted of the outside consultant, two members of the DP department, and two members of Marketing Research. The DP attitude was one of accommodation: by cooperating on this project, they hoped to defuse MR's criticism. Once the decision was made to acquire a Fourth Generation Language system (Chapter 10), the consultant was primarily responsible for assembling the overall system, establishing the quantitative component (Chapter 9) and the report generator formats for ad hoc queries by the user (Market Comparison Profiles, Time Series Analysis of sales trends, etc.). The DP group was responsible for data integrity and development of the programming code.

Implementation

Because the operating system was oriented toward batch processing, there were inherent problems in creating the user-friendly environment required for a decision-support application. Response time was also an issue. The system required five to 10 seconds for trivial tasks. When the user of the prototype system tried to access data and generate a report, the wait time escalated dramatically. The DP group had verbally committed to supporting the project but did not carry through in developing the necessary interactive computing features. Although a total conversational interface had been intended, it became necessary to de-emphasize the interactive processing aspect of the project in order to proceed.

As a fall-back position, a utility program called ISPF was chosen to provide a friendlier interactive environment. ISPF was used to build on-line help screens, query the user for choices, manage the process of submitting jobs, and so forth.

Unfortunately, even the "fallback" position of the ISPF program was unacceptable. The response time for even the simplest tasks prohibited any realistic attempt to create an interactive environment. The problem again centered around the lack of support from the DP group to create interactive facilities. The consultant encouraged the MR group to consider obtaining their own dedicated machine. A relatively inexpensive minicomputer could provide the interactive resources much better than the mainframe. Unfortunately, the MR Department lacked "clout" when it came to machine issues and its proposal to acquire an independent minisystem. The DP group maintained its age-old position (oriented toward large batch-processing machines) and won the battle. A machine three times more powerful than the current hardware was procured, yet the commitment to provide interactive processing facilities was still ignored. Even on the new equipment, marketing inquiries remained batch oriented with a minimum of 30 minutes turnaround time.

Because of the control the DP group had on the computer planning process, the interactive needs of MR were never allowed to enter into the decision process. MR attempted to circumvent the problem by using their own budget to develop microcomputer capabilities for some of the elementary tasks. Because of the relative isolation of the micro user from the large, rich corporate data base on the central computer (controlled by the DP group) this approach was also less than satisfactory.

Reflection

Data processing departments have historically been responsible for financial and accounting functions of large organizations. As a result, they are typically assigned the role of "keeper of the computer." Because of a batch-processing orientation and a focus toward hardware technology, such groups rarely have an appreciation for interactive capabilities or the quantitative expertise to deal with problems that are analytical by nature (sales analysis, forecasting, consumer research, financial planning, advertising and promotion). This causes a general conflict between the manager responsible for market analysis and the DP staff that is out of touch with the needs of a user-oriented system. The manager requires a fast, user-friendly access to analyze the corporate base of information in an interactive fashion. The DP group can live with a method of operation where the interval between data entry and output can be measured in hours or days with no ill affects. In the final tally, the hostile or passive participation of the DP department can doom a decision-support project from the start. To circumvent such a pitfall, the development team should strive for a consensus on hardware and software issues at the beginning and insure that, if the on site DP group participates, a commitment of support is more than just lip service.

STUDY 5

A DECISION SUPPORT APPLICATION IN THE RAILROAD INDUSTRY

Serendipity is the word coined by Horace Walpole in his fairy tale about three princes of Ceylon (Serendip) with the habit of making fortunate discoveries accidentally. Decision-support applications frequently evolve to support important functions which were not part of their original objective. This study describes a large DSS that has come to support an ever-broadening stream of applications that were not anticipated in its original development. In the multifaceted world of DSS tools, it is perhaps an endearing quality of information networks, that once justified in concert with a specific application, they continue to grow into primary management tools themselves. Indeed, as this study attempts to point out, there is no more fertile ground for producing a large crop of useful and varied DSS tools than an in-place information network that allows access to a large base of corporate data. This study illustrates how a decision-support application frequently depends on the existing foundations of a large scale Management Information System (MIS).

Topic contributed by:
Frank Di Gialleonardo
RAILINC Corporation

Introduction

The Association of American Railroads (AAR) is a trade association established in 1934 to represent the major freight railroads of the United States, Canada and Mexico. In the early 1960s, the various railroads, through the AAR, sponsored the conceptualization and development of a system called TRAIN (Tele-Rail Automated Information Network) in order to track the movement of railroad rolling stock throughout North America. The number of cars and units in this continental system totals over 2 million, with each potentially making several significant point-to-point moves each day, including interchanges of equipment from one railroad to another.

The TRAIN system tracks the movement of each car on a detailed basis through the reporting of sightings over telecommunication lines to a central computer complex operated by RAILINC Corporation, the AAR's data processing subsidiary in Washington, D.C. (Exhibit 12–5a). At this central site, the data is edited, processed and used to compile a series of reports and data bases for management use in either on-line or batch mode. These movements result in a daily volume of system transactions which averages over 700,000 and often exceeds one million per day.

The problem the TRAIN systems was conceived to originally address was the allocation of freight cars to different geographic areas. At that time, there were frequent shortages of freight cars by type and by location. Government's control of the railroads was much greater than today, and the shortage of cars was viewed as a national issue which could require government intervention and control. One can easily imagine the alarm engendered by an inadequate supply of hopper cars to move grain from the midwest to market at harvest time.

Facing the possibility of government involvement and being concerned with the provision of an adequate supply of cars to meet demand, the railroads sought to develop a system and procedure which could centrally monitor the supply/demand relationship and issue directives for the movement of selected cars from one location to another in order to avoid shortages of necessary rolling stock. The central point of control was the AAR, and the information system upon which it based its directives became the TRAIN system.

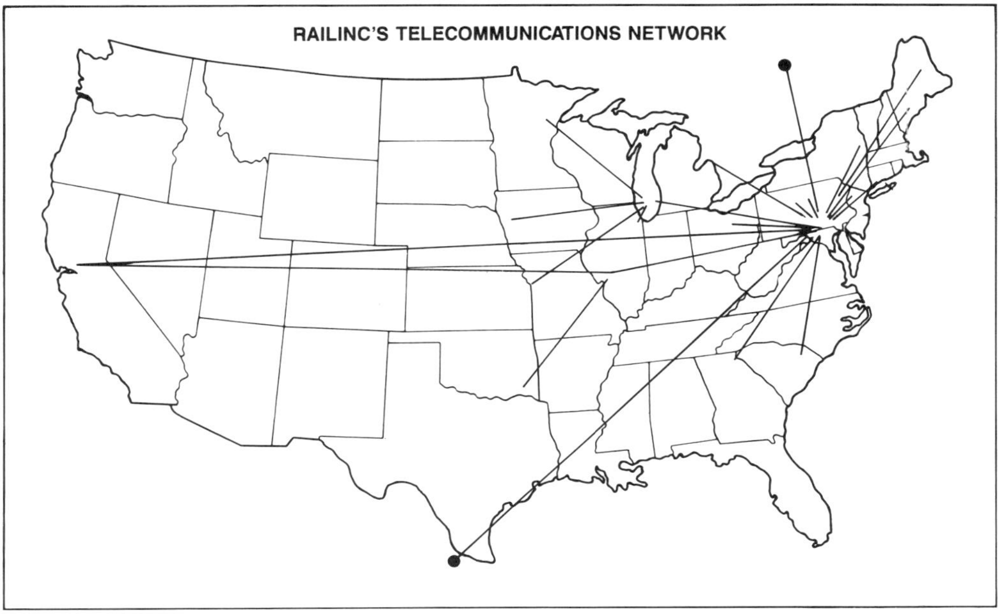

EXHIBIT 12–5a RAILINC's Telecommunication Network.

It is clear that the stakes in terms of lost business, deteriorated goods and agricultural products, and unfulfilled consumer demands was a strong incentive behind the creation and use of the TRAIN system. Without such motivation, it is not likely that the development of an electronic network linking the railroads would have received the financial and organizational backing necessary for successful development and implementation when it did. It was the TRAIN system and the problem it was conceived to address that brought about the development of a complex telecommunications network that today supports a wide variety of DSS and MIS applications.

The System and Its Use

Automation provides support through two primary activities (Chapter 2): information management and data quantification. In multinational operations, organizations typically rely on large scale data processing networks to maintain, transfer, and process large amounts of information. The major function of such MIS is to support the information management requirements of the operation. Decision-support applications often build upon the data made available via the MIS. In such situations the MIS and DSS aspects of automation are coupled to provide a more integrated framework to support the decision process. This section describes both aspects of the system to better understand the scope of the application.

CAR ACCOUNTING

Car owners, both private and rail, are paid for the use of equipment on a per diem and per mile basis administered through a complex set of payables procedures and rules. The point of junction between railroads demarcates the transfer of responsibility to pay for the "car hire." That is, Railroad A would be responsible for paying the owner up to the junction with Railroad B, after which Railroad B becomes responsible for the charges. Thus the point of junction or interchange is a key piece of information in calculating the car hire payable. Validation of a junction has been handled via a "junction slip." Soon after the establishment of the TRAIN System, it became apparent that this information could be sent over the network.

The effective use of this development required much more than the simple notion of conversion to electronic transfer. It also required the cooperation of railroad accounting organizations skilled in the arcane rules of computing car hire payables, acceptance by railroads of junction validation in electronic form, and the merger of electronic input to each railroad's payable system. While the initial purpose of the TRAIN System was to provide for *overall* monitoring and control by the AAR, individual railroads soon found the system to be useful in providing current information on the location of its own equipment on other railroads. This enabled better planning of equipment use and availability.

SHIPPER CAR TRACING

The recent interest in Japanese management techniques, particularly the minimization of inventory costs through "just in time" delivery of materials, has served to underscore one of the most important "unexpected" applications of the TRAIN network—car tracing for shippers. Each railroad traditionally supplied its shippers with location information to a greater or lesser extent. However, many shippers ship over several railroads and some shipments travel in this way every day, it is easy to appreciate the plight of shipper and railroad traffic departments in obtaining and providing up-to-date information on shipment status. Yet the importance of such information can also be seen. Think of the materials control officer in an assembly plant concerned with the timely arrival of short supply parts.

In response to this problem, shipper representatives in the form of the National Industrial Traffic League (NITL) and railroad industry traffic officers jointly proposed the use of the network for car tracing in 1978. As a result, a shipper assist messaging (SAM) service was born whereby a shipper could access the TRAIN network to obtain information on its "fleet" of shipments over all participating railroads. One electronic "call" replaced scores, even hundreds of phone calls and enables vast improvements in shipper service to their customers. Today, hundreds of shipper organizations are linked into the network through a variety of devices using dial-in or dedicated telecommunication lines.

ORDERING

Two types of ordering are currently performed electronically over the network. The first, Bill of Lading, represents the contract for railroad transportation service to transport a specific set of goods to a specified location. As a legally binding contract, the electronic transaction of Bills of Lading is significant in that both parties had to agree to jettison the usual contract "boilerplate" as part of the individual transaction and allow those contract provisions to function in the background as a general agreement between the parties under which individual electronic "contracts" would be governed.

A more recent development has been the use of the TRAIN network for transmission of purchase orders from railroads to their suppliers in electronic form (Exhibit 12–5b). The typical large railroad procures millions of dollars of supplies and equipment. The reduction of the multiplicity of purchase orders to electronic media is anticipated to eventually yield huge savings in the reduction of inventory stock needed on hand to avoid out-of-stock situations. A variety of quantitative forecasting procedures are used by certain participating railroads to predict the material supply requirements based on historical demand data.

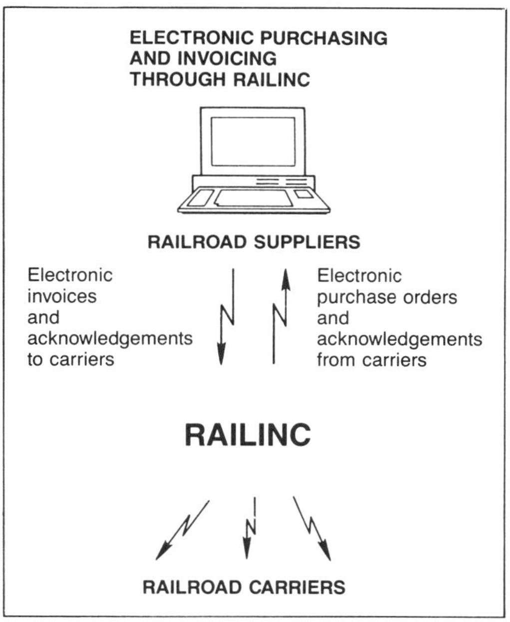

EXHIBIT 12–5b The Electronic Transaction Process for RAILINC.

OPTIMIZATION OF BACKHAUL

As in all transportation operations, the minimization of empty mile backhauls is a prime opportunity for reducing operational cost, increasing market share, and contributing to bottom line profits. The importance of minimizing backhaul distance is especially germane where very specialized equipment is used. This equipment is usually of high expense yet has few alternative uses (if any). For example, railroads have cooperated with auto manufacturers to optimize the routing of empty "multilevel" railcars used to ship autos from manufacturing plants to distributors.

Car location information streaming into the central computer via RAILINC's TRAIN network is funneled to a DSS which includes a linear programming application (Chapter 9) to recommend an optimal routing of the empty railcar to the nearest plant with a need. Other DSS applications are using car location information reported over the network to minimize the empty car miles in the overall rail system. Empty car mileage minimization translates into a reduced need for the amount of very costly equipment needed to support equivalent transportation services.

Reflections

The above examples are only a sampling for some of the more significant applications that have evolved from one initial concept, the establishment of the TRAIN system. Each is different in several respects but may share common development and implementation traits, which are summarized below.

PROMOTION BY AN ADVOCACY GROUP

Whether the group comes from outside of the organization, from within, or is a federation from both camps, the support of an advocacy group is usually an essential step in both the development and implementation of major business applications such as those described above (see "Power Base" in Chapter 11). Indeed, in order for effective implementation, it may be essential for the advocacy group to be intimately involved in the development process itself—especially where the application will change long standing procedures and traditions.

ADOPTION OF STANDARDS

A variety of standards groups have been involved in the applications on the TRAIN system. Long planning and painstaking attention to detail are necessary if such broad-based applications are expected to blossom in an interorganizational sense.

VIEW TO THE INVESTMENT

One cannot expect the corporation to invest large sums of money and resources without its perceiving either a substantial threat to its operations or significant profits or savings to be gained. Perhaps more importantly, an investment once made should be carefully husbanded so that its potential is fully utilized. The job of a DSS developer is hardly done when the application is completed. There must be evaluation and feedback of course, but there should also be thorough investigation of new opportunities that have been created as a result of the application and its supporting information framework. This was especially true with the TRAIN system. Follow-on applications were much easier to cost-justify because of the facility that was already in place.

LEGAL AND REGULATORY CONSIDERATIONS

Many large applications are, unfortunately, fraught with potential legal and regulatory issues (recall the "Layer of External Factors" in Chapter 3). For example, cooperation of companies within an industry to achieve overall economies might benefit both the participants as well as their customers through reduced cost and improved service. Yet those very actions could be construed as illegal collusion by federal or other regulatory bodies. A worthwhile application may have to await a long drawn out process of legal consideration and even petitions for exceptions from existing rules or legislation.

FOLLOW THROUGH FOR ACCEPTANCE

Even though the initial audience and approving management group may be "sold" on the application concept at the start, one must remember that most large scale applications will take a concerted sales effort at implementation time. A string of "road shows," question and answer sessions, and training support may be necessary to fully implement the application. Once changes in long standing methods and procedures are involved even the most malleable employee is likely to want to know why.

STUDY 6

SUPPORTING LARGE SCALE PRODUCTION/DISTRIBUTION DECISIONS

Decision-support tools are available today to help managers analyze the comlex issues associated with finding the best facility network for manufacturing and distributing goods to a large and diverse market. Although problems of great technical difficulty can now be solved, the measurement and reward structures of an organization can block successful implementation. Recall in Chapter 6 that not all decision-support applications result in executive operation of the system. In many of the more complex and large scale problems (Band 3 of Exhibit 2–1), the manager relies on the assistance of a team of experts to evaluate and analyze scenarios in question. This case study demonstrates the application of large scale optimization techniques to support the decision process.

Topic contributed by:
Dr. Richard Powers
INSIGHT, Inc.

Background

Plametco's Executive Committee was confronted with some disconcerting financial information. The company's senior managers were trying to generate alternative approaches to address several key issues:

- ☐ Distribution costs were growing faster than sales. In 1975 sales were \$238 million and distribution costs were \$13.8 million (5.8 percent of sales). By 1985 sales were up to \$800 million and distribution costs were \$64 million (8.0 percent of sales).
- ☐ Distribution costs were growing faster than manufacturing costs. In 1965 distribution costs represented 6.5 percent of the cost of goods sold. By 1975 the percentage was 8.2 percent, and by 1985 it was up to 11.4 percent, almost double the 1965 level.

- ☐ Inventory turns were down. Finished goods inventory turns were 7.5 per year in 1975; by 1985 turns were down to 6.0.

Plametco had been founded 60 years earlier in 1925. In 1985, the company was manufacturing a line of nondurable consumer goods using two separate production technologies. The original technology, dating back to the company's beginning, involved stamping and finishing metal goods. In 1930, the company was operating a plant in Hartford and a distribution warehouse in Chicago. In 1950, Plametco introduced a complimentary product line based on injection molded plastic. A plant to produce the new line was opened in Wilmington, Delaware.

The 1960s and 1970s saw a rapid expansion of Plametco's operations, stemming primarily from a very heavy emphasis on marketing. By 1980, the company was selling in all 50 states, supported by 17 warehouses throughout the country. Manufacturing capacity had also expanded. In addition to the original plant in Hartford, which still produced only metal products, a plant in Chicago produced both metal and plastic goods. The plant in Wilmington still produced only plastic, a plant in Atlanta produced only metal, and a plant in Houston produced only plastic.

With markets throughout the country served by 17 warehouses, the fact that all plants were east of the Rocky Mountains meant large freight costs to replenish the warehouses and high inventory levels at the warehouses to maintain desired service objectives. By 1985, distribution costs were $64 million, broken down roughly as follows:

Freight cost to customers	40%
Freight cost to replenish warehouses	35%
Inventory carrying cost	15%
Warehousing cost	10%

Plametco's management had been dealing with logistics issues on an ad hoc basis for several years. They recognized the significant dollars devoted to distributing their products, and they had taken action on several occasions aimed at influencing distribution costs and customer service. During the 1960s and 1970s, the period of the company's rapid market expansion, marketing executives had convinced top management that there had to be more warehouses to provide the customer service necessary to compete effectively. This was especially true for the western U.S. where there were five warehouses, four of which had been opened since 1970. Expanding the warehousing network did improve customer service and sales. It also reduced the freight costs to customers. At the same time, however, warehousing costs and inventory holding costs increased, as did replenishment freight costs. To deal with the increasingly higher replenishment freight expense, management decided to shift from trucks to much heavier use of rail replenishment for the warehouses in the west and southwest. This did reduce replenishment for the warehouses in the west and southwest. This did reduce replenishment freight costs, but it also increased warehousing costs and inventory holding costs, and had a negative impact on customer service.

Recognizing the increasing inventory levels as a drain on profits, management had decreed an arbitrary inventory reduction of 20 percent. This action did reduce inventory costs but at the same time driving transportation costs up, as well as decrementing customer service. While increased marketing efforts improved sales, the production facilities remained the same. To meet the greater demand, Plametco increased production capacity by converting what had previously been warehousing space at each of the five plant locations to supplemental production lines. As a consequence, finished products had to be moved out quickly, often to satellite warehousing locations in the same city as the plant. While production management was delighted with their continually decreasing unit production costs (to which bonuses were rated), distribution costs were adversely affected. Transportation, warehousing, and inventory costs had all increased.

Application Development

The executive committee knew something had to be done, but there was no agreement on what specific actions would yield the desired results. At this juncture the president of Plametco returned to first principles. He said, "We have a fundamental question we are trying to resolve. What production-distribution network will yield the greatest return on assets, given all the tradeoffs in our system?" The executive committee translated this overall objective into several specific issues:

- ☐ How many warehouses should there be, where should they be, and which customers should be served by each?
- ☐ Should new plant locations be opened and/or should the production mix among plants be changed?
- ☐ Which plants should provide which products to each warehouse, and what mix of transportation modes should be used?

It was recognized that to address the issues a huge amount of data had to be collected, integrated, and analyzed; such data as sales by customer by product for a year, transportation costs among all existing and potential network locations, warehousing and inventory holding costs, production costs, and capacity limits for various components in the network. Although Plametco's executives believed they could gather the necessary data, they did not believe they had the decision-support tools or skills to accomplish the effort internally. They decided to hire a consulting firm that was capable of modeling logistics systems. The consulting firm they selected specialized in optimization problems that required powerful data management software to make the quantitative models "user-friendly."

It took about six months to get all the data together and in the appropriate form. Another several months were devoted to using the modeling system to evaluate dozens of logistics network scenarios and "What If" questions. Based on the results, a set of recommendations was prepared for the executive committee, namely:

1. Acquire a new plant on the West Coast, preferably near Los Angeles. This plant should manufacture all product lines.

2. Add production capacity for plastic products to the Atlanta plant so that it could make the full product line.
3. Decrease the number of warehouses from 17 to nine, and make each warehouse a full line facility.

Implementation

By implementing the recommended changes, it was estimated that Plametco would save roughly $13 million a year in logistics costs. This represented a 20 percent savings in replenishment freight costs (only 6 replenishment lanes versus the original 22), warehousing costs, and inventory costs. Freight costs to customers was not expected to increase significantly even though the number of warehouses was cut almost in half. (With more effective warehouse stockage policies and clearly defined customer support patterns, fewer cross shipments between warehouse service areas would occur.)

Plametco's top management decided to gradually move toward the rationalized network indicated by the analysis. There was not complete agreement, however, about the savings potential for making all the recommended changes. The Vice President for Manufacturing was strongly opposed to opening a West Coast plant or to adding plastic lines to Atlanta. He argued that fragmenting production would result in inefficient production lot sizes, higher set-up and changeover costs, and thus, higher unit production costs overall (remember that the bonus structure was tied to production costs). The consultants suggested that perhaps the internal reward structure should be reviewed in conjunction with the network changes.

To date, some minor shifts have been made in production allocations, but no plastics production has been slated for Atlanta. A search is underway for a West Coast site, but no firm decision has been made to open a plant there. Two of the 17 warehouses have been closed, and the stockage and customer support patterns for each remaining warehouse have been changed. Although the most drastic recommended changes in the production-distribution network have not been made, Plametco is still expecting logistics cost savings of four to five percent with just the realignments which are being implemented.

Reflections

Integrating the huge mass of data inherent in complex production-distribution analysis virtually dictates a decision-support capability of some sort. In this case, optimization techniques (such as linear and integer programming) were used to support the decision process with substantial success. Although the tools were readily accepted by Plametco's management, when it came to implementing findings of the analysis, behavioral issues became dominant. Because the corporate reward structure was highly functional rather than integrative, opposition arose from those in the organization who felt threatened by the suggested changes. Until the fundamental organizational and reward system changes are made, it is doubtful that the full potential indicated by the analysis will be realized.

EXERCISES

1. For each case study, identify which quantitative models from Chapter 9 appears the most applicable (allocation models, distribution problems, activity scheduling, etc.).
2. Identify what level(s) of the decision process (Chapter 4) is being supported in each case study.
3. In each study, what software strategy was used (from scratch, composite approach, off-the-shelf)? If it is not clear which approach was used, state what strategy would appear the most appropriate.
4. In Chapter 2, we noted that an application does not always fall distinctively and completely into either the MIS or DSS domain. In many cases, the capabilities and uses of the system characterize a hybrid application (see Exhibit 2–2). In your opinion, which of the six case studies presented in this chapter appear to represent such a hybrid application?
5. At the end of Chapter 11, we discussed several typical roadblocks (rules of thumb) that led to an unsuccessful application. For each of the case studies that were estimated as unsuccessful (or not realized to their full potential) note which roadblock appeared to be at work.

13

On the Horizon—Future Direction in Decision Support

The rapid growth of modern technology can be attributed, in part, to the staggering rate of progress in the field of computer science. Today's innovations no longer have a life span measured in years but instead become obsolete in a manner of months. Advancements in capacity, speed, cost, and user interface will have significant implications in the area of decision support. The phrase "DSS" may be replaced by new terminology, yet decision-support applications will experience quantum leaps toward more effective and usable systems.

This chapter will explore some of the trends that are likely to influence future DSS capabilities and developments over the near horizon. Much of the research and innovation will focus on aspects of current systems that have precluded the concept of decision support from being applied to its full potential such as:

- ☐ Development cost and duration (productivity).
- ☐ Conversational user interaction.
- ☐ Increased longevity and life span (flexibility).
- ☐ User independence (through microsystems).

The material examines several initiatives that support these goals and play a key role in moving toward broader and more useful applications. Topics discussed include: implications of microcomputers; improvements in user interaction; the value of generic modeling systems; the implications of Artificial Intelligence as it relates to decision support; use of natural language processing; and advances in Expert Systems.

MICROCOMPUTERS

Computer science has seen more progress in less time than virtually any other technical field. Advances in automation capabilities have experienced not a linear but an exponential growth. Nowhere has this been more prevalent than with the creation of microcomputers [10,12,17,24]. Consider the advancement of chip memory capacity over the past few years. It took approximately four years to improve the 16K (16,000) bytes of memory to 64K, two years to advance to a 256K chip, and roughly one year later, the 512K chip went from the drawing board to specialized applications. This phenomenal rate of growth has resulted in many of the microsystems of today possessing both the speed and capacity of mainframes and the minisystems available in the 1970s, at only a fraction of the cost.

Economics has always been an important factor affecting trends in market development. During the era of mini/mainframe systems, the decision to invest in more innovative management techniques carried a substantial cost. In cases where hardware was already available, the organization still had to expend significant capital over the lifetime of a software package. Purchase or lease charges could range between $25,000 to $200,000 for the rights to use a proprietary system. With the advent of microcomputers the market potential for DSS applications has expanded significantly. With a broader customer base, vendors no longer need large price tags to cover development costs. Competition has also affected the tendency of companies to become complacent about user needs and financial fairness in their pricing strategies. Until recently the use of microcomputers for many decision-support applications was out of the question. The complicated mathematical procedures associated with analyzing complex and large scale problems exceeded the capabilities of microsystems. The analytical techniques used in many of the quantitative models are computationally intensive and require extreme speed and memory capacity. In the early 1980s, microcomputers with 128K of Random Access Memory (RAM) and less than one megabyte (one million bytes or characters) of disk storage were available for simple DSS applications but the more comprehensive problems remained unreachable.

By 1985, microsystems had been introduced with new chips (Motorola 68000) that provide speeds between five and 10 times faster, Random Access Memory (RAM) reaching 12 megabytes, and hard disk memory units with over 400 megabytes of memory: all for a price ranging between $6,000 to $50,000. For example, the stride microcomputer series introduced in 1985 is roughly six times faster than the original IBM-PC, and even exceeds the computational speeds of most minisystems (Exhibitg 13–1). Although the Stride series is aimed at specialized applications (engineering, software development, operations research, etc.), the more generalized business systems (like IBM-AT, HP150, Micro Vax 2, etc.) have improved significantly over systems available three years ago.

ERATOSTHENENES SIEVE PRIME NUMBER BENCHMARK*				
Machine (Chip)	**p-Code Pascal**	**Native Pascal**	**C**	**Assembly**
Stride (12 MHz 68000)	26.3	2.73	1.78	0.93
Stride (10 MHz 68000)	31.5	3.28	2.13	1.12
Sage (8 MHz 68000)	39.4	4.1	2.70	1.40
IBM PC (8088)	147.0	19.4	22.10	4.00
TRS-80 Mod II (Z-80)	274.0	n/a	n/a	n/a
Apple II (6502)	516.0	n/a	n/a	n/a
Macintosh (68000)	69.0	n/a	n/a	2.3
Wicat 150 (68000)	n/a	6.5	4.7	n/a
Charles River (68000)	n/a	n/a	6.3	n/a
PDP-11/60	n/a	4.5	n/a	n/a
VAX-11/750	n/a	n/a	3.1	n/a

EXHIBIT 13–1 Comparison of Computational Speeds. Numbers represent run time in seconds. The lower the value, the faster the computer. *Courtesy of* Stride Microcomputers, Inc.

For under $6,000, a common microcomputer can be obtained with two megabytes of RAM, 20 megabytes of disk storage, and a multitude of application and utility packages. These systems are also capable of using virtually every type of compiler for the higher order languages (FORTRAN, COBOL, APL, ADA, PASCAL, etc.) used to create a DSS (Chapter 10).

The increase of speed and memory capacity makes microcomputers a practical alternative for many large scale applications that had previously been possible only on mini/mainframe series computers. With the current rate of technological advancement, it is a safe assumption that by the early 1990s microcomputers will achieve RAM memory exceeding 50 megabytes and hard disk storage measured in the thousands of megabytes, all for the approximate price of what today's systems cost. Few (if any) of the potential areas for decision support cannot be satisfied by such capability.

The reason why microcomputers offer such great appeal stems from both cost effectiveness and the freedom provided by independent automation facilities. With minimal risk, virtually any organization can afford to "experiment" with between $5,000 and $50,000 depending on the application. Management also need not depend on assistance from in-house programming resources that often have great difficulty in appreciating the decision-making environment. Unlike mini or mainframes that bring all users to a halt when they fail, multiple microcomputer stations can function independently and in harmony. Microcomputers are so inexpensive that in areas of high dependence it pays to purchase additional systems for back up in the event of failure. Also, because of the significant market base, the number of commercially available low price DSS packages for microcomputers is expanding much faster than mini/mainframe systems.

THE USER INTERFACE

It has previously been noted that the interface between computer and user plays a key role to the value and success of a decision-support application. We will discuss several innovative approaches and market trends currently underway that will contribute significantly toward improving user interaction in DSS applications, specifically: more prevalent use of embedded help facilities and self-instructional aids, the advent of icon/window oriented displays, and the availability and use of Natural Language Processing. We will discuss the first two trends here and come back to "Natural Language Processing" in the section entitled "Artificial Intelligence."

User Assistance

Because of the associated development cost and state of the art, the majority of early DSS applications were built upon a command-oriented structure (Chapter 8) for user entry. The products relied upon significant user training, offline documentation, and continual familiarity in order to effectively utilize the systems capabilities. Today, however, the trend for many DSS products is to establish a more user-tolerant environment using help options, menu structures, on-line tutoring, conversational prompts, and so forth. Some of the older products (like RAMIS, IFPS and FOCUS) attempt to achieve this by providing optional modes of user interaction (succinct commands, menu driven, verbose prompts, English dialogue, etc.). Many of the newer products (like CLIPS, STATVIEW, DECISION-AIDE) have instead designed their user interface from scratch with a conversational interactive environment. This trend is likely to continue given the recognition and acceptance reflected by the user base.

Icon /Window Oriented Display

Early in the 1980s, a revolutionary approach to user-oriented computer applications was introduced to a broad-based market by Apple Computers, Inc. with their line of MacIntosh products.[1] The MacIntosh combines four innovative features that reflect an operational environment analogous to how humans think and that is conducive to user-

---

[1]Although XEREO was one of the originators of icon/window oriented displays, Apple Computer was the first to establish a broad-base microcomputer product (initially with its LISA product line and finally with the MacIntosh) that provided a multitude of software applications and features aimed at the novice.

oriented applications, namely: positioning and designation of user entities using a hand-held omni-directional roller device (referred to as a "mouse"); symbolic screen figures (called "icons") that represent system components and operations (such as the printer, files, disk drives, copy operations, etc.); continually available menus that visually open (into what are referred to as "windows") to highlight possible options; and a significantly cost effective-high resolution screen. Simply stated, the user coordinates the movement of a desk top mouse with a pointer on the screen to indicate what actions are to be taken (menu windows opened, options selected, files transferred, disk renamed, etc.) and where information is to be entered/stored. All interactions are accomplished via a pictorial representation that mimicks the physical world. Icon/window oriented displays can now be found in a variety of computer applications, for example: GEM (graphic representation on an IBM-PC/XT), INSIGHT's Micro Dispatcher (shipping and distribution operations), STATVIEW (statistical analysis), and JANUS (a two-dimensional combat simulation used to provide commander training).

GENERIC MODELING SYSTEMS

Most decision-support applications rely heavily on quantitative procedures to analyze complex problems. The traditional approach is to model the situation and to design the program around the structure of the particular problem. Terminology, names, prompts, display headings, and so forth, are coded into the program to satisfy the needs of the specific application.

There are certain classes of problems where the underlying structure and quantitative model is virtually equivalent. Network optimization (Chapter 9) provides a good example. In cases where network procedures apply, the mathematical model and formulation are essentially the same. Material distribution, production scheduling, inventory management, and similar problems can be easily modeled and solved with a network formulation.

With significant foresight and program planning, generic packages can be designed to satisfy a broad class of decision-support applications. Options are created within the program that allow the designer (or user) to fit the package to a particular problem without modifying the code. CONVERNET is one example of a generic system that can be applied to a multitude of complex decisions that can be modeled as a network. The user can alter what a node represents (cities, workstations, plants, warehouses, time periods, etc.), what an arc indicates (a route, pipeline, work assignment, investment, powerline, etc.); redefine what the characters of an arc are called (cost, profit, time, interest) and so forth. In this manner, the system can be tailored to the requirements of a particular problem.

Generic systems hold great promise for reducing both the time and cost for creating a successful DSS application. They are, however, extremely difficult to design. The effort to develop a generic system can be many times greater than a DSS created for a singular application. The programming code can also be significantly larger and require innovative programming procedures to fit within the confines of available memory space.

Nonetheless, generic systems offer an avenue for significant advancement and are likely to become more predominant in the near future.

ARTIFICIAL INTELLIGENCE

The General Prognosis

Artificial Intelligence (or simply AI) is the "in phrase" of the 1980s. AI tools and techniques have broad implications that spans from robotics to automated manufacturing and includes Natural Language Processing (NLP), Expert Systems, and that segment of decision support where a computer is used to emulate the human thought process. AI will eventually permit the user to ask:

> I WANT TO KNOW HOW I SHOULD INVEST NEW PROFITS FOR THIS YEAR GIVEN THREE DIFFERENT PROFILES OF RETAINED EARNINGS: 10 PERCENT, 25 PERCENT AND 50 PERCENT. CONSIDER A TIME HORIZON OF SEVEN YEARS. POTENTIAL INVESTMENTS ARE: STOCK OPTIONS ON XYZ INC., CAPITAL INVESTMENT THROUGH FLEET UPGRADE OR BUILDING A NEW PLANT, AND PURCHASE OF LONG-TERM BONDS. THE DATA FOR EACH OF THESE OPTIONS IS CONTAINED IN THE FILES CALLED "STOCK," "FLEET," "PLANT" AND "BOND," RESPECTIVELY. PROVIDE ANY ADDITIONAL SCENARIOS I HAVE MISSED OR OTHER INVESTMENT ALTERNATIVES THAT MAY OPTIMIZE LONG-TERM GAIN, ALONG WITH THE ASSOCIATED RISK.

The computer would analyze the manager's request, ask for any missing conditions or information, and then display the results for each alternative. The system would then suggest other alternatives to consider and inform the user of how these results would change under different conditions.

There is currently much confusion as to the real substance behind the concept of Artificial Intelligence. In the last few years, the phrase "Artificial Intelligence" has been applied across the total spectrum of automation. There is also disagreement as to the present state of the art [1,3,4,9,16,19,22,23,25]. Some feel that AI is far from a position where it exists in a practical form. Others advertise that we have already entered the realm where true AI applications exist.

It should be obvious that technology has a long way to go before we achieve the capabilities depicted in the previous example. Significant AI research, however, is underway. The AI market is expected to grow from roughly $700 million in 1985 to over $4 billion in 1990 [27]. With this investment, something is bound to happen. Systems that support the decision maker through simulated deductive reasoning should begin to appear in the next seven to 10 years, provided the profession recognizes the reluctance of management to tolerate concepts and technology that do not become applicable to real world problems. Much of the current expenditures and market for AI has been generated by the developers themselves. The field cannot afford many mistakes or it will be pushed aside for a new approach. Research must be aimed at satisfying the true needs of managers and not merely for the sake of research itself.

Natural Language Processing

Systems possessing the various user friendly features discussed in Chapter 8 are conversational by nature and easy for nontechnical users to apply. There is another plateau, however, that allows a user to communicate with the computer in a free form that emulates the natural language of the user. A natural language interface offers great latitude and promise for applying automation directly into the decision process [5,13,14,15,18]. The concept is to provide an unstructured and unconstrained interaction between the user and the computer. All instructions are entered in the spoken tongue in the same manner they would be stated verbally. For example:

> "LIST ALL SALES IN TEXAS FOR OUR WINTER PRODUCE LINE THAT OCCURRED BETWEEN NOVEMBER AND JANUARY. SORT THEM ALPHABETICALLY AND BY DEPARTMENT. THEN DISPLAY SALES BY DEPARTMENT IN A PIE CHART."

Although NLP systems are in their infancy, there are several commercially available products that allow the user to interact with the computer in a style that emulates his normal everyday language. The Le Courtier stockbroker system discussed in Chapter 5 is one example of a specific (domain dependent) application that provides a natural language interface with the user. Another would be the INTELLECT system marketed by Artificial Intelligence Inc. INTELLECT is an ad hoc data base query system that allows the user to state his requirements (for example, what information he wishes to see) in everyday English. Exhibit 13-2 provides a simple illustration of INTELLECT

Show me what percent of total salaries is for managers in each department.

PRINT A PERCENTAGE OF THE TOTAL ANNUAL SALARY IN EACH DEPARTMENT OF ALL EMPLOYEES WITH EEO=MANAGER.

DEPARTMENT	SALARY	PERCENT
ACCOUNTING	$25,560.00	1.94
ADMINISTRATION	$162,924.00	12.37
CUSTOMER SERVICE	$56,880.00	4.32
DATA PROCESSING	$224,808.00	17.07
FINANCIAL PLANNING	$45,000.00	3.42
HUMAN RESOURCES	$20,400.00	1.55
RESEARCH	$39,600.00	3.01
SALES & MARKETING	$368,820.00	28.01
STORES	$341,940.00	25.97
TRAINING	$30,909.00	2.35
OVERALL	$1,316,841.00	100.00

EXHIBIT 13-2 Example of a Natural Language Processor. Courtesy of Artificial Intelligence, Inc.

in action. The top line indicates what the user asks (types into) the system. The next two lines reflect what the computer echos back to the user to reveal its understanding of the question (task). The remainder depicts the results of the data base query. Another area of significant potential are portable NLP systems (programs that can be linked with other DSS components to provide a natural language interface for general DSS application). TEAMS (Transportable English Access Mechanism System) is an example of a portable NLP under development by SRI [1].

Many of the marketed Fourth Generation Language (4GL) based systems are beginning to recognize the potential behind NLP and are providing "natural language" capabilities with their DSS products. RAMIS II (from Martin Marietta Data Systems) and FOCUS (from Information Builders in New York) are two examples of 4GL vendors that now offer NLP features and options within long standing product lines [14]. Exhibit 13-3 illustrates how one 4GL product (RAMIS II ENGLISH) uses NLP to improve user interaction. Exhibit 13-3a shows a simplified application where the user asks

what products have been sold with a price of less than the unit cost?

PRODUCT

WORD PROCESSOR-1
WORD PROCESSOR-4

WHAT

how many of our accounts have purchased more than 500,000 dollars?

The answer is 1.

HOW MANY

when were they sold?

More than one field name associated with the word: WHEN
1=YEAR
2=MONTH
3=DAY
4=ALL OF THE ABOVE

Please enter the number of the fieldname to use
or (CR) to cancel the request:
4

YEAR	MONTH	DAY	PRODUCTS
83	2	21	WORD PROCESSOR-1
		28	WORD PROCESSOR-1
*	*	*	*
*	*	*	*
*	*	*	*

A REQUEST FOR CLARIFICATION

more than 300,000 dollars?

Referring back to the previous request.
Paraphrase of request.

COUNT THE UNIQUE CUSTOMER ENTRIES IF THE TOTAL VALUE IS GREATER THAN 300000.

Is this okay?
Please enter "YES" or "NO":
yes

The answer is 5

REFER BACK

EXHIBIT 13-3a Using a Natural Language Interface for a Simple Information Query. RAMIS II ENGLISH, *Courtesy of* Martin Marietta Data Systems.

KNOWLEDGE BASE
INCORPORATES SPECIAL VOCABULARY

give me a sales summary for our best customers

CUSTOMER	AREA	UNITS	REVENUE
ABN	EAST	1224	$588,750.28
ANDERSON CONTROLS	SOUTH	481	$325,008.85
INFORMATION, INC.	WEST	409	$326,360.85
SHANNON INDUSTRIALS	SOUTH	525	$330,741.29

SUPPORTS EVOLUTIONARY THOUGHT PROCESS

how many customers bought more than 10 furniture items last month?
the answer is 8.
more than 30?
the answer is 3.
list them and their salesreps.

SALESPERSON	CUSTOMER
REID	ROSS AND YOUNG INS.
WEISS	GENERAL UTILITIES
YOUNG	IF A SUPERMARKETS

ANY NUMBER OF SENTENCES

break that down by product type for the southern region, add column totals.

PRODTYPE	AREA	CUSTOMER	UNITS	REVENUE
ELECTRONICS	SOUTH	ANDERSON CONTROLS	59	$108,325.46
		SHANNON INDUSTRIALS	27	$46,325.00
FILES	SOUTH	ANDERSON CONTROLS	47	$30,196.37
		SHANNON INDUSTRIALS	65	$24,818.95
FURNITURE	SOUTH	ANDERSON CONTROLS	311	$93,742.73
		SHANNON INDUSTRIALS	348	$107,997.44
TERMINALS	SOUTH	ANDERSON CONTROLS	64	$92,744.10
		SHANNON INDUSTRIALS	95	$151,599.90
TOTAL			1006	$855,749.94

DEFINE NEW FIELDS

ASSUME THAT PROFIT IS DEFINED AS QUANTITY TIMES THE DIFFERENCE BETWEEN LIST PRICE AND UNIT COST. ALSO SUPPOSE THAT MARGIN EQUALS LIST PRICE MINUS UNIT COST. SHOW ME THE TOTAL PROFIT FOR EACH PRODUCT WHOSE MARGIN IS OVER 50.

PRODUCT	PROFIT
GRAPHICS DISPLAY	21,833
PERSONAL COMPUTER	182,337

EXHIBIT 13–3b A More Comprehensive Application of Natural Language Processing. RAMIS II ENGLISH, *Courtesy* Martin Marietta Data System.

four relatively simple questions in a natural language. Exhibit 13-3b depicts the evolution of a somewhat more comprehensive query of the system, but still in a form that emulates the everyday language of the user.

Although the general application of natural language processing is in its infancy, advancements over the next few years are likely to benefit the field of decision support significantly. Estimates indicate [27] that the $40 million spent on natural language initiatives in 1984 will grow to over $600 million by 1990. References [2,11] provide an extensive survey of NLP research and currently available systems.

Expert Systems

Virtually every discipline and organization contains a small core of experts that possess the accumulated knowledge and technical expertise necessary to analyze difficult problems. Consider the doctor trying to diagnose an illness, an avionics technician attempting to identify the cause for equipment failure, a mining exploration team evaluating samples for potential mineral deposits, or a lawyer searching for the best legal defense in a specific case. Each situation requires that a significant degree of operational experience, corporate memory and technical training be used to support a difficult decision. Chapter 5 introduced "Expert Systems" as a special class of automated support that allows individuals to draw on the experience and insight of specialists in a particular field. We will examine three areas were advances in Expert Systems will significantly benefit decision-support applications, namely: use as the front end of a 4GL; increased applications on microcomputers; and use of Expert System Generators (Chapter 5).

One of the shortfalls noted with 4GLs (Chapter 10) is the extent of training and user "preparedness" required to exercise the full capabilities of 4GLs. The knowledge base building capabilities of an Expert System will allow a user to define the problem and create the application more expeditiously and with less training [6,7]. The application of Expert Systems on microcomputers has been limited to relatively small problems because of the memory and speed required to transcribe human knowledge and experience into the computer. In large problems the knowledge base can be made up of literally thousands of different rules and conditions. Until recently, the capacity of microcomputers has been too restrictive for any practical large scale application of Expert Systems [8]. As noted earlier, high performance microsystems are now available with sufficient memory and speed to handle large scale applications on a selective basis. Over the next few years, the growth in memory capacity and computational speed will continue to spread into the general business microcomputers with a similar affect on the potential market for microbased Expert Systems.

Chapter 5 provided several examples of Expert Systems that were designed and structured around a specific application (medical analysis, maintenance support, tax accounting, etc.). The cost of developing such capabilities from scratch (Chapter 10) is significant. In the past few years, there has been an increased emphasis on "generator systems" that can be used to build an Expert System for virtually any application. An Expert System is still "built" and tailored for each situation, but not from scratch. The *builder* package is used to help a developer create an Expert System for a particular application by using the package's facilities to define the characters, features, requirements, and decision rules pertaining to the specific problem. Appendix A lists some of the commercial packages that can be used to build Expert Systems for microcomputers.

REFERENCES AND SUGGESTED READING

1. Andriole, S., "The Promise of Artificial Intelligence," *Journal of Systems Management,* July, 1985.
2. Alexander, T., "Artificial Intelligence," *Popular Computing,* May, 1985.
3. Bender, E., "AI On Micros Stirs Debate," *Computerworld,* June, 24, 1985.
4. Briggs, G., "Micro's Role Seen Expanding Greatly in AI World," *Management Information Systems Weekly,* April 17, 1985.
5. Bryant, S., "Talk Naturally," *Computer Decisions,* August, 1984.
6. Cobb, R., "Fourth Generation Languages: From Backwater to Mainstream," *Computerworld,* October 14, 1985.
7. Cobb, R., "In Praise of 4GLs," *Computerworld,* July 15, 1985.
8. Fertig, R., "Small Expert Systems OK—As Far As They Go," *Management Information Systems Week,* May 22, 1985.
9. Foster, E., "Artificial Intelligence," *Personal Computing,* April, 1985.
10. Foster, S., "Broadening Your Personal Computers' Horizons," *Computer Decisions,* January, 1984.
11. Gevarter, W., *Artificial Intelligence, Expert Systems, Computer Vision, and Natural Language Processing,* Park Ridge, N.J.: Noyes Publishing, 1984.
12. Goodman, D., "How Much Memory is Enough?," *PC World,* June, 1984.
13. Harris, L., "Teaching Computers English...," *Mini-Micro Systems,* December, 1984.
14. Johnson, T., "NLP Takes Off," *Datamation,* January 15, 1986.
15. Lehnert, W. and M. Ringle, *Strategies for Natural Language Processing,* London, England: Lawrence Erlbaum Associates, 1982.
16. Martins, G., "The Overselling of Expert Systems," *Datamation,* January, 1985.
17. Milden, C., "Capitalizing on the Microcomputer Software Boom," *Mini-Micro Systems,* September, 1984.
18. Miller, M., "Natural Language Interfaces," *Popular Computing,* June, 1985.
19. Rauch, W., "Artificial Intelligence: Coming of Age," *Systems & Software,* August, 1984.
20. Roberts, S., "Computers Simulate Human Experts," *Mini-Micro Systems,* September, 1983.
21. Roberts, S., "Artificial Intelligence," *Mini-Micro Systems,* December, 1983.

22. Seaman, J., "Artificial Intelligence: Out of the Lab into the Workplace," *Computer Decisions,* August, 1984.

23. Spoerl, J., "AI Environment Speeds Software Development," *Systems & Software,* August, 1984.

24. Stang, D., "Future Appears Bright For Micros," *Government Computer News,* June 7, 1985.

25. Tate, P., "The Blossoming of European AI," *Datamation,* November 1, 1984.

26. Ten Dyke, R., "Outlook On Artificial Intelligence," *Journal of Information Systems Management,* Fall, 1984, Vol. 1, no. 4.

27. "Toward the Fifth Generation," *Computerworld,* May 6, 1985.

Appendix A
Commercially Available Packages

All listed packages are interactive. Targeted audience varies for each package (technically naive, technically informed, technically oriented [Chapter 4]). Current events have demonstrated that the software market is quite volatile and unstable. The products and vendors were commercially available at the end of 1985.

TYPE	*PRODUCT NAME*	*VENDOR*	*HARDWARE*
Thought Structuring Systems Chapter 5)	LIGHTYEAR	Lightyear Inc. 1333 Lawerance Expressway Santa Clara, CA 95051	IBM-PC/XT
	DECISION-AIDE	Kepner-Tregoe Inc. Research Road, P.O. Box 704 Princeton, NJ 08540	IBM-PC/XT HP150 DEC Rainbow
	EXPERT CHOICE	Decision Support Software 1300 Vincent Place McLean, VA 22101	IBM-PC/XT
Conversational Linear/Integer Programming	CLIPS	MKSC P.O. Box 454 White Plains, MD 20695	IBM-PC/XT

TYPE	*PRODUCT NAME*	*VENDOR*	*HARDWARE*
Network Analysis (simulation, decision trees)	CONFIDENCE FACTOR	Simple Software 2 Pinewood Irvine, CA 92714	IBM-PC/XT HP150 DEC RAINBOW
	ARBORIST	Texas Instruments Inc. P.O. Box 1444 Houston, TX 77251	IBM-PC/XT TI
Conversational Network Optimization	CONVERNET	MKSC P.O. Box 454 White Plains, MD 20695	IBM-PC/XT
Project Management	PERTMASTER	Westminster Software 660 Hansen Way, Suite 2 Palo Alto, CA 94304	IBM-PC/XT HP150
	TIMELINE	Breakthrough Software 505 San Marin Drive Novato, CA 94947	IBM-PC/XT HP150
	PROJECTMASTER	Simple Software Inc. 2 Pinewood Irvine, CA 92714	DEC RAINBOW IBM-PC/XT
	VUE	National Information Systems Suite 130 20370 Town Center Lane Cupertino, CA 95014	HP3000, IBM DEC 20, VAX IBM-PC/XT
	WORKBENCH	ABT 6th Floor 365 Broadway New York, NY 10013	IBM-PC/XT
	PRO-JECT 6	Soft Corp. Inc. Suite 244, 2340 State Road Clearwater, FL 33575	IBM-PC/XT
	HARVARD PROJECT MANAGER	Harvard Software 521 Great Road Littleton, MA 01460	IBM-PC/XT
	MICROSOFT PROJECT	Microsoft Corp. 10700 Northrup Way Bellevue, WA 98009	IBM-PC/XT
	MACPROJECT	Apple Computer Inc. 20525 Mariani Avenue Cupertino, CA 95014	MacIntosh
Financial Planning/ Ad hoc query	EASY PLANNER	SORCIM 2195 Fortune Drive San Jose, CA 95131	IBM-PC/XT

TYPE	*PRODUCT NAME*	*VENDOR*	*HARDWARE*
	MICRO IMPACT DSS	MDCR Inc. 760 Highway 18 East Brunswick, NJ 08816	IBM-PC/XT DEC RAINBOW
	IFPS	Execucom 3410 Far West Boulevard Austin, TX 78731	IBMs, VAX, CDC DEC20,PRIME,HP3000 IBM-PC/XT
	EMPIRE	Applied Data Research Route 206 and Orchard Road Princeton, NJ 08540	IBMs, VAX DEC 20
	OZ	Fox & Geller Inc. 604 Market Street Elmwood Park, NJ 07407	IBM-PC/XT
	PROPHIT	Via Computers 7177 Construction Court San Diego, CA 92121	IBM-PC/XT
	FORESIGHT	Compro Financial Systems 6025 Corners Parkway Norcross, GA 30092	IBMs, PRIME VAX, HP3000
	FOCUS	Information Builders Inc. 1250 Broadway New York, NY 10001	IBMs, DEC20 VAX, Wang, IBM-PC/XT
	JAVELIN	Javelin Software Corp. One Kendall Square Cambridge, MA 02139	IBM-PC/XT
	EXCEL	Microsoft Corp. 10700 Northrup Way Bellevue, WA 98009	MacIntosh
	TRAPEZE	Data Tailor Inc. 1300 S. University Drive Fort Worth, TX 76107	MacIntosh
Statistical Analysis	STATVIEW	Brain Power Inc. 24009 Ventura Boulevard Calabasas, CA 91302	MacIntosh
	SYSTAT	SYSTAT Inc. 2901 Central Street Evanston, IL 60201	IBM-PC/XT MicroVax
	SAS	SAS Institute Inc. Box 8000, SAS Circle Cary, NC 27511	IBMs, VAX IBM-PC/XT
	EXEC*U*STAT	Exec*U*Stat Inc. Research Park 2 Wall Street Princeton, NJ 08540	IBM-PC/XT

TYPE	*PRODUCT NAME*	*VENDOR*	*HARDWARE*
	FORECAST MASTER	Scientific Systems Inc. One Alewife Place 35 Cambridge Park Drive Cambridge, MA 02140	IBM-PC/XT
	STATGRAPHICS	STSC Inc. 2115 East Jefferson Street Rockville, MD 20852	IBM-PC/XT
	STATPRO	Penton Software Inc. 420 Lexington Avenue New York, NY 10017	IBM-PC/XT
Packages to Build Expert Systems	TIMM	General Research Corp. McLean, VA	IBM-PC/XT
	M.1	Teknowledge Inc. 525 University Avenue Palo Alto, CA 94304	IBM-PC/XT
	EXSYS	EXSYS Box 75158 Contract Station 14 Albuquerque, NM 87194	IBM-PC/XT
	EXPERT EASE	Human Edge Software Palo Alto, CA 94304	IBM-PC/XT
	KDS	KDS Corp. Wilmette, IL	IBM-PC/XT
	RULE MASTER	Radian Corp. Austin, TX	IBM-PC/XT

Appendix B
Answers to the Exercises

CHAPTER 1

1. a. There are at least three potential causes for the mismatch between user needs and many of today's promoted systems:
   - ☐ *Misrepresentation.* Whether it is intentional or not, many of the marketed DSS products oversell their capabilities and features. Many vendors rely on the fuzzy nature of ecstatically pleasing terms like "user-friendly" or "Natural Language Interface" to catch the eye of a potential customer in a highly competitive market.
   - ☐ *Divergent Perspectives.* Historically, those involved in the construction of information systems are accustomed to dealing with complex procedures and a technically-oriented syntax. Managers have neither the time nor the inclination to struggle with a syntax that is anything but tolerant to the user and communicates with the manager in his terms.
   - ☐ *Different Environments.* Managers deal with a multitude of diversely different problems and tasks each day, often with little time to respond with a decision. Systems' designers are typically in a more controlled environment. Although they work on many projects at one time, the fundamental principles and structures are essentially the same. The designer is adept to a computer interface because he must deal with it on a continuous basis. The computer is the focal point of the designer's profession. On the other hand, computer support to a manager is viewed

as an auxilliary tool that he may use on occasion. There are usually significant gaps between sessions when the system is used (sometimes weeks or even months). The manager cannot afford the luxury to relearn and become familiar again with using the system. In Chapter 8 we discussed some of the features that should be built into a DSS to help a manager use the system in his environment at his pace.

b. There are numerous defense mechanisms discussed throughout the text that help protect against purchasing a system that will eventually lead to dissatisfaction. To summarize:

- ☐ Whenever possible, ask for a free trial period or a demonstration unit. Vendors with a good product have confidence that the product will sell itself and are usually willing and prepared for such an arrangement.
- ☐ When this is not possible, try to purchase a users manual by itself. Examine its contents to see whether it suits your needs and is easy to follow.
- ☐ Some of the periodical literature on information systems are oriented toward users and often provide surveys or articles on the pros and cons of current systems, or major causes for user dissatisfaction. The references at the conclusion of each chapter provide examples of such periodic literature.

3. Microcomputers have had a positive effect on expanding the user base of decision-support applications. Additional benefits include:

- ☐ Broadening the scope of DSS products and markets by encouraging small firms to apply their expertise in a particular area, or to go commercial with a tool designed specifically for their organization or client.
- ☐ Improving the cost effectiveness of DSS applications by reducing the cost of associated hardware and software.
- ☐ Reducing the risk of costly mistakes by allowing organizations to evaluate (or prototype) a new approach to a particular problem at minimal cost.
- ☐ Reducing the overhead and operating expenses for using automated support.

Although the advent of microcomputers will continue to benefit the field of DSS, there are certain negative "side effects" that an organization can experience and should take into account:

- ☐ At present there is no industrial standard that insures the microcomputer hardware (and software) supplied by various vendors will be operationally compatible with one another. Without proper planning and acquisition control, an organization can frequently find itself with a large number of applications that cannot interact or work with one another.
- ☐ Because of the low cost of microcomputer based applications, the process for defining the requirement, justifying the need, and evaluating various products is often ignored. This increases the likelihood of failure.
- ☐ The cost associated with a mini/mainframe application provides incentive for an organization to commit the personnel resources and administrative policies to institutionalize operation of the system. Because of the minimal investment required for a microcomputer based application, systems are often distributed across the organization without a logical, controlled and consistent implementation plan.

4. a. A computerized *product* for controlling and managing a manufacturing process.

   b. An *application* for planning and managing personnel resources.

c. A mathematical *technique* used in many DSS.
d. A *technique* used to manage the phased implementation of an information system.
e. A quantitative *technique* incorporated into various applications.

CHAPTER 2

1. The following noted applications are DSS used at various levels within the organization to evaluate complex situations and formulate a preferred course of action: b, c, e, g, h, i, j.

2. a. Automation of any sort is a tool, and any tool that increases a managers work, without some corresponding benefit, will not be used. Remember that a DSS provides the decision maker with more latitude as to the alternatives he can choose from and greater insight as to the affects on his actions. In many cases the freedom and ease with which a user can examine and evaluate alternative situations enlarges the scope of the decision process and, as a result, increases the effort a manager must concentrate on any particular problem.
   b. Shedding more light and knowledge as to the implications of various alternatives carries the associated benefit of more effective and less risky decisions with fewer surprises.
   c. When a decision maker uses a DSS in a setting where management objectives are subjective, or there is significant uncertainty as to the exact conditions and factors that play a part in influencing the outcome, then a greater range of possibilities must be considered. When, in addition to finding better solutions to how an operation should be carried out (production scheduling, product distribution, etc.), the system reduces the manual effort that would be necessary without automated support, then the result is not an increase in workload but an offset in savings.

3. b. Operations planning and management.
   c. Workload and demand forecasting.
   e. Resource allocation and acquisition.
   g. Operations planning and management.
   h. Workload and demand forecasting.
   i. Resource allocation and acquisition.
   j. Process evaluation and analysis.

CHAPTER 3

1. a. *External*—Legal repercussions*, loss of political support, loss of support from financial institutions for future capital, government pressure*, etc.

   Organizational—Local public image, labor/union reactions, established disaster response policy, potential cost of repeated incidence*, customer reactions, etc.

   Operational—History of previous instances, plant recording instrument measurements just before the explosion, files on recent preventive maintenance or equipment failures, observations from plant survivors, production capacity of other plants to carry the overload if similarly upgraded operations are shut down, etc.

b. *External*—Market share*, financial options for obtaining capital*, stability and history of other companies, etc.

Organizational—Return on investment, existing experience of your organization in that market area, opinions from the board of directors*, etc.

Operational—Current production capabilities, option to use existing warehouse facilities, revision costs* (retooling, new equipment, . . .), etc.

c. *External*—Projected changes in the market, financial options to reduce cuts, supply of each staff discipline for eventual replacement, etc.

Organizational—Layoff cost*, minority impact statements, affirmative action quotas for federal contracts*, personnel policies, seniority rules, customer dissatisfaction, etc.

Operational—Unit performance*, current workload densities, potential areas of surplus, professional to support staff ratios, contract bit to award ratio, increases in order backlog, existing inventories and contracts, revenue certainty from each product line, etc.

2. a. ☐ Prevent costly system technology obsolescence from overstocked (unsold) items (economics, operational, numerical, clear).

☐ Minimize risk of customer dissatisfaction because of delivery delays from out-of-stock conditions (performance, external, subjective, fuzzy).

☐ Reduce lost investment opportunity from dormant capital (economics, operational, numerical, fuzzy).

☐ Minimize risk of periodic workforce layoffs from overproduction and excessive inventory (survival, organizational, subjective, fuzzy).

3. a. ☐ *Uncertainties*—Time to diagnose cause of failure, likelihood that incident resulted from the revisions, public reception of the incident or your action, etc.

☐ *Potential Losses*—Lost revenue from reduced output, future clients, strikes and community rebellions, severity of legal actions, etc.

b. ☐ *Uncertainties*—Your share of the market, return on investment, success of marketing programs, etc.

☐ *Potential Losses*—Significant financial losses, company stability/survival, management or leadership reorganizations, etc.

c. ☐ *Uncertainties*—Future market for software, bid to award ratio, affects/benefits of staff cuts, etc.

☐ *Potential Losses*—Morale/attrition problems, reduced capability for providing high caliber products, customer dissatisfaction, etc.

4. a. *Political*—Labor/management arbitrations require that each group reach an acceptable compromise.

b. *Organizational*—The manager will be concerned with performing well on those projects with the most executive visability, not violating legal restrictions on contract funding expenditures, conforming to personnel policies, etc.

c. *Rational*—The decision will be based on straightforward comparison of quantitative factors (cost, performance, etc.).

CHAPTER 4

1. b. Measured in days, local, operational.
   c. Measured in days, local, operational.
   e. Months to years, internal, both tactical and strategic.
   g. Measured in days, local, operational.
   h. Measured in months, internal, tactical.
   i. Months to years, internal, tactical.
   j. Years, internal, both tactical and strategic.

CHAPTER 5

2. b ☐ How will additional staff affect our response time?
   ☐ To what extent will overtime help with our backlog and how much will it take/cost?
   ☐ When will a client's vehicle(s) be completed?
   ☐ How much will our productivity improve using new diagnostic equipment and how long before it pays off?
   c. ☐ Is adding new delivery vehicles cost effective?
   ☐ How much oil do we need to order (or retain on hand) in each time period?
   ☐ Are current storage facilities sufficient or would new satellite facilities be cost efficient?
   ☐ How will cuts in staff affect delivery times?
   e. ☐ When should I sell selected investments?
   ☐ What is my optimum portfolio?
   ☐ At what interest rate is it economical to acquire capital for a particular set of investments?
   g. ☐ What are the most cost effective routes?
   ☐ Where should additional storage or distribution centers be located?
   ☐ Where will an increase in vehicle capacity be most profitable?
   h. ☐ Where is our marketing campaign working the most (and least) effectively?
   ☐ Where do we need to shift inventory levels between regions and retail centers?
   ☐ Are distribution and retail centers adequate (or excessive) for projected demands?
   ☐ Are there selected items where production needs to be increased (or decreased)?
   i. ☐ Where do I need to commit more resources?
   ☐ Where is there slack in the organization?
   ☐ How will a resource cut in certain areas affect output and the operating cost?
   j. ☐ What will be the affect of cuts to specific safety programs?
   ☐ Where do we need to increase resource commitments (safety inspections, training, etc.)?
   ☐ Is our safety program effective?
   ☐ Are there positive (or negative) trends in selected branches or regions?

3. See Exhibit B–1.

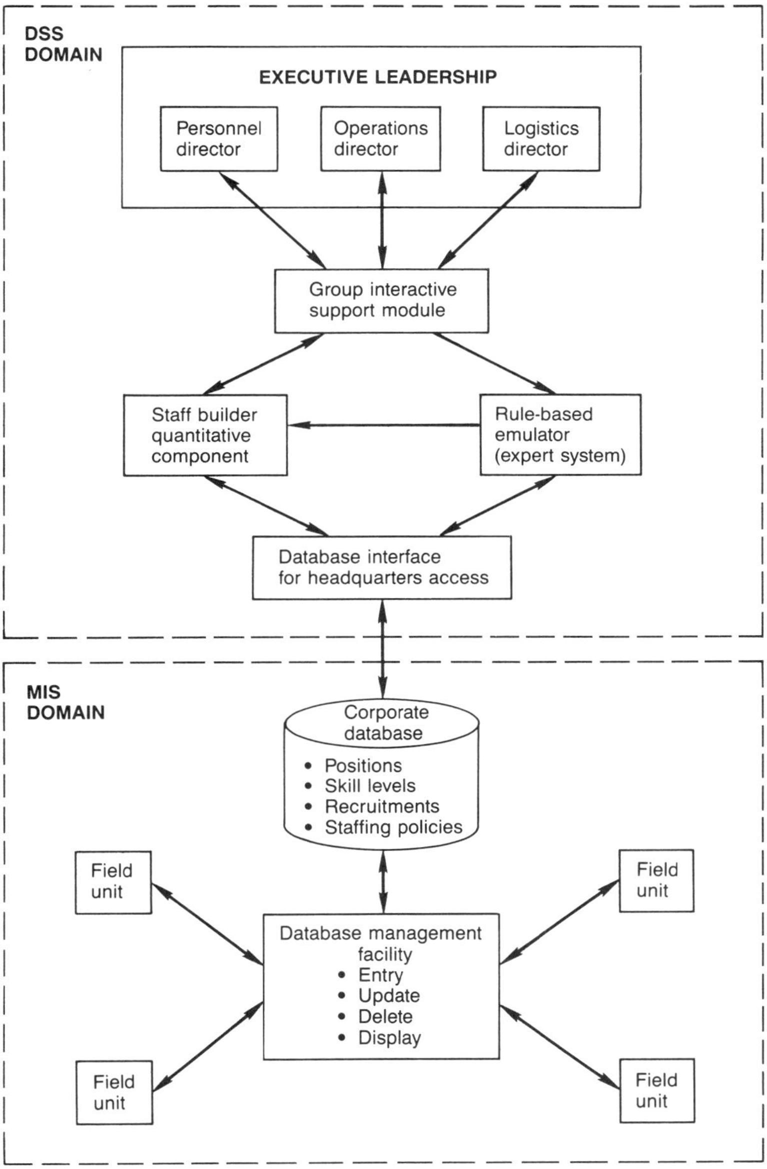

EXHIBIT B–1 Diagram of the System Described in Exercise 3 of Chapter 5. This represents one way of depicting the described system. This application would:

—support strategic decisions
—represent a multi-site application
—support a single function (manpower planning and management).

CHAPTER 6

Exhibit 12–1A provides the figurative model of an organization's workforce. In order for the workforce level to remain constant, the flow of personnel into the organization (from recruiting actions) must be equal to the flow out of the organization (due to attrition). In other words aW=hR. This relationship could be used to get a rough idea of how much recruiting would be necessary for a given workforce level, attrition rate, and hiring rate (for example, R=aW/h).

CHAPTER 7

1. Exhibit B–2 provides one possible layout of a relational database for a vehicle rental tracking system.
2. Exhibit B–3 is one possible representation of a hierarchical data base for a project management system.
4. See Exhibit B–4.

CUSTOMER							
NAME	COMPANY	ADDRESS	TYPE VEHICLE REQUESTED	PICKUP POINT	DROP OFF	ASSIGNED LICENSE	VEHICLE MILEAGE READING
Joe Doe	Self	XYZ St., Boston, MA	Midsize	LA	San Fran	KX 103	10890
Jane Smith	DOD	Pentagon, Wash. D.C.	Compact	Texas	Texas	D70FZ	14292
Jim Jones	ABC Inc.	Elm St., San Diego	Fullsize	Portland, OR	Portland, OR	1096M	06778

EXHIBIT B–2 Relational Database for Tracking Vehicle Rentals.

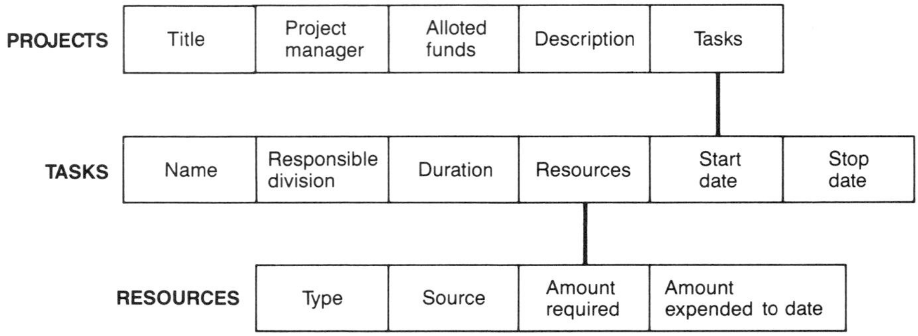

EXHIBIT B–3 Heirarchical Database for a Project Tracking System.

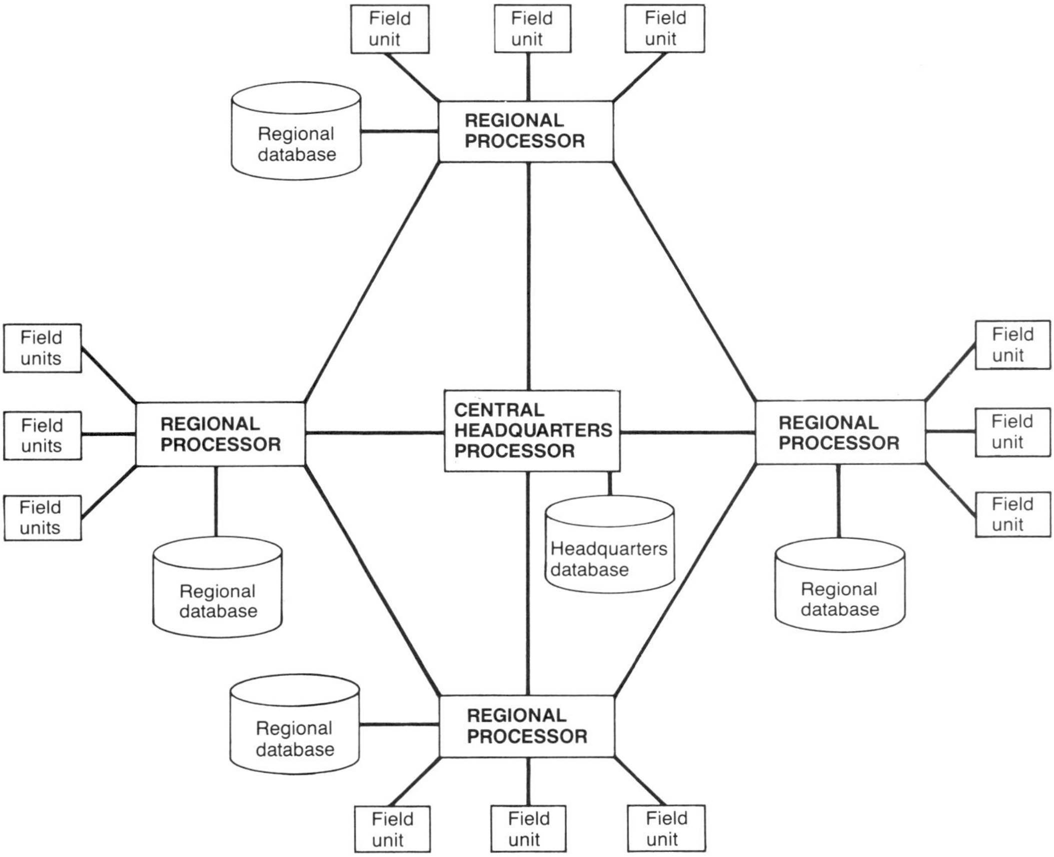

EXHIBIT B–4 A Distributed Architecture for the Application Described in Exercise 3 of Chapter 5.

CHAPTER 8

2. Training should never be used as a substitute for a user interface oriented toward the background, comfort, and preferences of the user. Often system's proponents view user training as a means of circumventing the additional cost of systems development and as a method to compensate for the lack of a user-oriented interface. As discussed in Exercise 1 of Chapter 1, managers have neither the time nor the inclination to struggle with anything that is not conversational and does not provide complete instruction and guidance along the way. Although DSS used to support operational decisions are often used on a routine basis, the support provided at higher levels (tactical and strategic) is often of a less continuous nature. Under such conditions, managers rarely have the opportunity to refamiliarize themselves with a system built upon the philosophy that the prime ingredient to user acceptance is training.

3. *Benefits*
   - ☐ Improves chances that the system will become an integral part of the decision process.
   - ☐ If done properly, a well-designed system allows the user to learn as he goes, thus reducing the transition time to becoming operational.
   - ☐ Reduces operator error and apprehension.
   - ☐ Simplifies user documentation.

   Impacts on the Development Process
   - ☐ Larger program code.
   - ☐ Increases development time and manpower costs.
   - ☐ Requires significantly more "test-bedding" to debug the system.

4. Samples of actual user-oriented systems that exhibit the characteristics and properties discussed in this chapter are provided in Chapters 2, 5, 8 and 9. Not all agree that such "elaborate" measures are necessary or warranted (obviously the author does). As a general goal, truly user-oriented and friendly systems should reflect the following features and capabilities:
   - ☐ *Conversational*—The system should communicate in words and terms that parallel the user's background. Terminology must conform to the users world (terms like PARAMETER, NODE, INTERFACE, etc., are not typical everyday terms to the technically naive audience).
   - ☐ *Guidance and Self-Instruction*—The user should be able to operate the system from ground zero. Instructions and guidance should be available to the user at any point in the system (instructional prompting, help options, self-tutoring facilities, etc.). The user should be able to answer questions about the system directly during the session. The user should be provided several levels of instruction so that, as he becomes a veteran, guidance does not become a nuisance.
   - ☐ *Error Proofing*—With the exception of a power failure, the system should never "hang" or bomb because of user actions. Data should be evaluated by the system for validity (logical dates, positive weights, etc.).
   - ☐ *Flexibility*—The system should allow the user to define his own abbreviations and aliases. The user must also be provided the provisions for tailoring the DSS to his particular preferences and application environment.
   - ☐ *Consistency*—Procedures should be consistent throughout the system. The system must communicate with the user in clear nonambiguous terminology, comply with accepted human stereotypes, etc.
   - ☐ *Advise*—In the more sophisticated applications, the system should advise the user as to the potential interpretations of the results (high likelihood of a cost overrun, there is a significant negative trend in Region 4, etc.), and likely avenues and directions for future evaluations (where to distribute unused resources, what factors improved a solution the most, etc.)

CHAPTER 9

1. ☐ The technique must conform to the structure of the problem.
   - ☐ Complexity of the application (linear versus nonlinear).

- ☐ Computation speed can be an important factor.
- ☐ Designer background and experience.
- ☐ The availability of existing software oriented toward a specific quantitative procedure.
- ☐ The required precision of the application.

2. b. Activity scheduling.
   c. Demand/resource forecasting.
   e. Resource allocation.
   g. Distribution problem.
   h. Demand/resource forecasting.
   i. Both resource allocation and demand forecasting.
   j. Decision/risk analysis.

3. a. Statistical analysis (possibly time series analysis).
   b. Markovian analysis.
   c. Event simulation.
   d. Network optimization.
   e. Mathematical programming (possibly linear or integer programming).

CHAPTER 10

1. FORTRAN
2. APL
3. An acceptable Fourth Generation Language
4. Pascal or ADA
5. The properties, capabilities and productivity of the various programming language options are important to a manager who is responsible for the construction of a DSS from scratch, provided he has the latitude of which language to choose from. Consideration of the pros and cons of each language can help in the system specification phase to minimize the risk that the final product will run poorly, require excessive revision for transfer to other hardware, or is difficult (and costly) to modify for future expansions or unforeseen changes. The author is reminded of one application where, because of unfamiliarity with the general properties and performance characteristics of different programming languages, the manager provided no guidance as to what facilities were permissible, nor any restriction on acceptable run times. As a result, the contractor selected, beat out other proposals by using an interpretative language. The delivered product required four hours to evaluate one scenario. Since this was unacceptable, another contract was required to reprogram the system. Although the final product provided an acceptable run time of 10 to 20 minutes, the organization ended up paying virtually twice as much for the product.

CHAPTER 11

1.

	Pros	Cons
Off the shelf	☐ Often a demonstration version is available to try before you buy ☐ Least expensive approach for initial cost ☐ Quickest payoff	☐ May not satisfy total requirement ☐ Usually cannot be revised
Composite approach	☐ Less expensive than developing from scratch ☐ Allows use of best features from each component package	☐ Often difficult to account for all interface problems in mating components ☐ Not easy to find compatible components
From scratch	☐ Can be designed to satisfy total requirement ☐ Typically can be upgraded more readily	☐ Most costly ☐ Requires greatest time frame ☐ Greatest chance of lost interest due to organizational changes

2. ☐ Staff time for training, initial reduced efficiency, system operation, etc.
   ☐ Software maintenance for revision/upgrades.
   ☐ Lease charges for software, telecommunication network, etc.
   ☐ Hardware maintenance.

5. *Biology*—The study of how a cell takes input (nutrients, oxygen, neurological instructions, etc.) and processes it into a specific product (muscle cells provide motion; brain cells provide reasoning, motor control, etc.).

   Automotive Engineering—How an engine uses air, gasoline, electricity, etc. (inputs), transforms them (air/fuel mixture from carborator, voltage amplification in the coil, etc.) and finally produces power at the wheels.

   Macroeconomics—Many of the macroeconomics models are based on viewing a country as a process where supplies (inputs such as labor, funds, material, etc.) are converted to satisfy demands (output in the form of services, products, etc.).

CHAPTER 12

1. 1. Demand/resource forecasting.
   2. Activity scheduling and resource allocation.
   3. Activity scheduling.
   4. Demand/resource forecasting.
   5. Distribution problem.
   6. Distribution problem.

2. 1. Tactical
   2. Operational
   3. Operational
   4. Tactical
   5. Operational and tactical
   6. Strategic
3. 1. From scratch
   2. From scratch
   3. From scratch
   4. Off-the-shelf
   5. Composite
   6. Off-the-shelf
4. Case Studies 4 and 5

Index